Learning Teaching from Teachers: Realising the Potential of School-based Teacher Education

Developing Teacher Education

Series Editors: Hazel Hagger and Donald McIntyre

The focus of this series is on teacher education, with particular reference to the problems that research has revealed in established approaches to teacher education, to solutions that have been offered to these problems, and to elucidation of the underlying processes of teachers' learning on which effective solutions must depend. While different countries have inherited different systems of teacher education, and are therefore faced with different problems, all countries are faced with the same dilemmas of helping beginning and serving teachers to teach as well as possible within their existing schools while at the same time mobilizing their critical and creative thinking so they can contribute to the development of better schools for the future. Authors in this series explore such opportunities and challenges and seek to understand and explain how the processes of professional learning and of facilitating that learning can be understood.

Published titles:

John Furlong, Len Barton, Sheila Miles, Caroline Whiting and Geoff Whitty:
    Teacher Education in Transition
Les Tickle: *Teacher Induction: The Way Ahead*

Learning Teaching from Teachers: Realising the Potential of School-based Teacher Education

Hazel Hagger and
Donald McIntyre

Open University Press
Maidenhead · New York

Open University Press
McGraw-Hill Education
McGraw-Hill House
Shoppenhangers Road
Maidenhead
Berkshire
England
SL6 2QL

and Two Penn Plaza, New York, NY 10121-2289, USA

email: enquiries@openup.co.uk
world wide web: www.openup.co.uk

First published 2006

A catalogue record of this book is available from the British Library

ISBN 10: 0335 202 926 (pb)   0335 202 934 (hb)
ISBN 13: 978 0335 202 928 (pb)   978 0335 202 935 (hb)

Library of Congress Cataloging-in-Publication Data
CIP data has been applied for

Typeset by BookEns Ltd, Royston, Herts.
Printed and bound in Poland by OZGraf S.A.
www.polskabook.pl

Contents

Series editors' preface

The task of writing this series editors' preface is a rather strange one, since it is for our own book that we are writing the preface. It is, however, good for us to have to step back after writing this book to consider again how it fits in to the series' broader task of exploring ways in which teacher education can fruitfully and effectively be developed.

We can usefully start by quoting the opening paragraph of our preface to an earlier book in the series, *Teacher Education in Transition*, by John Furlong and his collaborators, published in 2000:

> During the last decade, initial teacher education in England has been the subject of massive change. At one level, this change can be seen as a long overdue recognition of the capacity of schools, and especially of the teachers who work in them, to make a major contribution to the professional education of those entering the profession. How this can best be done, against a background of almost a century in which teachers have had very little such involvement, but in which both what is sought from schooling and our understanding of schooling have expanded greatly, is a highly exciting question. What problems, and especially what opportunities, it will involve we are only beginning to discover. One of the aims of this series is to contribute to the exploration of the opportunities and to the solution of the problems.

Teacher Education in Transition has, as we predicted, come to be regarded 'as the authoritative text on what happened in English teacher education in the 1990s'. Among other things, it told us, as we said in our preface, that the Nineties had 'seen some significant achievements in initial teacher education, which we would be very foolish to ignore, and also that the immense potential of real partnership between schools and higher education (was) generally very far from being realised.' Six years later, in 2006, the situation is in our view not greatly different: while there are still significant achievements to be celebrated, the potential of partnership in ITE between schools and higher education is still very far from being generally realised. England certainly led the world in moving towards a partnership approach to ITE; but the way in which it was initiated at a national level in 1992, and has since been maintained, through unilateral government imposition, has not led to widespread or vigorous exploration of its potential. Nor has this imposed system attracted admiration, far less emulation, elsewhere in the world.

Yet the case for a more school-based approach, and for carefully developed partnership in ITE between schools and higher education, was and remains an impelling one, both in England and elsewhere. The limited nature of the success described in *Teacher Education in Transition* was due to the particular limited and misconceived versions of these ideas that have been promoted by successive English governments. This book, in contrast, is about the potential of school-based initial teacher education.

As is explained in the first chapter, this book starts from an acceptance of the inherent inadequacy both of a largely university-based approach to initial teacher education and of the theory-into-practice rationale on which such an approach was based. On the other hand, it starts from an equal discontent with the current government-imposed system in England, concerned only with beginning teachers' attainment of a large set of untheorised and bureaucratically determined 'competences'. There is no room for doubt about our basic premise that effective teaching depends upon all teachers engaging for themselves in what we call 'practical theorising'. While viewing the contribution of higher education institutions to ITE as vital, the book recognises schools as the places where beginning teachers' core professional learning has to be located, and also the places where there is most need and scope for new positive developments. It therefore concentrates on the school-based elements of ITE programmes, and is aimed at developing a fuller, clearer and better theorised account of what school-based ITE could fruitfully be like than has previously been available.

As is always the case in attempts to develop new and better practices, it is important both to appreciate what we already know and to recognise how much has still to be found out. In Chapters 2 and 3 of this book, we consider the implications of several different fields of research for what initial teacher education should be trying to help beginning teachers to achieve, and for how it can best do this. As these chapters reveal, there is a great deal to be learned from previous research that has not as yet had much influence on the design of teacher education programmes. On the other hand, since only very limited versions of school-based ITE have previously been tried, there is still a great deal to learn about how it can best be done. One of the main messages of this book is that we can best learn about what high-quality school-based ITE involves through a variety of relatively modest, but carefully conceived and evaluated, initiatives. Part B of the book reports one such initiative and makes clear how much we did not know when we started it, but instead had to learn from it. In particular, this initiative taught us about the crucial importance of *planned curricula for school-based ITE*, a concept that we have not encountered elsewhere. In the final section, Part C, we develop this concept and consider some of the practical implications of moving forward in this direction.

If, as we very confidently believe, we are broadly right in what we argue for in this book, then there is a great deal of very exciting work to be done in the early twenty-first century, developing and perfecting school-based ITE. We are in no doubt that beginning teachers will benefit from initial professional education that is both intellectually challenging and highly practical and that is led by professional school-based teacher educators. But schools, too, will benefit greatly from taking on such a responsibility not just for leading the 'practical' aspect of ITE, but for leading beginning teachers in their *thinking* about education and their own part in it. And university departments of education will benefit greatly if their role in ITE can be more coherently conceived as following from their proper concern to use their research and scholarship to help schools and teachers to think in critical and informed ways about their work. What matters most, of course, is that we should all be both imaginative and realistic about how we can best contribute to the quality of the educational experience of school students.

Hazel Hagger
Donald McIntyre

Acknowledgements

Everything in this book has depended on our learning from other people, and especially from working with other people. We are deeply grateful to all the school-based and university-based teacher educators and student teachers with whom we have worked in various contexts over many years, and also to the many researchers on teaching and teacher education from whom we have learned. Our particular thanks are due to the teachers, student teachers and colleagues who participated in, or helped with, the study reported in Part B of the book. It was from their collaboration and thoughtful contributions that this whole book grew. And two individual people especially deserve our thanks. One is Sally Brown, since the research reported here built very heavily and fruitfully on the earlier research with her. And the whole project, from beginning to end, depended on Louise Gully, who managed us and amazingly maintained meaningful order among the sporadic successive drafts and changing structures of the book. Thank you, Louise.

Hazel Hagger
Donald McIntyre

Tables and figures

Part A

The Case for School-based Teacher Education

1 Changing teacher education

The purpose of this book is to consider the kind of initial teacher education (ITE) that is needed for the twenty-first century. It will ask what can be learned from the very different approaches that have been tried in the past and from the now considerable body of research into such approaches. It will consider the assumptions upon which teacher education programmes can safely be planned and the goals towards which they might wisely be directed. It will conclude that, internationally, there are as yet no satisfactory models of teacher education practice which meet the needs of the education systems in which they are embedded, far less models which might be developed or modified to suit the varying needs of different national educational systems. While recognizing the amount of work still to be done, we shall seek to articulate a coherent and realistic vision of the kind of approach needed for ITE in the coming years.

The problem is not that there has been too much complacency in recent years about ITE. On the contrary, there has been marked discontent in many countries, notably from governments. There have been many proposals for radical change, much heated debate, and some fundamental changes. Two common elements seem to have led to all this discontent and questioning. One has been a growing belief in the importance of schooling for the civilized quality of societies and for the success of national economies, a belief that we shall not seek to dispute. The other has been an assumption that the quality of schooling is heavily dependent, primarily dependent, on the quality of its teachers and their teaching. That is an assumption that we are confident is correct; and it follows that any system of schooling that has an annual intake of thousands of committed, eager and able beginning teachers needs to give them the best possible preparation and start. But we shall shortly want to look more closely at precisely what ITE can sensibly be expected to contribute to the quality of schooling.

Beyond these common assumptions, however, there has been little international consensus. Partly, that has been because different countries, while inheriting very different ITE systems from the past, have been inclined to find fault with these inherited systems. Thus the many countries (including virtually all English-speaking countries) which had relied in the twentieth century on higher education institutions (HEIs) to prepare teachers have tended to identify the same central problem, namely a lack of practical focus in too much of what was done in these institutions. The solution was assumed to lie in a stronger role for schools with tighter accountability. In England, this culminated in the early 1990s in radical moves to reduce the dominance of the universities and to give a much bigger role to schools. In contrast, at precisely the same time, France initiated an equally radical reform in the opposite direction by establishing the Instituts Universitaires de Formation des Maîtres (IUFM) and a new national pattern of ITE for which these university bodies were to be responsible (Judge *et al.* 1994; Moon 1998).

Even where the diagnoses have been similar, as in those countries where greater practicality has been sought, the outcomes have been very different. In the USA, throughout the twenty years since the National Commission on Excellence in Education's *A Nation at Risk* (1983), debates have raged, innumerable new pilot programmes have been initiated, and a diffuse movement of professional development schools (Darling-Hammond 1994) has been active; but it is not apparent that any significant structural changes have taken place. In Scotland, proposals for major structural changes were more explicitly rejected. In England, in contrast, the sweeping changes in the early 1990s included a major shift of responsibilities and resources from higher education to the schools (Department for Education and Science 1992; Department for Education 1993), complemented by steadily increased bureaucratic governmental controls (e.g. Department for Education and Skills 2002) ever since. In the Netherlands, even more radical changes are under way, with ITE for all novice teachers being provided while they are already in full-time employment (Snoek 2003). Such absence of any international consensus does not give one great confidence in any of the national solutions.

This background of international discontent, questioning, debate and change provides the context for this book. Inevitably, however, we as authors are especially aware of the English system, which arguably has hitherto seen the most radical change. The aim of the book is to build on what can be learned from the recent and the more distant past. It will seek to show that research and experience have enabled us to identify many of the key elements from which a satisfactory approach to ITE could be constructed; but it will also suggest that the most important kinds of thinking needed for effective ITE have yet to be undertaken.

One of the central controversies about ITE in most countries has been the question of how much responsibility and time should be allocated to HEIs, and how much to schools and teachers. In many countries, the nineteenth century was dominated by school-based approaches to ITE while, in contrast, the twentieth century was dominated by higher education-based approaches. Towards the end of the twentieth century, however, as we have already noted, there was growing discontent with the higher education-based approach and, in England in particular, a reversion to a much more school-based system. After more than ten years of this bold English initiative, we need to ask how successful it has been in resolving the fundamental problems of ITE, and again what lessons can be learned. On the basis of the conclusions which emerge from these explorations of the past, we shall pose the key questions on which we must focus in our efforts to find a more satisfactory future for ITE.

In order to establish criteria for assessing the strengths and limitations of past systems, we must first examine the assumption that we mentioned as being made by governments, that ITE is an important determinant of the quality of schooling. Is it important? If so, how is it important? And, therefore, what is it that we should be seeking from ITE?

What should ITE contribute to the quality of schooling?

The obvious and, in our view, incontestable purpose of ITE is to ensure, if at all possible, that prospective teachers should become able teachers.

Clearly teachers need many different kinds of knowledge and expertise. Most evidently, they need a thorough and rich knowledge of the subject-matter that they are teaching. Unless teachers feel secure about what they are teaching, they tend to teach in a defensive way, sticking to a set, pre-planned script, concentrating on communicating what they know and avoiding as much as possible thoughtful questions from pupils. Teachers who have a wide, deep and confident knowledge of the subject can afford to promote investigations by pupils and wide-ranging discussion among them, sure in the knowledge that they will be able to respond in an informed way to whatever issues arise. It is such teachers too who are best equipped to offer helpful examples, applications, metaphors, analogies and connections to illuminate their explanations and in response to pupil questions. And from a pessimistic perspective, it is such teachers who are least likely to allow or even to promote persistent false and misleading understandings among their pupils. We should be in no doubt about the central importance of subject knowledge.

That, however, is just the beginning. And, for graduate student teachers with appropriate school and university qualifications, it can often be the kind of knowledge about which teacher educators can be most confident: these student teachers have probably spent at least 16 years acquiring such knowledge. It is other kinds of knowledge which they may lack in very fundamental ways.

In a very sensible and informed book confronting precisely this question of what kinds of knowledge beginning teachers need, published for the American Association of Colleges for Teacher Education (Reynolds 1989), each of 24 chapters was devoted to a different kind of knowledge, subject knowledge being only one of them. Included among such kinds of knowledge could be: knowledge of aspects of the school system, how it works, the curricula and examination requirements it imposes, and the duties, legal obligations and rights it gives teachers; knowledge of other national systems and the alternatives they suggest; knowledge about, or based on, what are often seen as the 'foundation disciplines' of education, philosophy, sociology, history and psychology; knowledge about learners of different kinds, and of different ideas about learning, different learning processes, and different kinds of learning outcomes; knowledge of the contexts in which different sections of society live, of different cultures, different child-rearing practices, and the educational impacts of differences in power, status and wealth; and knowledge of the different needs pupils will have for different kinds of occupations. A very good case can be made for beginning teachers needing all these and many other kinds of knowledge.

Given such a rich range of persuasive and attractive possibilities, it is always necessary to be selective, to prioritize. This need is especially obvious and acute in those systems where only one year is allowed for professional ITE. It is not a matter of contesting the potential value of any of these different kinds of knowledge; it is instead a matter of deciding which is most essential. In these circumstances, it makes sense to start from the target situation – the school and, in particular, the classroom – and to ask about the kinds of knowledge that beginning teachers need in order to do well the job they will be asked to do there. This does not by any means resolve the problem, but it narrows it by asserting that priority must be given to classroom teaching expertise. It is quite consistent too with the idea that there may be other lesser priorities, to which some time and attention must be given. It suggests, however, that the main curriculum issue for ITE is that of enabling beginning teachers to develop classroom teaching expertise. That will be a central assumption of this book.

Another fundamental assumption, for which we shall argue at some length in Chapter 2, is that classroom teaching expertise is necessarily complex, subtle and sophisticated. Even in a stable system, where the tasks schools are asked to undertake do not change, a high level of such expertise cannot be attained quickly; and where schools are under constant pressure to innovate and to improve, the challenge is inevitably greater. This being so, it is clear that initial teacher educators have to construe their work as involving three main tasks. The first, and no doubt the most urgent, is that of enabling student teachers to acquire the thorough, if basic, classroom competence which will allow them to qualify as teachers and to do satisfactory work in their first teaching posts. The second task is to prepare them for a situation in which they will need to go on learning, primarily on their own initiative and on the basis of their own classroom experience. As Zeichner (1996b: 217) comments, 'unless the practicum helps to teach prospective teachers how to take control of their own professional development and to learn how to continue learning, it is miseducative, no matter how successful teachers might be in the short term'. And the third task is to prepare beginning teachers to respond intelligently and critically to demands for innovation and improvement. Thus ITE's concern must be for student teachers not only to learn to do the job of classroom teaching competently, but also to learn how to *learn* to do it better.

What, then, should ITE be expected to contribute to the quality of schooling? Clearly it should contribute competent, confident teachers who have the knowledge and the commitment necessary to become expert classroom teachers within a few years. But what should its contribution be to improving the school system? That is a critical question because it is clear that many governments see ITE as a key lever for bringing about rapid school improvement, and because it is equally clear that governments can easily deceive themselves into making naïve and over-optimistic assumptions about this.

It is of course vitally important that student teachers should be equipped with as much cutting-edge knowledge as possible not only about developments in their subjects but also about well-tested and useful new developments that can contribute to the improvement of schooling, for example in the use of information and communication technologies. Not only will this help them to develop their own teaching quickly and effectively as their schools gain the necessary resources; it will also make them useful colleagues for more experienced teachers who have to learn on the job to use these new tools effectively. However, both experience and research (e.g. Lacey 1977; Zeichner *et al.* 1987) strongly support what common sense would suggest, that it is generally counterproductive to expect the least expert and least established members of organizations such as schools to be the key agents of change. Beginning teachers generally feel a strong need to establish their credibility both with their students and with their colleagues, and any attempts that they make to challenge accepted school practices are likely to make this task more difficult. The most probable outcomes of anything other than the most cautious attempts at change are likely to be disillusionment and even a loss to the teaching profession of talented and enthusiastic practitioners.

Governments are right to see ITE as crucial to the development of the teaching profession and so to the improvement of schools. They would, however, be profoundly wrong if they were to believe that they could, by using novices as change agents, either solve or bypass the problems of persuading and enabling established teachers to accept radical change.

For our part, we need to ask how adequately past and present approaches to ITE have prepared beginning teachers to be competent classroom practitioners, to learn how to improve their teaching, and to be able to contribute to the critical evaluation and assimilation of new ideas for the improvement of schooling.

Lessons from schemes for learning to teach on the job

We noted earlier that the nineteenth century was dominated internationally by school-based approaches to ITE. Historically, that was the high
point of *apprenticeship* systems. The best-known and best-respected British
apprenticeship scheme for teachers was the pupil-teacher scheme, which
dominated the second half of the nineteenth century and lasted into the
twentieth. The pupil-teacher scheme seems to have exemplified very well
the strengths and weaknesses of the apprenticeship approach; and, a century later, we should be taking care to learn from it.

The pupil-teacher scheme seems to have had two main strengths. First,
it was a scheme based on respect for, and reliance on, the expertise of
practising teachers. The importance of this respect for teachers' expertise
is apparent when one compares it with what came next. During the twentieth century, instead of gradually refining our understanding of how best
beginning teachers could learn from the expertise of their experienced
colleagues, we largely ignored that expertise. Now, at the beginning of the
twenty-first century, we have no tradition of ITE which draws strongly
and effectively upon the expertise of practising teachers. One of the central messages of this book is that we need to redevelop such a tradition.
(We should not, however, romanticize the respect in which the expertise
of experienced elementary school teachers was held in the pupil-teacher
scheme: it was a respect tempered about by a concern that those teachers
from working-class backgrounds should not be allowed to control the culture or the future of their profession; and, as Gardner (1993) explains, it
was this concern that lay behind the gradually increased provision of college training to complement the pupil-teacher experience.)

The second main strength of the pupil-teacher scheme was that it
seems to have effectively developed the practical competence of beginning teachers. It may not always have done this in thoughtful ways, but
five years of teenage apprenticeship, with daily practical experience both
of observation of experienced teachers and of practice in the teaching
tasks judged appropriate, seems to have developed teachers whose practical competence was recognized. At worst, as one former pupil teacher
recalled, 'You sank or swam. Either you could "hold" a class of thirty, fifty
or sixty boys or you could not' (Spencer 1938: 75). When later this
scheme was supplanted by a system of secondary education followed by
professional training in colleges, the craft skills of pupil teachers would be
judged to be 'mechanical' and 'narrow'. Colleges tended to be on the
defensive when the practical competence of their products was compared
with that of those who had gone through the pupil-teacher system, but
Gardner (1993: 34) notes that 'however well prepared in other respects,
new generations of young teachers were now emerging from the colleges
with but a tiny fraction of the practical experience of earlier cohorts'.

The weaknesses of apprenticeship are also well exemplified by the
pupil-teacher scheme. Two such weaknesses may be highlighted. First,

although the practical learning of apprenticeship is often complemented by a more wide-ranging college-based learning agenda, it is generally very difficult to plan effectively for these two kinds of learning to interact. In the pupil-teacher scheme, no attempt was made to connect the practical learning in schools with subsequent college-based learning. The practical learning of how to do things in the classroom was not therefore normally related to any more general ideas, nor examined critically in relation to any broader principles of good practice. In that sense the judgement that the skills developed by pupil teachers were 'mechanical' and 'narrow' was probably justified. The system lacked any incentives or guidance for thinking critically about one's teaching, for questioning its quality or for planning for its further development after the achievement of basic competence. And it did not prepare teachers to know how to evaluate critically, nor where appropriate to implement, subsequent suggestions for the improvement of their practice.

A second weakness of apprenticeship is that it tends to be heavily dependent on the individual master-craftsperson to whom one is apprenticed. In a mass system where many thousands of such master-craftspeople are necessarily involved, the quality both of the practice to which apprentices are exposed and of the training they are offered is often a matter of luck.

> The system depended upon the wholehearted and consistent support of individual headteachers. Many rose to the challenge admirably but others often fell short of expectations. Right from the start of the pupil-teacher system complaints abounded about the widespread abuses and weakness of the apprentice-practitioner model suggesting that, in practice, it was fundamentally flawed.
>
> (Robinson 2004: 34)

The two main suggested sources of variation in quality, were, first, the tendency for pupil teachers to be used as cheap labour, to the neglect of their training, and second, the variation in the capacity of the headteachers to undertake the task effectively. These variations in quality seem to have been very apparent in the pupil-teacher scheme.

The pupil-teacher system was discontinued only gradually, with an intermediate period around the end of the nineteenth century in which 'pupil-teacher centres' took over much of the training role of the headteachers (Robinson 2004: 36–42). Despite its distinctive merits – its respect for and reliance upon the expertise of practising teachers, and the extensive practical classroom experience it gave novices – it was abandoned for good reasons. We shall need something that is a great deal more thoughtful and sophisticated for the future.

Higher education-based ITE in the twentieth century

In striking contrast to the nineteenth century, in the twentieth century an overwhelming emphasis was given in many countries to approaches to ITE based in, and largely controlled by, HEIs.

Much of this emphasis on higher education was concerned with teachers' knowledge of the subjects that they were to teach in primary and secondary schools. As we have already noted, there can be little doubt that, other things being equal, the wider and deeper teachers' knowledge is about what they are teaching, the better their teaching is likely to be. So from our perspective this emphasis on teachers' subject expertise was and remains entirely commendable. Our concern here is with teachers' *professional* preparation and its twentieth-century location in, and control by, HEIs.

Teachers' initial professional education throughout the twentieth century appears to have been based, in the UK and in most Western countries, on the premise that beginning teachers should first understand about good teaching, and should then put that understanding into practice. Good teaching, from this point of view, stems primarily from an intelligent moral vision of the processes of teaching and of learning, of the relationship between teacher and learner, of the kind of people one is trying to help learners become, of the study of one's subject, of the kind of society to which one's teaching is contributing, and most usually some combination of such ideals. Teacher educators' visions were of many kinds, and drew on many sources. For much of the century, they were primarily moral visions, with an emphasis on persuading beginning teachers of the rightness of certain educational ideals and related classroom activities, norms and purposes. Often, however, the emphasis was more on the intelligence of the vision, and on the beginning teachers' theoretical understanding of what teaching, learning, classrooms and schools involve. Both elements were always there in some measure.

This focus on the rightness and intelligence of the educational and social visions underlying good classroom practice had much to commend it. Underlying any classroom practices, there must be explicit or implicit understandings and ideals about what teaching does and should involve, and about what it should be directed towards; and it is surely desirable that teachers should have thought about, questioned and consciously espoused the understandings and ideals implicit in their teaching. What is less obvious is whether the kind of classroom expertise which teachers need can be derived primarily from idealized views of teaching. On the contrary, the twentieth-century experience suggested that, whatever teacher educators intended, developing understandings and ideals about teaching was not in itself of much help in developing such expertise. Generations of student teachers have discovered, often painfully, that the disciplined scholarly understandings which they may have developed in higher education contexts, and the ideals to which they may have become deeply committed, are quite inadequate as a basis for effective classroom functioning.

It was only slowly and with considerable reluctance, if at all, that twentieth-century teacher educators recognized that this theory-into-practice conception of ITE was inherently flawed. There was much debate about the kind of theoretical or idealized knowledge that was most appropriate, with the 'foundation disciplines' of psychology, sociology, history and philosophy, more topic-based analyses of aspects of education and schooling, and subject curriculum or methods courses vying for space and frequently being taught in parallel. Right up to the end of the century there were those who saw the problem as being less with the theoretical content than with the credibility of those who delivered it, and sought solutions for example through including practising teachers in university teaching teams (e.g. Cope and Stephen 2001). Others saw the central problem as being that the immensely difficult task of translating theory into practice was too often left for the novices themselves to resolve. So they devised means to guide and support students in this translation process, such as 'microteaching', developed at Stanford University in the 1960s. Towards the end of the century, increasingly detailed schemes for connecting students' school practice or 'practicum' activities to their university courses were also developed.

We shall argue in Chapter 2 that classroom teaching expertise cannot in principle be derived from theoretical or idealized views of teaching. In practice, however, it was the accumulating weight of research and inspection evidence that in England was crucial in demonstrating the unacceptability of a primarily university-based approach to teacher education. It gradually became apparent that while most student teachers engaged conscientiously in their theoretical university-based studies, they found that using these studies as a basis for thinking about their teaching while in schools was not only very difficult but also unnecessary. Lacey's (1977) study remains the one which most fully reveals the sophisticated strategies which student teachers adopted, in school and university contexts, to deal with the demands of teacher educators. He showed, in particular, how they used the division of their work between university and school contexts to cope effectively with each. In the same way, more recently in Scotland, the great majority of student teachers find it easiest to forget about their theoretical studies once they get into schools and are working with teachers who do not approach their work in such theoretical terms (e.g. McNally *et al.* 1994; Stark 2000).

Research thus gradually made clear how misguided it was to believe that teaching expertise could be learned effectively by using theoretical knowledge to shape classroom practice. Related beliefs that most of student teachers' time could most usefully be spent in HEIs, and that the relatively limited time spent by them in schools should also be supervised by HEI-based teacher educators, were equally discredited. The most politically important evidence of these errors came in England from two surveys by Her Majesty's Inspectorate (HMI) in the 1980s (HMI 1982, 1988) which showed that headteachers, student teachers and inspectors themselves were highly critical of the courses and of the adequacy of the preparation for teaching which they offered. If the most important purpose of ITE was to develop competence in classroom teaching, this was most likely to be achieved through working primarily in schools under the supervision of experienced teachers.

The English reform: back towards school-based ITE again

In suggesting that the ITE methods of the twentieth century were not well conceived for the development of classroom teaching expertise, we are clearly following in the steps of the English government more than a decade ago, when it introduced radical changes in the structuring of ITE. The government's intention, and achievement, was to shift the centre of gravity of ITE from higher education into the schools. The move could well be seen as reverting to something more like the nineteenth-century approach.

The thinking behind the 1992 decision by the then Conservative government to make ITE much more school-based was in part, as expressed in the barrage of right-wing pamphlets which preceded it, an opposition to what were rightly seen as egalitarian, inclusivist, progressive and multicultural emphases in university teacher education courses. The move was justified primarily, however, by the belief that classroom teaching was a fairly straightforward business and that, so long as one had a good command of *what* one was teaching, learning to teach should mainly be just a matter of practising (e.g. Lawlor 1990; O'Keeffe 1990; O'Hear 1988). Giving schools a major responsibility for ITE was not therefore seen or represented as a considerable new task for schools, and certainly not as a challenge for them. All they had to do was to provide the contexts in which beginning teachers could get the practice which they needed. No extra resources were seen to be needed and certainly none were provided, either for schools to undertake this new task or for them to think out what it might involve, although schools were to negotiate with universities to get a share of their teacher training income.

From the beginning, then, neither the resources nor the rhetoric were such as to encourage schools to be innovative in their teacher education thinking or practices. Nor has that changed significantly over the intervening years. It is true that the government has, through the Teacher Training Agency, become more demanding of school-based teacher educators; but the demands have rarely been for them to develop or pursue innovative approaches to facilitate the development of classroom teaching expertise. On the contrary, the demands have been for increased conformity to a central government agenda, focused on what beginning teachers should learn and especially on their assessment. In view of the problem of widely varying standards that we have noted in relation to the pupil-teacher scheme – a problem which continued in another guise during most of the twentieth century, in that each training institution pursued its own distinctive agenda – we would not wish to contest the importance of quality assurance and control. Nor would we argue that the standards against which all student teachers in England have to be judged are unreasonable. However, we do not believe that it is a sensible use of school-based teacher educators' limited time for them to spend much of it collecting evidence, for each of the specified standards, to justify their decisions about which boxes to tick for each student teacher.

What have been the consequences of this professionally minimalist but bureaucratically demanding regime? The impact of the government reforms has been very informatively studied through two successive surveys by the Modes of Teacher Education (MOTE) research team (Furlong *et al.* 2000). From their complex and sophisticated analysis, we select four key themes.

First, perhaps most obviously, they note that 'Teachers were ... being asked to take on much more responsibility in relation to the developing of students' practical teaching competence' (Furlong *et al.* 2000: 86). They quote typical teachers involved in these new 'mentoring' roles:

> Up until a couple of years ago the class ... you just had a role as the class teacher really and supported them and talked about how they'd done and gave suggestions and advice, whereas now it's much more a tutoring role because we're a partnership school ...
>
> (Furlong *et al.* 2000: 86)

> I find it quite demanding but I also find it quite rewarding. Erm, I really enjoy it. It gives me a kick up the backside quite honestly when I see what some marvellous ideas they come up with ... We spend a lot of time talking ...
>
> (Furlong *et al.* 2000: 86)

Other research and our own experience strongly confirm both the substantial new roles that teachers have taken on and also the frequency with which they as mentors have felt the stimulating and empowering sense communicated in the second of the above quotations. Teachers' expertise has clearly been used as never before, or at least not since the nineteenth century, and many teachers have been delighted to be able to contribute in this way. Yet it should be noted that it was most clearly in the area of assessment that Furlong and his colleagues found teachers being given primary responsibility; and we have already mentioned the increasingly tight control by government, and its considerable demands, in this area. Empowerment of teachers in ITE, respect for their expertise and reliance on it, have been hedged around by central government priorities, as well as by the limited time which teachers have been allowed for such work.

A second area on which the MOTE team focused was satisfaction with the outcomes of the new system. So far as possible, they replicated the HMI surveys of the 1980s which had had such a decisive influence in preparing the way for reforms. They found that, by the mid- and late 1990s, student teachers and newly qualified teachers were reporting almost universal satisfaction with their courses and with the adequacy of their own preparation for teaching, and that headteachers were even more positive. In most respects the majority of student teachers saw both school and university elements of their courses as having contributed to the development of their professional competences and understandings. From this evidence, there can be no doubt that the practical effectiveness of courses has been greatly enhanced by the shift to a more school-based pattern.

A third area explored was what course teams saw themselves as trying to develop. In both surveys, course leaders were asked whether any particular philosophy of professionalism informed their courses and if so, what it was. In both cases, the majority responded 'yes', and dominant among the philosophies identified was that of 'the reflective practitioner'. As the team comment, 'the dominant model of professional learning advanced by teacher educators has changed from the receiving of theory to "theoriz*ing*" through reflection' (Furlong *et al.* 2000: 137; emphasis in original). Accordingly, they asked students about whether they recognized and valued 'reflection' as a key part of their professional development. They found that 'many (though not all) students recognized the importance of reflection within their course' and 'considered themselves well prepared in this area' (Furlong *et al.* 2000: 137). As to what 'reflection' meant, they found:

> For some students … reflection … implied a critical process, reviewing personal experience in the light of other forms of professional knowledge (descriptions of practice; principles derived from practice; the findings of research; theoretical insights derived from the 'foundation' disciplines etc.). For the majority, however, it seems that reflection was much more of a 'lay' activity where trainees struggled to come to terms with their own experiences by articulating them and sharing them with others. … if reflection remains only this, rooted in particular practical experiences, then its implications for professionalism are significantly different from when trainees are systematically provided with opportunities to engage with other forms of professional knowledge.
>
> (Furlong *et al.* 2000: 138)

Thus, despite the considerable benefits of the new system in enabling student teachers to develop practical competence as teachers, severe reservations were being recorded about whether they were acquiring the necessary critical abilities to develop real teaching expertise. While the inadequacy of the university-based system in preparing competent class-room practitioners seemed to have been overcome, the new approach did not seem to be effective for the two other basic purposes which we iden-tified, those of student teachers learning how to improve their teaching, and learning how to evaluate and assimilate new ideas for the improve-ment of schooling.

Finally, one of the MOTE team's particular interests was the nature of the partnerships being formed between universities and schools within the new dispensation. They found a few partnerships which approxi-mated to the 'collaborative partnership' model exemplified by the Oxford Internship Scheme (Benton 1990; McIntyre 1997), based on sustained critical dialogue between the different kinds of expertise which teachers and university lecturers could bring as equal partners to considerations of teaching expertise. The most common type of partnership was, however, one which they had not anticipated and which they described as the 'HEI-led model'. In partnerships of this type, under the influence of increasing government control and severe financial constraints, the HEI played primarily a managerial role:

> The aim, as far as course leadership is concerned, is to utilize schools as a resource in setting up learning opportunities for students. Course leaders have a set of aims (often set out as a set of compe-tences) that they want to achieve and this demands that schools act in similar ways and make available comparable opportunities for all students. Within this idealized model, quality control – making sure students all receive comparable training opportunities – is a high priority.
>
> (Furlong *et al.* 2000: 117)

Two aspects of this finding may be highlighted. First, the consequences of such managerially oriented partnerships, complementing as they did the lack of either resources or rhetoric to encourage schools or teachers to develop new approaches, were predictable. It is not difficult to under-stand, for example, why such limited success was noted in the novice teachers' development of the skills and orientations for reflective practice. Second, we noted earlier that in any apprenticeship system, where the responsibility for training the apprentices is necessarily widely dispersed, issues of quality control are likely to present difficulties. In a system where priority is placed overwhelmingly on the learning and assessment of centrally specified competences rather than on the expertise that the many experienced practitioners involved have to share, such problems of quality control are likely to assume a dominating importance. Is adequate advantage being taken of the move towards school-based ITE if such lit-tle importance is being attached to the expertise of experienced teachers?

It is perhaps a little alarming to find that the strengths and weaknesses of the current English system revealed by the MOTE study are so reminis-cent of our earlier analysis of the pupil-teacher scheme. The analogy should not be pressed too far, but in both cases we have found qualified strengths in that

• the expertise of the experienced teachers is (within quite severe limits) recognized and relied upon,
• beginning teachers generally acquire basic practical competence,

but limitations in that

• beginning teachers frequently do not learn how to critically evaluate and improve their own practice,
• official concerns are focused more on a pervasive regime of quality control than on the development of learning opportunities within the system.

The way forward

We have in this chapter represented the history of ITE, at least in England, as a kind of political ping-pong, with moves back and forward between predominantly school-based and higher education-based ITE, each with its characteristic strengths and limitations. We believe this to be a fair, if simplified, representation of that history. It is not, however, a fair representation of what it has been possible to learn from research and experience about ITE. On the contrary, we believe that teacher educators internationally are now considerably better placed than ever before to plan high-quality ITE programmes. To achieve this, however, we need to stand back from the politics which has dominated debate in most countries, and to consider how best, in what contexts, with whose help, and through what diverse processes beginning teachers can best learn what they need to learn.

By the 1980s it seemed clear, from the massive international accumulation of evidence throughout the second half of the twentieth century, that there was a need for schools to play a much larger part in ITE. Student teachers needed to spend more time in schools and practising teachers needed to be involved much more in planning students' learning experiences and in actually helping them to learn. We knew a great deal then – and know more now – that could help us plan highly effective ITE curricula of a more school-based kind. Unfortunately, the development of such curricula was inhibited by politicians with very different agendas. Whether successful in imposing a move towards school-based ITE, as in England, or unsuccessful, as in Scotland, the politicians effectively prevented the improvement that was needed.

The Conservative government's imposition in England in the early 1990s of more school-based ITE was justified primarily by the belief that classroom teaching is a fairly straightforward business and that, provided one has a good command of what one is teaching, learning to teach should just be a matter of practice. Our own rationale for a predominantly school-based approach is very different. It is that the task of classroom teaching is so complex that one cannot afford to use very much of the limited time available for learning about anything other than classroom teaching; that the best place to do most of one's learning about the complexities of classroom teaching is where that teaching is happening; and that the best people from whom to learn most about these complexities are those who are engaged with them on a daily basis.

We have suggested that the most important task of ITE is to enable beginning teachers to develop classroom teaching expertise; that an important second task is to prepare them for a situation in which they will need to go on learning, primarily on their own initiative and on the basis of their own classroom and professional experience, thus generating new elements of their practice; and that the third important task is to prepare beginning teachers to engage intelligently with ideas for innovation and improvement.

We noted that the move in England in the late twentieth century towards a more school-based ITE has led to widespread satisfaction with what is being achieved in relation to the first of these tasks: beginning teachers do generally seem to acquire basic practical competence. We do, however, have doubts about the adequacy of this improvement. These doubts stem first from the overwhelming dominance within this new regime of a concern for 'standards' (Department for Education and Skills 2002; Furlong *et al.* 2000) as a way of thinking about quality in ITE, and a consequent neglect of the ITE curriculum and of the quality of student teachers' learning experiences. Our second major reservation relates to the simplistic and entirely untheorized understanding of classroom teaching competence and expertise that informs these 'standards'. In our view, the planning of high-quality ITE is impossible if one has not first reflected in an informed way on the nature of classroom teaching expertise. For that reason, Chapter 2 of this book is devoted very largely to a consideration of what research can teach us about teaching expertise.

As regards our suggested second and third tasks for ITE, preparing student teachers to go on learning, primarily on their own initiative and on the basis of their own classroom experience, and preparing them to respond intelligently to proposed innovations, the available evidence (e.g. Furlong *et al.* 2000) suggests that the current English arrangements frequently do not help student teachers to learn how to critically evaluate and improve their own practice. On balance, it seems that there is still enormous room for improvement in this new more school-based approach to ITE.

It is not difficult to understand why this is so. The shift to a primarily school-based approach to ITE was not accompanied by any suggestion that those involved were faced by a major task of rethinking the methods by which beginning teachers could best learn how to teach. Nobody – in schools or elsewhere – was asked to consider how the enormous potential advantages of a largely school-based approach to ITE could most fully be realized. Far less were people given the necessary time and resources. And so, as a result, we have a move back towards something like an apprenticeship system, but of a kind which minimizes the changes from the twentieth-century theory-into-practice system. Much the most significant change, apart from that of location, is that school-based teacher educators (mentors) have largely taken over the role that teacher educators from HEIs (supervisors) used to fulfil in schools. Mentors are very well placed to fulfil that role much more effectively; but it is not at all apparent that they have been asked or encouraged to develop this or indeed new roles and strategies in ways that take full advantage of their positions, knowledge and expertise. If this had been done, and done thoughtfully, we are in no doubt that very much more success would have been achieved in relation to all three of our suggested tasks.

There have been sustained efforts by successive English governments since the early 1990s to introduce even more thoroughly school-based programmes, through various initiatives such as School-Centred Initial Teacher Training schemes, Training Schools and Graduate Teaching Programmes. But however useful such initiatives may or may not have been for teacher recruitment, the evidence (e.g. HMI 2003, 2005, 2006) does not suggest that any of these schemes have led to significant innovation in terms of the nature of student teachers' learning experiences in schools.

The main aim of this book is to contribute to the rethinking work that so unfortunately was not undertaken earlier. What teaching and learning strategies are likely to be realistic and useful elements of a largely school-based ITE programme that effectively contributes to the three major learning tasks that we have identified? What principles and considerations should inform the planning and construction of the school-based components of ITE curricula?

In Chapter 2 we shall consider more fully, on the basis of previous research, what it is that student teachers need to learn. In Chapter 3, we shall consider the rich range of opportunities which schools and practising teachers can provide for beginning teachers' professional learning; and we shall consider too what we know about beginning teachers' learning processes. Finally, we shall identify a set of broad principles which should, we believe, inform the planning of the school-based component of ITE curricula.

Part B (Chapters 4 and 5) will then be concerned with exploring in practice what is involved in planning and successfully implementing one important component of the new kind of school-based ITE curriculum which we envisage.

Chapters 6 and 7 form the third and final part of the book in which we shall consider the kind of school-based ITE curriculum that is needed, and that could realistically be developed. In Chapter 6 we shall first reflect on what can be learned more broadly from the successes of the initiative described in Part B and from the difficulties it faced. We shall then re-examine and develop further the framework of principles outlined in Chapter 3, offering a set of general organizing ideas for the construction of a school-based ITE curriculum of high quality. In Chapter 7, we shall focus on more particular ideas, outlining specific elements that could contribute to a planned school-based curriculum. The book will end with an exploration of some of the considerations and processes involved in developing the kind of curriculum we are advocating.

2 Understanding the practice of good classroom teaching

Different approaches to initial teacher education reflect in large measure the different goals and purposes which are prioritized. Such different goals as that teachers should be generally well-educated people, that they should have a good understanding of educational theory, or that they should be competent classroom practitioners have been prioritized at different times and in different places. We have already made clear our view that priority in initial professional teacher education should be given to the classroom teaching expertise of beginning teachers, including both their initial competence and also their capacity for continuing development through their own personal learning and through their critical engagement with suggested innovations. What such priorities imply for the nature of teacher education programmes will depend heavily on how good practice in classroom teaching is to be understood; and so it is to an exploration of this issue that this chapter is devoted.

How good practice in teaching is best understood is a highly contested matter. To some degree differences in ways of understanding good practice tend to reflect the positions people occupy and their needs in these different positions. Thus teachers themselves have to find ways of understanding their lives in classrooms which are realistic and sustainable and which also give them some sense of satisfaction in what they do. On the other hand, politicians and educational managers often feel a need to understand good practice in ways that allow them to hold teachers accountable for the quality of their practice; and that can lead to very different ways of thinking about good practice. One might expect researchers to have less of a vested interest since their task is simply to understand good practice, but they have an obligation to give accounts of practice which are explicit and which make sense to different audiences;

and even such obligations can lead to distinctive ways of representing good practice.

Fortunately, there are other and more objective grounds on which understandings of good practice can be evaluated. Important among these are the quality of the evidence available to support any one way of making sense of good practice, the comprehensiveness with which it takes account of the available evidence, and the coherence of the account of good practice which it offers. Furthermore, while it is tempting to see different ways of understanding good practice as conflicting and mutually incompatible, it is perhaps likely that a best understanding will result from drawing on the strengths of several different approaches.

In what follows, we shall outline the nature, strengths and limitations of three successive ways of thinking about good practice. We shall try to show how the strengths of each can be harnessed, and the limitations overcome, by assimilating each to its successor.

Good practice as what demonstrably 'works'

The simplest way of thinking about classroom teaching is to view it as a task with fairly obvious goals, with the problem being to identify and to pursue the most effective means for achieving these goals. The goals of teaching are of course those of pupils' learning, and so good practice is directed towards optimising pupils' learning. If we can identify, describe and follow those practices which best facilitate pupils' learning, we shall be engaging in good practice.

Although that is the simple core of this way of understanding good practice, everyone would surely agree that usefully implementing this way of thinking would be a very complex undertaking. The goals of classroom teaching are never straightforward: the relative importance to be put on the many different goals of any curriculum, on immediate learning as opposed to developing interest and enthusiasm for learning, on social as opposed to academic educational goals, and on the diverse learning needs of the different members of any class, all present teachers with frequent tensions and dilemmas. Furthermore, in order to pursue such learning goals effectively, one needs to identify and to attain many key intermediate goals, for example of order, attention, motivation, review of prior knowledge and especially of establishing appropriate ways of working.

Nor is it obvious that there is always one best way of achieving any given goal. If there is one best way, it is likely in many cases to be best only within a particular range of teaching circumstances – a particular age group, accustomed to particular school and classroom practices, with particular kinds of prior achievements and attitudes towards learning, dealing with a particular kind of subject content. Circumstances, experience suggests, are likely to be important in determining what will work best.

There is also a need to recognize that teaching, like other social activities, cannot be reduced simply to means and ends. The ways in which teachers act towards their pupils are not, and could not be, merely instrumental towards the achievement of goals. Embedded in classroom teaching activities are values – relating, for example, to human relationships, subject disciplines and institutional norms – which have to be understood less in instrumental terms than as expressing what is cared about by teachers and within the school, subject, professional and local cultures which inform their practice.

The extent of these difficulties should not, however, be exaggerated. There is a high level of consensus among teachers and other interested parties, we believe, about educationally valuable goals and also about necessary intermediate goals, such as orderly classrooms and motivated pupils. There is probably greater diversity among teachers about what they believe to be effective means for achieving these goals; but that is surely something on which research ought to provide guidance.

How much help can research offer on this? Especially during the 1970s, there was a great deal of research concerned with precisely such questions, especially in the United States, but also in the UK and elsewhere. Since then such research has been rather less popular; and, as Hargreaves (1996), for example, has complained, in the UK there has been very little research indeed of this kind, concerned to identify effective patterns of classroom teaching and learning, during the last twenty years. Why has that been?

It is not that research of this kind was unproductive. For example, in one authoritative review, Brophy and Good (1986) summarize some of the replicated and reliable findings concerned with patterns of classroom teaching which maximize pupils' achievements. Those relating to 'giving information' are summarized as follows:

> *Structuring* Achievement is maximised when teachers not only actively present material, but structure it by beginning with overviews, advance organisers, or review of objectives; outlining the content and signalling transitions between lesson parts; calling attention to main ideas; summarising subparts of the lesson as it proceeds; and reviewing main ideas at the end. Organising concepts and analogies help learners link the new to the already familiar. Overviews and outlines help them to develop learning sets to use in assimilating the content as it unfolds. Rule–example–rule patterns and internal summaries tie specific information items to integrative concepts. Summary reviews integrate and reinforce the learning of major points. Taken together, these structuring elements not only facilitate memory for the information but allow for its apprehension as an integrated whole with recognition of the relationship between parts.

Redundancy/Sequencing Achievement is higher when information is presented with a degree of redundancy, particularly in the form of repeating and reviewing general rules and key concepts. ... In general, structuring, redundancy and sequencing affect what is learned from listening to verbal presentations, even though they are not powerful determinants of learning from reading text.

Clarity Clarity of presentation is a consistent correlate of achievement, whether measured by high-inference ratings or low-inference indicators such as absence of 'vagueness terms' or 'mazes'. Knowledge about factors that detract from clarity needs to be supplemented with knowledge about positive factors that enhance clarity (for example, what kinds of analogies and examples facilitate learning, and why) but in any case, students learn more from clear presentations than from unclear ones.

Enthusiasm Enthusiasm, usually measured by high-inference ratings, appears to be more related to affective than to cognitive outcomes. Nevertheless, it often correlates with achievement, especially for older students.

Pacing/Wait-Time 'Pacing' usually refers to the solicitation aspect of lessons, but it can also refer to the rate of presentation of information during initial structuring. Although few studies have addressed the matter directly, data from the early grades seem to favour rapid pacing, both because this helps maintain lesson momentum (and thus minimises inattention) and because such pacing seems to suit the basic skills learning that occurs at these grade levels. Typically, teacher presentations are short and interspersed with recitation or practice opportunities. At higher grade levels, however, where teachers make longer presentations on more abstract or complex content, it may be necessary to move at a slower pace, allowing time for each new concept to 'sink in'. At least, this seems to be the implication of wait-time data reported ...

(Brophy and Good 1986: 362)

Such findings surely offer a very valuable guide to good practice. More research, which provided more such authoritative guidance, would surely be useful. Some recent commentators would go much further and suggest that it is exactly this kind of research that is needed if good practice is to be shared and to develop:

Specifically, I believe we need to
 (1) Develop the technology of teaching by more research, in order to give us the teacher behaviours that are appropriate for children of different ages, subjects, catchment areas and districts ...

(2) We need to ensure that all preservice teachers receive the technology of their profession, as would any other group of professionals. ... All teachers must practise these effective methods or the consequences are disastrous.

(Reynolds 1998: 28)

There are probably few teachers or researchers who would share Reynolds' view, but it offers a good starting point from which to consider the limitations of the 'what works' approach to good practice, as well as its neglected merits.

The idea of a 'technology of teaching', with scientifically established rules of good practice which teachers would be obliged to follow, is not attractive. But the idea is not simply unattractive; it is also wrong. Its success would have to depend on there being a body of totally reliable and generalizable scientific laws by which one could predict the effects upon pupils' thinking and learning of whatever teachers did. Not only would this body of scientific knowledge have to be immense, to take account of all the complex variations in the tasks and circumstances with which teachers are faced; it would also have to be as precise and reliable as, for example, the Newtonian physics which underpins civil and mechanical engineering. But because pupils are thinking, creative and imaginative beings, all living in distinctive and constantly developing cultural contexts, we know that they are not, and could not be, that predictable. Generalizations such as those of Brophy and Good quoted above offer, we believe, useful guidance for teachers, but with the following reservations:

1 They are generalizations about what is probable, telling us what is likely to happen, other things being equal.
2 They are generalizations formulated in very abstract terms, and therefore need a great deal of interpretation in order to be useful in a specific context.
3 They are generalizations derived from research in specific cultural contexts and therefore, while probably generally valid for most other contexts, are not necessarily so.
4 They are generalizations about the thinking and activities of human beings, who sometimes decide to behave differently.

We certainly do not have here, then, a basis for a 'technology of teaching'. What we have (and could usefully have much more of) is evidence about how the practices of teachers seem to make systematic differences to the attainments of their pupils. It is evidence about good practice, evidence from which teachers, and especially beginning teachers, could very usefully learn. It is not, however, and could not be, a comprehensive basis on which to describe or prescribe good practice. And it has probably been the recognition that such evidence could only tell a limited part of the story that, more than anything else, has led British educational researchers in recent decades to do very little research of this kind. We believe that this is unfortunate, and we hope that more of this very useful kind of research will be done in future.

The recognition that it was not going to be possible to develop a science of teaching, through which good practice could be established as a set of laws connecting appropriate teaching behaviour to high pupil achievement, was sensible, even though it unfortunately led researchers to lose interest in research on 'what works' for the next quarter-century. The good outcome was that, recognizing that what lay behind effective patterns of classroom teaching and learning were thinking teachers and pupils, researchers turned their attention to trying to understand the thinking involved in good practice.

Good practice as expert pedagogical thinking

There has during the last twenty-five years been a great deal of useful research into teachers' thinking. Some of that research has been undertaken with the specific purpose of identifying characteristics of expert teachers' thinking, frequently in direct comparison with novice teachers' thinking. It is on such research that we shall focus in this section, before going on in the next section to look at some of the research on teachers' thinking undertaken with rather different purposes in mind.

Much of the research comparing the thinking of expert and novice teachers has drawn deliberately on other work within a cognitive psychology tradition aimed at understanding expert thinking in other contexts (e.g. Chase and Simon 1973; Chi et al. 1990). One important and influential programme of this kind, directed by David Berliner and Kathy Carter at the University of Arizona, reflected that tradition also in that most of the research was focused on carefully designed and controlled laboratory tasks on which the performances of expert, beginning and totally inexperienced high school teachers were compared. The experts were teachers nominated as excellent by school principals and whose classroom teaching was judged to be excellent by knowledgeable observers. Berliner (1987), for example, describes a simulated teaching task in which the teachers were asked to take over another teacher's task in mid-year. Having been given information of various realistic kinds about the class and what had been done with them, they were asked to plan the first two days' classes, to take any notes that would be useful and to prepare for a debriefing. The experienced teachers were much more selective in the information of which they took note, not for example showing interest in individual pupils, but rather assimilating the given information to rich existing schemas about types of students, and about classroom activities and events; and their attention seemed to be much more functionally focused on what they needed to know in order to select and develop appropriate types of instructional plans for pupils' work, again derived from existing schemas.

Another task, concerned with visual information processing (Carter *et al.* 1988), showed a similar distinctively selective focus on classroom work systems by experts as they viewed a series of classroom slides. They alone reacted quickly and predominantly to stimuli indicating whether or not pupils were working well. In a third example of this team's research (Sabers *et al.* 1991), expert, beginning and novice teachers were asked to express their thoughts as they viewed simultaneously three television monitors, each focusing on a different work group of a junior high science class. The aim here was to simulate the simultaneity, multidimensionality and immediacy of classroom events (cf. Doyle 1980). Experts were found to be able to monitor and interpret events in more detail and more analytically. They attended to the multidimensional nature of the classroom differently, dividing their attention more evenly across the three monitors, attending more to the instructional language used, and focusing more on the possible causes of and possible solutions for inappropriate behaviour, and less on the behaviour itself.

Much of the research comparing expert and novice teachers has been more focused on subject-specific aspects of teaching. An outstanding contributor to such work (on mathematics teaching) has been Gaea Leinhardt of the University of Pittsburgh. Like Berliner and Carter, Leinhardt's work draws explicitly on cognitive psychology, but her research has been on real classroom teaching, thus discarding both the artificiality and the control offered by laboratory studies. Her selection of experts has also been done differently, the criterion used being that of consistently high levels of attainment in mathematics by their pupils. We quote an example of her summary of conclusions from one paper about expert elementary school teachers of mathematics who teach in a relatively didactic style:

> Expert teachers use many complex cognitive skills. This paper will focus on only a few of them. Expert teachers weave together elegant lessons which are made up of many smaller lesson segments. These segments, in turn, depend on small, socially scripted pieces of behaviour called routines that teachers teach, participate in and utilise extensively. Expert teachers have a rich repertoire of instructional scripts which are updated and revised throughout their personal history of teaching. Teachers are precise, flexible and parsimonious planners. That is, they plan what they need to but not what they already know and do automatically. Experts plan better than novices do in the sense of efficiency and in terms of the sharable trace that they operate from. From that more global plan – usually of a unit of material – they take an agenda for a lesson. The key elements of the agenda are available as mental notes the teacher has before teaching. The agenda serves not only to set up and co-ordinate the lesson segments but also to lay out the strategy for actually explaining the mathematical topic under consideration. The

ensuing explanations are developed from a system of goals and actions that the teacher has for ensuring that the students understand the particular piece of mathematics.

(Leinhardt 1988: 47–8)

Leinhardt's elaboration of these and other concepts, based on the observation and videotaping of teachers at work, and detailed interviews with them, and especially of the nature of the explanations offered and of the thinking underlying them, gives a rich insight into expert teaching of mathematics in elementary schools. Much other interesting and useful research, contrasting the thinking and practices of expert and novice teachers of different subjects, has been reported, a large proportion of it emanating from Shulman's (1986) emphasis on the importance of what he has called 'pedagogical content knowledge' (e.g. Ball and McDiarmid 1990; Grossman 1990).

Some of the most interesting research on expert teachers' thinking and practice has derived from a concern with the ecology of classroom teaching. From this perspective, the nature of the expertise required for classroom teaching derives in large measure from the conditions of teachers' work. Most strikingly, as Dreeben (1970: 51) put it, 'The most obvious characteristic of schools is their division into isolated classrooms, each containing aggregates of pupils under the direction of one teacher. This fact itself determines much of what happens in classrooms'. It was from such a perspective that Kounin (1970) conducted his groundbreaking study of the expertise involved in classroom management. He found that teacher qualities associated with high levels of pupil work involvement were 'withitness' ('having eyes in the back of one's head'), 'overlapping' (being able to attend to several things at once), group rather than individual focus, and maintaining momentum and a flow of classroom events.

Doyle (1980) has argued that intrinsic features of the classroom environment, which create constant pressures that shape the task of teaching, include the following:

1 Multidimensionality, which refers to the large quantity and diversity of events and tasks in classrooms.
2 Simultaneity, which refers to the fact that many things happen at once in classrooms.
3 Immediacy, which refers to the rapid pace of classroom events.
4 Unpredictability, which refers to the fact that classroom events often take unexpected turns.
5 Publicness, which refers to the fact that classrooms are public places and that events, especially those involving the teacher, are often observed by a large number of the students.
6 History, which refers to the fact that classes meet for five days a week for several months and thus accumulate a common set of experiences, routines and norms which provide a basis for conducting activities.

One of the main foci of research on expert teaching from this perspective has understandably been on the task of creating and sustaining order, and specifically on 'work systems'. Doyle (1986) suggests that the key to order in classrooms is programmes of action which make clear the kind of order appropriate for specific periods of time and which direct pupils along identified paths. Carter (1990: 302–3) summarizes the expertise which research has shown to be necessary for successful classroom management in these terms:

> First, successful managers, defined by indicators of work involve-
> ment and achievement, design sensible and context-sensitive work
> systems for their classes. In other words, they prepare in advance for
> how students will be organised to accomplish work and what rules
> and procedures will govern movements about the room and routine
> access to resources and materials. Second, successful managers com-
> municate their work systems clearly to pupils through explanations,
> examples, practice and feedback. Finally, successful managers mon-
> itor classroom events to make sure that the work system ... is oper-
> ating within reasonable limits and to notice early signs of potential
> disruptions. By monitoring the flow of classroom activity, they
> reduce the need for frequent reprimands and other interventions
> and maximise the opportunity for students to engage in working
> with the curriculum.

These, then, are some examples of research designed to offer a more adequate understanding of classroom teaching expertise by studying not simply what successful teachers do in classrooms but also the thinking underlying it. It is clear that such research need not limit itself to a focus on teachers' thinking, but can fruitfully combine a detailed focus on teachers' thinking with an equally detailed focus on their classroom practice. It is also clear, we hope, that the findings from such research can provide insightful, sensible and useful guidance for teachers aiming to develop their expertise; and that the limited examples which we have mentioned offer only a small sample of the useful guidance that such research can already provide, far less of what it could potentially provide in future.

Good practice as professional craft knowledge-in-use

So far, we have looked at examples of the research on teachers' thinking which has sought to identify the distinctive characteristics of expert teacher thinking. Much research into teachers' thinking, however, has been undertaken with the equally appropriate purpose of understanding more adequately the kinds of thinking which generally inform teachers' classroom practice. Such understanding does not necessarily provide any guidance as to what is good practice, but it certainly can help one to think more intelligently about good practice and especially to avoid making false assumptions about it. Clark and Peterson (1986), for example, reviewed a number of investigations of teachers' classroom decision-making during interactive teaching and concluded that several of the preconceptions which had informed earlier models, including their own, had been misconceived. These misguided assumptions had included, for example, the idea that decisions would generally involve choices among alternatives and the assumption that decisions would generally be provoked by judgements about pupils and their behaviour. Similarly, their review of research on experienced teachers' planning prior to interactive teaching led them to conclude that the widely prescribed linear rational planning model, according to which decisions about learning objectives lead on to decisions about content, activities, and so on, was not generally followed by teachers.

In our discussion of teachers' practical thinking, we shall follow Jackson (1968) in distinguishing teachers' thinking in the 'preactive' phase of teaching, when they are not actively engaged in the classroom, from their thinking in the 'interactive' phase when they are so engaged. The importance of this distinction should not be exaggerated, since there is of course a very high degree of similarity and continuity in teachers' thinking between the two phases. Nonetheless, there is one important difference in that during the preactive phase teachers can think in a more deliberative way – on occasion, for example, engaging in collaborative thinking and planning with colleagues – than is generally possible during classroom teaching. Schön's (1983) accounts of professionals' problem-formulating and problem-solving of the kind that he describes as 'reflection-in-practice' are much more reminiscent of teachers' thinking during this preactive phase than of any thinking that teachers can commonly do during classroom teaching.

This preactive or planning phase is clearly important for teachers, precisely because it is then that they do have time for deliberative thinking. The findings of research on teachers' thinking while planning have been well summarized by Calderhead (1996), who concludes that 'research on teachers' planning has taken several different methodological approaches but consistently has highlighted six main features of the processes involved' (Calderhead 1996: 713). These six features are:

1 *Planning occurs at different levels.* Teachers plan on different time-scales, such as yearly, termly, for particular units, weekly, daily and for particular lessons. 'Teachers' planning, therefore, … may be seen … as a continuous process of re-examining, refining and adding to previous decisions' (Calderhead 1996: 714)
2 *Planning is mostly informal.* Teachers generally do not find it helpful to produce formal written plans. They plan, often at odd times of the day, by mentally focusing on issues that need their attention. We have

already noted how Leinhardt (1988: 47) described teachers as 'parsi-
monious planners ... they plan what they need to but not what they
already know and do automatically.'

3 *Planning is creative.* Teachers' planning rarely follows a 'rational' model,
working from specified objectives to activities designed to attain them.
Instead, teachers tend to look for good ideas, for ways of seeing the task
or for formulating and then solving a problem, and then for ways of
translating these ideas into workable classroom activities.

4 *Planning is knowledge-based.* Teachers need to be able to draw on many
different kinds of knowledge and to be able to orchestrate these different kinds of knowledge in the process of planning.

5 *Planning must allow flexibility.* Calderhead suggests that 'a feature of
effective planning may be to prepare teachers to be able to adapt
planned activities to suit a variety of situations that might emerge
(Borko and Livingstone, 1989; Clark and Yinger, 1987)'. He suggests
that it is because 'experienced teachers ... possess a large repertoire of
plans in memory – clear conceptions of how particular types of lessons
are acted out, or of how particular topics are taught ... [that] it may be
possible for them to be more adaptable to particular contexts'
(Calderhead 1996: 714).

6 *Planning occurs within a practical and ideological context.* Among the various factors that are likely to influence the nature of teachers' planning
are policy expectations at school, district or national levels, the text-
books or other materials they are using, and their own conceptions of
the subject they are teaching.

Teachers' thinking during interactive teaching is necessarily framed by
decisions made in their planning; and as we have already suggested, there
is a very high degree of similarity and continuity between the two phases
in teachers' thinking. Thus, all the above features of thinking in the preactive phase – continuity with previous decisions, informality, creativity,
orchestration of many kinds of knowledge, flexibility and responsiveness
to context – also characterize teachers' thinking during the interactive
phase. We want to focus especially here, however, on teachers' thinking
while engaged in interactive teaching, because it is this thinking which is
necessarily most distinctive and because any adequate consideration of
good practice in teaching depends crucially on understanding the distinctive features of this kind of thinking. Perhaps most obviously, such thinking is tacit, in that teachers tend to be fully engaged in overt activities
involving interaction with pupils and have neither a need nor an opportunity to articulate to themselves the thinking embedded in their overt
actions. There has been considerable controversy as to how best to characterize this tacit thinking. Some (e.g. Clark and Yinger 1987) have
argued that it is helpful to construe teachers' thinking, even during this
interactive phase, as involving the use of what Schön (1983) describes as
knowledge-in-practice for routine tasks and also occasional reflection-in-

practice for more problematic tasks. Others, following Dreyfus and Dreyfus (1986), suggest that what most clearly distinguishes expert professionals from others is that they have reached a stage where they can respond effectively to patterns which present themselves holistically and intuitively, without any conscious reflection at all. As we have already seen, cognitive theorists such as Leinhardt emphasize the rich repertoires of schemas and scripts which teachers gradually develop for making sense of, and acting appropriately in, the various situations which confront them. Still others, such as Olson (1992), put less emphasis on the psychology of individual expertise and stress instead the professional communities of practice, and the shared moral frameworks within which individual teachers gradually learn good practice; the emphasis here is on the classroom practice itself, with thought and action seen as inseparable facets of the same thing, rather than on thinking as something that underlies practice.

Each of these perspectives seems to us to offer useful insights; and we are not concerned to stress the merits of any one of them in contrast to the others. Our concern is rather to emphasize that there is a high level of consensus on the fact that classroom teaching does involve a great deal of tacit thinking and/or judgement, that the expertise of teachers is very closely bound up with this tacit thinking, and that in the normal course of events teachers very rarely have either the opportunity or the need to make explicit this tacit expertise.

A second important characteristic of the thinking involved in teachers' practice is that it is highly personal. The work of Clandinin and Connelly (1986; Clandinin 1985; Connelly *et al.* 1997), for example, shows very clearly how the thinking and practice of individual teachers are given coherence by the 'images' which inform them. Past experiences, present patterns of teaching and future plans are shown to be held together in personally meaningful unity, experience being continually reconstructed as personal practical knowledge of a narrative kind which in turn shapes the individual's practice. They offer as an example a primary teacher with an image of 'classroom as home', a powerful metaphor that impacts on how she perceives her work and which, therefore, affects her interactions with the children in her class, ways in which she manages the class, and the kind of physical environment she creates. A substantial body of similar research now demonstrates very clearly the individuality of the thinking embedded in teachers' practice, and how individuals' practice is given coherence by their distinctive repertoires of images and metaphors (Munby 1986; Russell *et al.* 1988; Grant 1992).

The third characteristic of teachers' practical thinking to which we wish to draw attention is its immense complexity. While a great deal of qualitative research work is now available with which we could demonstrate this point, it will be convenient for us to discuss it with reference to the research by Brown and McIntyre (1993) which provided the starting point for the research described in Chapters 4 and 5 of this book. Brown and McIntyre's study focused on the nature of 'good teaching' of four primary school teachers and 12 secondary school teachers, 'good teaching' defined as aspects of the teaching judged to be good on the particular occasion by the individual teacher and his or her pupils. Each teacher was observed teaching a unit of work of 2–6 hours' duration. Following each lesson and again at the end of the unit, the teachers were asked to talk about 'those aspects of their teaching which had particularly pleased them, they felt they had done well or had given them satisfaction' (Brown and McIntyre 1993: 32). The researchers described the rich and varied ways in which the teachers evaluated and talked about their teaching in terms of four main generalizable and interrelated concepts, as shown in Figure 2.1.

Figure 2.1 The concepts which teachers use in evaluating their own teaching (Brown and McIntyre 1993)

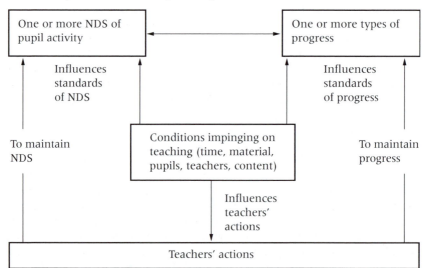

The teachers evaluated their teaching in relation to various types of progress by the pupils and to the attainment and maintenance of steady states of pupil activity that they had learned to recognize as appropriate for particular kinds of lesson or task – summarized by the researchers as 'normal desirable states of pupil activity' (NDSs). The teachers' actions and the standards they felt were appropriate for evaluating the extent to which their goals were achieved were both profoundly affected by a variety of conditions, the most numerous of which were those relating to pupils. While each teacher appeared to structure their teaching in terms of a quite limited set of individual goals (NDSs and types of progress), each seemed also to have a large repertoire of kinds of action which could be taken in order to attain these goals, with the actions used on specific occasions being chosen according to the incidence of an even larger number of potentially relevant conditions.

Following the initial study of the 16 teachers, the researchers carried out a more detailed study of the teaching of five of them, with the aim of refining their initial understandings. They found that teachers rarely took single actions to attain single goals, but rather that goals and actions were interdependent in complex ways:

> Actions would ... be chosen with several goals in mind, and several actions might be taken with the same goal in mind. Goals, and therefore the actions to attain them, might be dependent one on another, or mutually compatible, or in conflict ... teachers were choosing actions from extensive repertoires in view of a large number of possible conditions; they were also choosing various kinds of combinations of actions to attain various kinds of combinations of goals.
>
> (Brown and McIntyre 1993: 112)

Studies such as that by Brown and McIntyre do not help us to distinguish between expert teachers and others. They do tell us, however, that teaching expertise must lie in very subtle judgements about what standards to set, what actions to take and what combinations of goals can realistically be sought in the light of a multitude of potentially relevant conditions. We also know that these complex judgements are made more or less instantaneously, that they are made tacitly, and that they are made by different teachers according to their own distinctively personal 'images' of classroom teaching.

This leads us to a very simple, but enormously important, conclusion about understanding good practice in classroom teaching. It is this: teaching expertise is so subtle, so complex, so individual and so context-related that it can only adequately be understood in relation to particular practice, not in general. This means that research-based knowledge about teaching can take us only a limited way towards an understanding of good practice. It can, as we have seen in the previous two sections of this chapter, offer a great volume of very valuable generalized insights into expert practice. But since at the core of such expert practice is the need to make the kinds of subtle judgements we have described about how to act in unique situations, knowledge construed in such general terms must always fall short of offering a full understanding of, or guide to, expertise. As we promised earlier, and as we shall explain more fully shortly, we shall argue that the kinds of research-based views of expertise outlined previously will need to be taken into account and used; but our central assertion at this stage is that expertise must basically be understood in a way that takes account of the particularity of practice, as research-based knowledge cannot do.

We are, then, suggesting that teaching expertise must be understood as it is found, embedded in the practice of individual teachers. The term we use to characterize this way of understanding expertise is *professional craft knowledge*, with the following intended connotations:

- This is a kind of knowledge embedded in everyday practice.
- Each individual teacher will have a distinctive craft knowledge, although many features will be common across teachers.
- The teacher craftsperson can be expected to draw on an individual repertoire of craft knowledge for appropriate use in each specific situation.

Craft knowledge can, however, have other connotations, which we do not intend. For example, it is used by some (e.g. Elliott 1989) with pejorative connotations, craft knowledge being contrasted unfavourably with other more reflective and artistic kinds of professional knowledge-in-use. We also need to distinguish our meaning clearly from that on which Tom and Valli (1990) quote Scheffler:

> In discussing teaching as a practical art analogous to cooking or coaching, Scheffler (1960) echoes the concerns of many about the craft, or practical arts, tradition. This tradition, he notes, generates rules of practice out of knowledge that is derived from 'the heritage of common sense, or folklore, or the accumulated experience of practitioners' (p. 73). … he argues that we need a scientific basis for teaching so that we can increasingly 'judge and choose procedures on the basis of theoretical understanding, rather than their mere conformity to cookbook specifications embodied in the lore transmitted by previous generations' (p. 74).

If, like Scheffler, we were to understand craft knowledge as 'rules of practice', we should be equally dismissive of it. For us, however, professional craft knowledge is not rules of practice, but is instead all the complex, largely tacit knowledge that informs the contextualized professional judgements made by individual teachers in their everyday practice. Tom and Valli (1990) rightly warn that there is little consensus about what 'craft knowledge' means and that there is therefore a need for great care in using the term. Our own meaning is much closer to that of Tom himself, who in an earlier book, *Teaching as a Moral Craft* (1984), attempted very impressively to describe and to celebrate the sophisticated art of teaching.

We also, however, need to distinguish our view of how professional craft knowledge relates to expertise from another point of view which has been highly influential. It was McNamara and Desforges (1978) who in the UK were most influential in leading others to see the importance of professional craft knowledge. It was they who inspired the work of Brown and McIntyre (1993), for example. What McNamara and Desforges were advocating at that time was the 'objectification' of teachers' craft knowledge, the 'capturing' by researchers of this knowledge in an abstracted propositional form, which could then be shared easily with others. It was with such an aspiration that Brown and McIntyre (1993) initially undertook their work. Their conclusion and our view now, however, is that most of the expertise embedded in professional craft knowledge, and especially the subtle, fluent processes of making judgements in and for unique situations, would inevitably be lost in such abstraction and codification. It is true that we lack an adequate, or shared, theoretical understanding of the nature of that knowledge; and studies like those of Tom (1984) and Brown and McIntyre (1993) are important in helping us towards better understandings. Our claim, however, is that even if we had a much better theoretical understanding of professional craft knowledge, the subtle, personal particularity of that knowledge is such that it can never adequately be coded or formulated as a body of propositional knowledge. It is, and must remain, knowledge-in-use.

It is, then, primarily in terms of professional craft knowledge, thus understood, that expert teaching must in our view be understood. Yet in making that assertion, we are still left with a problem in that, as we have made clear, our general account of professional craft knowledge has not offered any way of distinguishing between expert teachers and others. So far as research has revealed, the practices of expert teachers and those of other reasonably experienced teachers tend generally to share the features of tacit, immediate, personal, highly complex and particular judgements and actions which characterize professional craft knowledge. These seem to be essential features of expert classroom teaching, but not distinguishing features. It is, we believe, appropriate to construe expert teaching in terms of professional craft knowledge-in-use, but this is not sufficient as a way of identifying expert teaching. What else is necessary and possible?

The answer would seem to be that, in order to assess the level of expertise involved in any person's practice as a teacher, one has to ask critical questions about that practice. At first sight that may seem like going back to the beginning again; but it is not. Instead of looking for a blueprint for expertise, and asking how well an individual teacher's practice fits that blueprint, we are saying that it is first important to recognize the individuality of the practice, and then to ask critical questions about it. What goals is the practice, on any given occasion, directed towards attaining? How appropriate and significant are these goals? How effectively are they achieved? How significant, given the context, is this achievement? Are the goals directly concerned with pupil learning? Are they construed in terms of all the pupils' learning? Are they successfully attained for all the pupils? If not directly concerned with pupil learning, how clearly and persuasively do they indirectly contribute to pupils' learning? In so far as positive answers to such questions appear merited, then this seems likely to be expert practice.

Among such critical questions, we should place a high level of importance on those deriving from the two other conceptions of good practice and expert teaching which we considered earlier, those which involved research aimed at identifying the classroom practices and thinking distinguishing expert teachers from others. How does any given practice relate to research findings about effective patterns of teacher and pupil classroom activity, and to teachers' ways of classroom thinking, relevant to the attainment of goals such as those being sought? If the practice is not consistent with what these research findings would suggest, are there good reasons for this? And, given such divergence, is there strong contrary evidence that this nonetheless is indeed good practice? Thus the kinds of propositional generalizations which research can offer about good practice, although themselves not adequate for the generation of good practice, can contribute significantly to the critical thinking through which it is possible to recognize some cases of professional craft knowledge-in-use as being expert practice.

Conclusion

We have concentrated in this chapter on articulating a point of view about the knowledge necessary for expert teaching. We have suggested that such knowledge is necessarily professional craft knowledge, including the knowledge used by teachers in their planning, but also the subtle, tacit knowledge embedded in the practice of experienced teachers, and much too complex to be abstracted from that context and expressed in propositional form. On the other hand, we have made clear our view that not all professional craft knowledge is expert knowledge, and that a claim that any particular teacher's practice reflects expertise can be sustained only by subjecting that practice to critical examination. Furthermore, while research-based generalizations about effective teaching practices or about expert teachers' thinking cannot on their own provide definitive knowledge about how to teach well, such research-based knowledge should play a very important and useful part in the process of judging claims of expertise.

This is not, we recognize, a tidy, complete or even very satisfying answer to the question of what classroom teaching expertise involves, far less that of what the beginning teacher needs to learn. It is above all an open answer in that, while we believe it does offer some important guidance, it also leaves room both for much more to be discovered and for many different specific answers. Although we very firmly wish to reject an uncritical acceptance of all claims to expertise, we equally recognize that good practice will be different in important respects in different cultural contexts, for different purposes, for different learners, under different conditions, and even at different stages in any teacher's professional learning. And even for any one specific situation, there will often be more than one equally good way of teaching. Furthermore, if our schools are to improve as they ought to, new kinds of teaching expertise will need to be developed during the coming decades: there are no grounds for complacency about our present performance.

Nonetheless, the view of teaching expertise which we have offered suggests some very important premises for our consideration of what ITE should involve:

- It will be primarily in the practical contexts of schools and classrooms that student teachers will be able to learn good practice as teachers.
- There are, however, very important research-based kinds of knowledge which it will be vital for student teachers to acquire.
- Almost certainly the primary source from which student teachers can learn is the craft knowledge of experienced teachers.
- Since the craft knowledge of experienced teachers is largely tacit and embedded in their practice, they may have to work quite hard to make it accessible to student teachers.
- There is a danger that both experienced teachers and student teachers may content themselves with the latter gaining access to only the more superficial elements of teachers' craft knowledge, thereby neglecting the rich veins hidden underneath.
- Good practice will not be developed by student teachers through learning any easily accessible standard practices.
- Student teaching can only be the first phase of a long process of developing classroom teaching expertise.
- Since classroom teaching expertise involves a very different kind of knowledge from that which student teachers are accustomed to learning in their academic studies, they are likely to need considerable help in learning how to learn it.
- It is not obvious that we have inherited carefully and appropriately conceived ways of helping student teachers to learn classroom teaching expertise.

In Chapter 1 we suggested that priority in initial professional teacher education should be given to three tasks relating to the classroom teaching expertise of beginning teachers:

- the development of an initial level of teaching competence sufficient to make them satisfactory classroom teachers;
- the development of their capacity for continuing development through their own personal professional learning; and
- the development of their capacity for critical engagement with suggested innovations in classroom practice.

What does the understanding that we have articulated of good practice in classroom teaching imply for the ways in which these three tasks should be pursued in ITE programmes?

The craft of interactive classroom teaching is dependent for its necessary fluency and for its effectiveness on very personal and intuitive judgements, on holistic schemas, on selective perceptions and on thinking and knowledge which are overwhelmingly tacit and barely conscious. The acquisition of such craft expertise is generally difficult and can be painful, since novices necessarily have to spend considerable time engaging in the task of teaching while lacking both much of the knowledge on which effectiveness depends and most of the characteristics that make fluency possible. The temptation to somehow, anyhow, and as quickly as possible achieve sufficient competence to 'get by' is enormous. 'Getting by' means performing in such a way that one's students, mentors and examiners do not make one's life even more difficult. Learning to 'get by' is possible, for example, through sustained practice and using occasional suggestions about how to meet the official 'standards'. The account by Furlong *et al.* (2000) to which we referred in the previous chapter seems to imply that this is how many student teachers currently complete their courses.

Our analysis of what good practice implies suggests, however, that such 'getting by' is quite inadequate in relation to each of our three tasks. Even the competence necessary to be a satisfactory beginning teacher depends on a level of craft knowledge that involves a modest repertoire of different ways of attaining any desirable goal, an awareness of the need to take account of many different circumstances in order to draw appropriately on this repertoire, and some initial capacity to make such judgements soundly. Even to have reached this basic level of competence, and certainly to be able to go on learning from experience, student teachers need themselves to have developed the skills, understandings and dispositions to evaluate their present practices and their craft knowledge against a wide range of practical, theoretical and research-based criteria, and to use these evaluations as a means towards further development. Similarly, they need to have learned to use the same range of criteria, confidently and constructively, in order to respond intelligently to suggested innovations.

We would emphasize, furthermore, that it is a teacher's craft knowledge, and the practical thinking that depends on it, not only the teacher's overt practice, that needs critical examination. It is of course possible and useful for observers to explore with teachers the craft knowledge and thinking that have informed the observed teaching; and such collaborative exploration is likely to be a crucial contributory factor in any beginning teacher's learning. But the people who can most usefully, most effectively and potentially most critically examine the thinking underlying teachers' practices are the individual teachers themselves. And it is this, we believe, that has to be at the heart of all three of the key tasks we have suggested for ITE. All three tasks will be successfully undertaken if and only if student teachers develop the confidence, the commitment, the analytic expertise and the habits necessary for critically examining their own developing craft knowledge and thinking. It is primarily this that will enable them to achieve a satisfactory level of initial competence, and it is this that will enable them to go on learning from their professional experience and to develop new expertise throughout their careers. Above all, such abilities and habits will enable them to examine analytically the implications of proposed innovations, and to assess the potential of these to undermine, or possibly to improve, their existing classroom practices.

The view of classroom teaching expertise that we have outlined in this chapter has one broad implication, therefore, for the construction of ITE curricula aimed at fulfilling the three tasks we have suggested. This is that the priority must be not only to enable student teachers to develop fluency and practical competence in their classroom teaching, but at the same time to teach them the understandings, skills, attitudes and habits they will need if they are to engage systematically in informed examination of their own developing craft knowledge. In Chapter 3 we shall turn our attention to a consideration of what that might involve.

3 Towards a planned school-based curriculum for ITE

The title of this chapter reflects the radically new enterprise with which we are concerned, that of developing the neglected and underdeveloped school-based component of the ITE curriculum. We are not arguing for a greater proportion of time to be given to school-based work than is currently the case in England. We are indeed quite satisfied with roughly the current proportions. Nor are we arguing about the merits of different 'routes' into teaching, such as the Graduate Teaching Programme in England, or of schools with special status, such as Training Schools. Our concern is instead with the planning of ITE curricula in schools.

We shall not be examining in detail the university-based component of ITE although, since the school-based component cannot satisfactorily be considered entirely in isolation, the nature of the university role in relation to the school context will have to receive some attention. Our central concern is with what is done within the school component, which should not be viewed as merely 'school experience' or 'school placement', but rather as a planned school-based curriculum, planned and structured with at least as much care and thought as the university-based curriculum. But of course, since schools offer a very different learning environment from universities, what that means will be something very different.

In this chapter, we shall consider the rich range of opportunities which schools and practising teachers can provide for beginning teachers' professional learning. We shall aim to identify some key principles that should inform the planning of the school-based component of ITE curricula and also some important questions that need to be explored.

We start by reminding ourselves of our conclusions from the first two chapters. In Chapter 1, we emphasized that our rationale for wanting ITE to be more school-based – in striking contrast to that of the English

Conservative government of the early 1990s – is that the task of class-room teaching is so complex that one cannot afford to use very much of the limited available time for learning about anything other than class-room teaching; that the best place to do most of one's learning about the complexities of classroom teaching is where that teaching is happening; and that the best people from whom to learn most about these complex-ities are those who are engaged with them on a daily basis. Because of the contemptuous attitude of that early 1990s government, nobody at the time was asked to consider how the enormous potential advantages of a largely school-based approach to ITE could most fully be realized. It is cer-tainly the case that teachers have replaced supervisors from higher edu-cation institutions as the people who, in the new role of 'mentor', give students feedback on their observed teaching and monitor their progress towards meeting the 'standards'. And in the intervening years, teachers in their thousands have unquestionably developed their expertise in fulfill-ing this new role, through experience, through individual and corporate reflection, and in many cases through undertaking courses of study about this specific role. Beyond this, however, there has been hardly any devel-opment of new roles and strategies for facilitating student teachers' pro-fessional learning through taking proper advantage of their presence in schools. We explained that the main task of this book is to contribute to the rethinking work that so unfortunately was not undertaken earlier.

We argued that one very important starting point in planning an ITE curriculum was the articulation of as clear as possible an understanding of the nature of classroom teaching expertise. And so that was what we sought to do in Chapter 2. We emphasized the centrality of the complex, tacit, sophisticated, situated, personal nature of the craft knowledge embedded in the practice of each individual teacher. We also emphasized the need for each beginning teacher to be supported, enabled, empow-ered and motivated to engage critically in the development of their own craft knowledge. This, we suggested, was the core prerequisite for the ful-filment of all three of the priority tasks that we suggested for ITE: the development of satisfactory initial competence; learning how to learn from professional experience; and learning how to engage intelligently with suggested innovations.

Now we need to start examining what might be involved in planning to optimize such learning. Our most central concern will be with the dis-tinctive opportunities that schools offer as contexts for learning to teach. We need first, however, to address two important preliminary themes. The first of these is one about which we have learned a great deal from research in the last quarter-century: the nature of student teachers as learners and of their learning processes. Any thinking about curriculum planning for ITE will be the poorer if it is not informed by this research-based learning. The second theme is that of 'work-based learning': school-based teacher education is of course only one example of the many work settings in which learning occurs and is relied upon. We need to consider what we can learn from knowledge about work-based learning more generally.

Focus on the learners

When beginning teachers embark on training, they are no more empty vessels than are children as they enter classrooms. It is now widely accepted that the personal knowledge and beliefs they bring with them are both complex and influential. This influence is exerted first through their individual agendas, including what they choose to learn or not to learn about teaching, and how they choose to set about that learning. These agendas – which may develop substantially or very little – are active and influential throughout the period while they are being formed as teachers. In addition, individuals' own values, preconceptions and concerns shape their interpretations of everything they encounter and the criteria by which they judge their success in every task that they undertake.

Lortie (1975) is generally given credit for having first drawn the importance of student teachers' prior learning to our attention. He plausibly suggested that it is young people's long 'apprenticeship of observation' while they are students at school that has a much greater influence on them than has their later professional education as student teachers. There has been much useful research since that time, but it has not yet determined the relative importance of 'the apprenticeship of observation' and of other prior influences on student teachers' preconceptions and agendas. As Hagger (2002: 3) notes: 'In addition to this extensive experience of teaching–learning interactions, they also come with knowledge of people, of making and sustaining relationships, and they have theories – albeit private ones – about how people do and should behave.'

Student teachers' agendas are influenced, of course, by the official expectations and demands of the professional education programmes they undertake. They make efforts to learn what they are taught and they generally seek to perform well in their assessed work. But these official expectations and demands can go with or against the grain. They can come close to coinciding with what student teachers believe they need to learn in order to become good teachers or, at the opposite extreme, they can be mere hurdles to be surmounted, without the concomitant learning having any lasting influence on their teaching.

Student teachers' agendas for what and how they should learn have tended to receive a somewhat negative press from researchers and teacher educators. That may, however, be because of their lack of match with these commentators' expectations. For example, student teachers have generally not been very ready to see their task in schools as being one of putting the theory taught in universities into practice, being more inclined to approach learning to teach as learning by doing and by trial and error (Younger *et al.* 2004). More specifically, they have typically failed to implement in schools the innovative and progressive ideas taught by university lecturers, finding it easier and more acceptable to implement the more familiar practices that they generally find being followed in schools. On the other hand, while their practice in schools has frequently been conformist, they have nonetheless often privately held on to their own individual beliefs, thus avoiding the learning that could follow from bringing their ideas into the open and putting them to the test of more experienced teachers' discussion and of practice. As Wang and Odell (2002) note, even when student teachers' agendas coincide with those of their mentors in seeing the latter's role as being primarily to give them emotional support, they have generally been seen by university-based commentators as having got it wrong.

Similarly, student teachers' preconceived beliefs about teaching have widely been perceived as problematic, being perceived both as generally wrong and as highly resistant to change. Again, this can best be understood as reflecting researchers' and teacher educators' own preconceptions about what beginning teachers should believe. For example, Wang and Odell (2002: 487) note that research findings tend to show that 'preservice teachers' beliefs about knowledge, learning and teaching often mirror the prevailing picture of teaching as a process of transferring information from teachers to students', beliefs that university-based teacher educators have typically wanted to change, yet have apparently frequently failed to change. But, as Wideen *et al.* (1998: 143) conclude, 'other studies suggest caution in accepting any generalised notion of the entry beliefs of beginning teachers'. They go on to comment:

> most recent studies on learning to teach focus on changing the beliefs of beginning teachers. However, it seems pointless to seek to change beliefs if evidence supports their enduring quality. A less problematic alternative appears to be the perspective taken by Feiman-Nemser and Buchmann (1989) and Calderhead and Robson (1991), who suggest that the alternative to changing beliefs is to build on the beliefs that already exist.
>
> (Wideen *et al.* 1998: 144)

In recent years, research reports such as that of Pendry (1997) have increasingly emphasized both the diversity of beginning teachers' preconceptions and the short-sightedness of viewing them in a negative way. Burn *et al.* (2000: 275), for example, were struck by the 'early awareness' on the part of the student teachers they studied 'of the complexity of teaching, and their capacity to take into account a wide range of impinging conditions in deciding what to do'. Reviewing such evidence, Hagger (2002: 4) concluded that student teachers' initial 'understandings and ideals cannot summarily be dismissed as naïve, misleading or unhelpful. We need to take them and their thinking very seriously.'

How much has student teachers' thinking tended to change under the influence of their training courses, and in what ways? One of the most influential theoretical accounts of how beginning teachers' thinking develops is that constructed by Fuller (1969; Fuller and Bown 1975) in terms of 'concerns'. Fuller suggested that the concerns of prospective teachers generally move 'outwards', with initial concerns about themselves and their own 'survival' gradually giving way to concerns about classroom situations and tasks, with these in turn ultimately being replaced by concerns about students and their learning.

Many research studies have explored the validity of this general picture, with somewhat conflicting results; and there has also been much questioning of the centrality given by Fuller to the notion of 'concerns'. Conway and Clark (2003), for example, point out that the Fuller model privileges concerns and anxieties over novice teachers' aspirations and hopes in a puzzling and inappropriate way. In their own study of six student teachers' developing concerns and aspirations during a one-year internship programme, Conway and Clark found no simple overall patterns, although there was an 'outward' shift away from self in the most prominent of the hopes and fears reported. These findings are similar to those of some other recent studies, such as that of Furlong and Maynard (1995), who found some tendency, though far from a universal one, for concerns to shift in the direction Fuller had predicted. Pendry (1997: 84), who found such shifts as occurred in student teachers' thinking to be much more subtle, varied and complex, sums up her own findings and also, we think, the general situation as follows:

> Whilst there may be common themes that can be useful to us in understanding beginning teachers' learning – for example, that their preconceptions, of whatever nature, are likely to profoundly influence them – each individual is likely to develop in different ways, even when they are engaged in the same programme.

Although Fuller's linear development model is too simple, it does often seem to be the case that student teachers' concerns with themselves and their own 'survival', in situations where they are in danger of being humiliated through their lack of competence, may need to be resolved as a necessary condition for more constructive learning to occur. Haggarty's (1997) study exemplifies this point well. Of the ten student teachers whom she studied, five recognized classroom control as a matter of concern to them from the beginning of the year. Therefore, during the more sheltered first half of their course, they took full advantage of available opportunities to learn about this aspect of teaching and so were well prepared for it when they first had regular whole-class teaching responsibilities. The other five, believing for various reasons that classroom control would not be an issue for them, rejected these early learning opportunities, were therefore taken by surprise when they had difficulties in managing whole-class teaching, and as a result, for varying periods of time thereafter, were overwhelmingly concerned with their own 'survival'.

More generally, the interaction of student teachers' preconceptions and agendas with the learning opportunities that they perceive to be available to them is likely to be of major importance in determining how successfully they attain the various goals towards which ITE should be directed. The fruitfulness of such interaction must surely depend heavily in the first instance on the extent to which a student teacher's own ideas are articulated, recognized, discussed and taken into account. It follows, therefore, that both the agendas and the preconceptions of student teachers should be taken as important starting points for negotiation of the successive learning tasks that they are asked to undertake as they progress.

When we relate these thoughts and findings about student teachers' prior understandings to our concern with a school-based curriculum for ITE, one of the most striking things is that, in the twentieth century, university-based teacher educators tended first to ignore student teachers' ideas and then to think only about trying to change them. It will be crucially important not to make either of these mistakes in relation to a school-based curriculum. Another even more directly relevant consideration is that it has been especially in their school-based work that student teachers have 'gone underground' with their ideas when they have judged these ideas to be unacceptable to school authorities. Where this has happened, it has meant that their school activities have had relatively little impact on their thinking about how to teach, with the consequence that the efforts of their school-based teachers have to a considerable extent been wasted. Thinking about how to take more effective account of student teachers' ideas in a school-based curriculum will be a considerable challenge.

Work-based learning

In many ways, the advantages of work-based learning are self-evident. The workplace is where the relevant action is. That is where expert professionals can be seen to be engaging in their expert practice, and where the novice is most likely to have easy opportunities for informal but purposeful conversations with them. The workplace is also usually where one's potential clients, in all their diversity, can be met. For anyone wishing to learn to teach, it is in schools that all the young people who are obliged to be there may be seen and met and studied, in classrooms and in more informal settings, in groups and as individuals. In schools, education is not just talked about; that is where people work to make it happen. And in schools, people have to confront and to deal with all the complex, messy difficulties which make education a demanding real-world task. For those who are in schools learning to teach, what they learn will generally be about this real world that they will themselves have to face.

In contrast to much professional learning, learning that is primarily work-based has an enormous further advantage in that it need not incorporate problematic distinctions between theory and practice. Whenever learning is based in a university or college, the problem arises of transferring what is learned there to the different world of practice, and of relating the theoretical to the practical. One almost inevitable consequence of this problem, for example, as Eraut (1994) points out, is that professionals learn both kinds of theory distinguished by Argyris and Schön (1974), the 'espoused theory' in terms of which professional practice is ideally conceived and publicly defended, and the 'theory-in-use' which actually informs practice. As these authors have clearly shown, the co-existence of two such different kinds of theory tends to be highly dysfunctional. But if professional learning is framed within the activities of the workplace, such dysfunctional dichotomies can perhaps be avoided.

In addition, we have benefited in recent years from very helpful theoretical and research-based accounts of work-based learning. Lave and Wenger (1991), for example, have very influentially elucidated the social learning processes that characteristically occur within 'communities of practice' for new or junior members of these communities through their 'legitimate peripheral participation' in the communities' life and work. The incumbents of such roles are enabled and obliged, in their apprentice-like roles, to make the modest contributions of which they are capable to the communities' work and also gradually to learn the craft expertise of their seniors. Perhaps most crucially, they effortlessly and incidentally learn, through living as full members of the communities, the rules, customs and culture of these communities. One can imagine the rich and powerful learning of this kind from which pupil teachers benefited in the nineteenth century through their extended participation in the work of schools. And there can be no doubt of the even greater depth and value of such benefits for a student teacher in the much more complex schools of today. Learning the daily routines of schools, the range of events that typically occur, the patterns of behaviour that are expected in different contexts from both students and staff, the sources of satisfaction and of irritation that teachers and students experience, and much else, is not only easily possible for the observant student teacher but also immensely valuable in becoming attuned to the life of schools and the work of teaching.

Yet, even in this simplified account, we have found it necessary to make distinctions between very different kinds of learning processes. There is the incidental learning through which much social learning is effortlessly achieved; also the deliberate learning of skills that have to be acquired; and then the more subtle and less easily described learning by the individual of his or her own very gradually developing role and professional identity. Work-based learning is far from uniform, nor easy to understand as a whole.

It is, however, the incidental learning that people do in the workplace that can be seen as most characteristic of work-based learning, since it fits well with the idea that the primary reason for being there is to work and that other benefits, such as learning, are incidental. For our part, how-

ever, we are very cautious about relying in school-based teacher education on such incidental learning. There are five major considerations that
lead us to this view.

The first consideration is that, as we have already noted, the knowledge and thinking on which experienced teachers primarily rely is tacit,
rarely made explicit even to themselves. Even the most experienced of
observers can make only very inadequate guesses when observing teachers at work and trying to work out what they are trying to do and especially why they are doing whatever it is they are doing and at that
particular time. Student teachers frequently report themselves to be bored
when asked to observe experienced teachers at work: what they see
seems 'obvious'; and they generally have no idea of all the important
work embedded in the thinking that is guiding the observed teacher's
practice, which they cannot see. So there is the problem that incidental
learning does not generally give one access to tacit expertise.

The second consideration is that expert teachers, like most experts,
tend to take their expertise for granted: to them, most of the thoughtful,
skilful things they are doing are obvious and need no explanation. So
they, the only people who can reveal what they are doing and why, tend
not to make any effort to reveal their tacit knowledge or thinking to
novices, because it seems 'obvious'. Hargreaves *et al.* (1997) encountered
a very similar phenomenon in their study of advanced medical education.
There was a general consensus, they found, that it was from experienced
consultants at work on the wards that junior doctors' most valuable
learning could occur; but, quite consistently, the junior doctors were left
guessing about the grounds on which the consultants had made their
clinical judgements, because the consultants took these judgements for
granted and did not 'incidentally' offer explanations for them. Hargreaves
et al. eventually concluded that the junior doctors themselves had to take
the responsibility for bravely asking their consultants for explanations. In
schools, too, incidental learning does not give access to experts' expertise,
because the experts tend to take that expertise for granted.

The third consideration is that when people do incidentally talk about
their work, they may do so in misleading ways. It is 'espoused theories'
rather than 'theories-in-use' that in many circumstances are more likely
to be articulated, and such espoused theories are likely to be misleading.
More generally, as Eraut (2000: 120) suggests,

> there is also the possibility that language used in the workplace may
> serve purposes other than making knowledge or actions explicit ...
> for example ... the latent functions may be to keep clients happy ...
> to tell managers what they want to hear ... In general, discourse in
> many settings helps (1) to provide a defensible account rather than
> a description of professionals' actions and (2) to create an impres-
> sion of professional control over situations which inspire confidence
> in them as persons. It may seek to disguise rather than to share
> uncertainty and risk-taking.

The fourth consideration stems from our account in Chapter 2 of the nature of expert teaching. Incidental learning, and especially learning through 'legitimate peripheral participation', is immensely valuable in enabling one to learn about how things are done in an established community, including many of the skills involved in a community's work. It is entirely appropriate for newcomers whose participation is legitimate but peripheral to ask questions, as part of their informal learning about what is happening, so that they can better understand. What is not appropriate, and is indeed highly problematic, is for such novices to question what happens, asking critical questions about established practice. Few communities would welcome such questioning from naïve and low-status newcomers; and the professional communities of schools are no different in this respect. Yet we have suggested in Chapter 2 that the only possible basis on which beginning teachers can develop teaching expertise is through not only developing their own craft knowledge but also subjecting it to sustained critical examination. It is evident that in developing their craft knowledge, they have an enormous amount to learn from the established practices of teachers in their schools; but it is equally evident that in critically examining their own developing knowledge and practice, they could very easily be critical of experienced teachers' practices. Where such dangers are present and such care and delicacy are therefore needed, one certainly cannot rely on incidental learning.

The fifth consideration relates to the social relations between teachers and pupils in schools. Student teachers, junior and unestablished as they are, unambiguously need to see themselves, and to present themselves, as members of the teacher community. They are therefore automatically outsiders to the rich and complex world of pupils; and it is not even as peripheral members of their community, but only as observant outsiders, that they can learn about the pupils' worlds. Given that even established teachers do not normally or routinely gain access to the pupils' perspectives on life in schools, what student teachers can learn about these perspectives through incidental learning is quite limited.

We are in no doubt, then, of the very great value of the incidental learning in which beginning teachers can engage through legitimate peripheral participation in the work of schools; but equally, we are in no doubt that much of the learning in which they need to engage cannot be dependent on such incidental learning, but must be systematically planned, guided and facilitated. In other words, we need planned school-based curricula for their learning.

In a useful contribution to the clarification of different kinds of learning in the workplace, Eraut (2000) distinguishes first between 'formal' and 'non-formal' learning. He defines 'formal learning' as occurring where structuring frameworks of the following kinds are in place: 'a prescribed learning framework; an organised learning event or package; the presence of a designated teacher or trainer; the award of a qualification or credit; the external specification of outcomes' (Eraut 2000: 114). A very large amount of the work-based learning in which beginning teachers need to engage is unambiguously formal. There should, we believe, be deliberate planning for each of the many kinds of learning from which we would want student teachers to benefit in schools, at the very least in that time should be allocated for each kind of learning and in that there should be explicitly shared understandings of the nature of each kind of learning and of why it is valued. Furthermore, each type of learning should be recognized as contributing to student teachers' professional education and, notionally at least, to their certification; and there should be designated educators who should ensure that the necessary conditions are in place to facilitate each kind of learning. So virtually everything that we are concerned with, including even the incidental learning, has to be viewed as 'formal learning'. We would indeed go further: it is just the kinds of structuring that for Eraut characterize formal learning that for us are crucially necessary for school-based ITE and to which we refer when we talk of a 'systematically planned school-based curriculum' for ITE.

There is another sense, however, in which the very essence of work-based learning is that it should not be structured for learning purposes. What distinguishes work-based learning is that it is the work itself that gives shape and meaning to everything that happens, and that whatever learning takes place follows from the nature of the work. It is of the greatest importance that the normal realities of how work is organized and of how people do their work should not be distorted by the ways in which learning tasks are structured. Otherwise the learning could more sensibly and conveniently be conducted in laboratories or lecture theatres. The whole point of work-based learning is that the learning is about the realities of the work. Unlike learning through 'case methods' (Merseth 1996) or in laboratories and lecture theatres, work-based learning has the distinctive and immensely important strength of being learning evidently attuned to the real world. To impose arrangements that undermine that strength would be to defeat the purpose of work-based learning.

Why then do we assert the need for, in Eraut's terms, 'formal learning'? This is because there are, in our view, two equally important facets to the learning that are needed, two facets for which there are contrasting requirements. On one hand there is the *content* of what has to be learned, and that content should, we believe, be concerned primarily with the realities of schooling and teaching, minimally distorted by learning structures. On the other hand there are the *processes* of learning, which involve gaining access to, and developing an understanding of, the realities of teaching. As we have explained, these processes present many serious difficulties; and student teachers need all the help they can get if they are to achieve the necessary understandings in the limited time available. So for that reason we are in favour of strong and carefully planned learning structures. A key principle in the planning of a school-based curriculum for ITE is therefore that work-based learning needs to be structured as much as is necessary to maximize learners' cognitive access to the full normal realities of doing the work, but must not distort these realities.

Eraut (2000) also distinguishes various kinds of work-based learning in terms of 'the level of intention to learn'. On that dimension, he distinguishes 'implicit learning' at one extreme from 'deliberative learning' at the other (with a third category, 'reactive learning', between the two). From our perspective, all of these are important in workplace learning and have to be recognized, valued, facilitated, attended to and accredited in ways that make them formal kinds of learning. This is true even of implicit learning, defined as 'the acquisition of knowledge independently of conscious attempts to learn and in the absence of explicit knowledge of what was learned' (Eraut 2000: 115).

Implicit learning is of the greatest importance in the learning of all teachers. Eraut, following Horvath *et al.* (1996), suggests that implicit learning occurs, in the first instance, through personally experienced events being stored in 'episodic memory'. Learning occurs through such memories informing practice, either directly through new situations being recognized as being similar, or in more complex ways through, for example, the construction of more generalized representations. The gradual building up of repertoires of recognized types of situations, with variations, seems, as noted in Chapter 2, to be a crucial part of the development of fluency and expertise in teachers, as in other professionals.

At the other end of the spectrum of 'the level of intention to learn', Eraut (2000: 116) includes, under the general category of 'deliberative learning', three subcategories distinguished by their relationship in time to the learner's actions:

Past episodes: review of past actions, communications, events, experiences; more systematic reflection.
Current experience: engagement in decision-making, problem-solving, planned informal learning.
Future behaviour: planned learning goals; planned learning opportunities.

It may be noted that these different kinds of deliberative learning not only reflect very obviously the kinds of planned school-based learning which we are suggesting is needed, but also are structured in ways designed to take advantage of the ongoing work without changing the structure of that work. Retrospective deliberative learning is actively seeking to learn from the work done, including the learning implicit in it. Deliberative learning from current experience is using engagement in the work not only to get the work well done but also to learn from it. And deliberative planning for future learning is thinking about how, in doing the work effectively, the learner will also have useful opportunities for purposeful learning. It is in such ways that learning can effectively and fruitfully be structured without the nature of the work itself being distorted.

We have in this section recognized the very valuable incidental learning from which student teachers can benefit through being in the school as a workplace and through being accepted as participants, albeit peripheral participants, in the professional teaching community of a school. We have also, however, emphasized various ways in which incidental learning is limited and constrained, and we have argued for the importance of planned structures to facilitate all the many different potentially helpful kinds of workplace learning. But, of course, that must be done without undermining the inherent distinctive advantages of workplace learning. In the next section, we go on to consider more fully the nature of such advantages in the particular case of ITE.

Distinctive opportunities offered by schools as contexts for learning to teach

Learning to be skilful teachers

At the core of the work of teachers is the socially complex task of classroom teaching. Social psychologists such as Tomlinson (1995) rightly emphasize both the demanding social skills required of classroom teachers and also the need for all these different social skills to be orchestrated into complex integrated activities. The skills involved in engaging effectively in such activities are certainly social skills, but they are also in very large measure thinking skills and are heavily dependent on the understandings that underlie them. How do people learn to engage effectively in such complex social activities?

It is helpful to think of the learning of these complex, socially skilled activities as being dependent on the same three basic processes that are involved in learning any skills. Just as in learning a simple skill like driving a car, learners need *models*, to establish helpful symbolic or concrete mental pictures to guide all or part of their activities. They also need *practice*, repeated opportunities to try out activities for themselves, to try to get them right. And they need *feedback*, reliable evidence that tells them how far they are getting the activity right and in what respects they are getting it right or wrong. One of the biggest advantages of ITE being much more school-based, and more especially under the control of school-based teacher educators, is the enormously enhanced opportunities that this creates for both the scale and the quality of these three processes in helping people to learn to teach.

Modelling

The school-based teacher educator has the enormous advantage of being able not only to explain to student teachers what they need to do but also to show them. Modelling at its best always involves demonstration of what is involved, explanation of how to do it, and drawing attention to key elements; and all this can be done very much more easily and realistically in a school context than elsewhere. Teacher educators can, for example, draw attention before a lesson to the key social arrangements, ways of structuring pupil tasks, patterns of discussion, and transitions between lesson phases; and after the lesson they can, where appropriate, focus the discussion on these same themes. Through such *cueing*, in advance or afterwards or both, whatever is especially important for a particular student teacher's learning at that time can be highlighted. If necessary, for that stage in the student teacher's learning, the key aspect of the teaching can be presented in a very simple way; or, at a later stage, the same aspect can be presented in its full complexity, with due attention to context and to how the teacher adapted the action to meet the needs of that particular context. The school-based teacher educator can focus on very specific elements of the teaching, such as specific questions, examples or words of praise, or on much more complex elements, such as a whole-class teaching and learning strategy. Nor is the school-based teacher educator dependent on his or her own practice. Where appropriate, student teachers can be shown a multiplicity of models for an important aspect of teaching, such as getting pupils interested in a theme, drawing on the practice of several experienced teachers. Or they can be shown a model of one teacher chosen because he or she is especially expert in doing that particular thing.

The scope for the flexible use of modelling in curriculum planning is enormous for school-based teacher educators who know their own school contexts and the rich possibilities that they offer. Student teachers can get very much more help than they have traditionally been given through both being shown key examples of the art of teaching as it happens in the real world, and having these explained to them by the teachers observed, examples appropriately chosen to meet their own learning needs at different stages of their learning. (The extended example of school-based ITE that is explored in Part B of this book focuses especially on some of the issues involved in giving student teachers access to expert modelling of aspects of teaching which especially concerned them.)

Practice

Nobody will argue with the idea that student teachers need lots of practice if they are to learn to be good teachers. But it is only too easy to have a lot of practice of a kind that does not assist learning. Indeed, many teachers will remember practice experiences when they were student teachers that, far from helping them to learn, left them simply confused.

So, what matters about practice is not simply the amount of it but its appropriateness for promoting learning. As with most learning tasks, the need is for practice tasks that are meaningful and challenging to the learner, but that can with effort be successfully undertaken. They are not impossibly difficult tasks, from which the learning is unpredictable and may well be counter-productive. So at each stage of a student teacher's learning, the teacher educator ideally needs to devise practice teaching tasks calculated to meet his or her learning needs.

Teacher educators who are also classroom teachers are ideally placed for this task. The regular challenge they face is that of using the student teacher as a classroom assistant in a way that will be helpful to pupils, and in a way that also provides the student teacher with a valuable learning opportunity. Often at early stages this will involve them in undertaking specific tasks with small groups of pupils, such as helping them to formulate and share good ideas, or checking their understanding of a newly explained idea. At other times, the student/assistant will be given responsibility for a part of the lesson, such as managing a question-and-answer session, introducing a new concept, or demonstrating an experiment. While such activities should always be designed as real parts of the class's work that are useful to the pupils, they should also be planned to meet identified learning needs of the student teacher at that stage in his or her development.

Teachers have always, of course, used student teachers as classroom assistants, and have generally done so very sensibly. For the school-based teacher educator, however, the immense value of being able to plan student teachers' practice of teaching using tasks that are considerably less demanding than that of complete responsibility for a whole class, can hardly be overestimated. In the 1970s, many teacher educators put an enormous amount of effort into exploring an idea called *microteaching*, developed at Stanford University (Allen and Ryan 1969; Brown 1975; McIntyre *et al.* 1977) and concerned with giving student teachers focused practice in the use of important teaching skills in simplified and sheltered conditions. At its best, microteaching worked very well, or did so except for the problem of transferring skills learned in the microteaching laboratory to the very different environment of the school classroom. Although microteaching was a well-conceived idea, the scale of the transfer problem often proved too great. The focused learning of teaching skills needs to be done in the classroom, and as part of the ordinary real work of the classroom, but still with simplified and protected conditions for the novice student teacher. The problem in the 1970s was not only that the teacher educators were neither in nor responsible for the school classrooms but also that the classroom teachers were not expected to be teacher educators. Now things have changed, and now it is possible for thoughtful school-based teacher educators to plan for their student teachers to have just the kinds of practice tasks from which they will learn most at each stage of their development.

As Burn (1997) has shown, this kind of simplified practice for student teachers within the framework of experienced teachers' lessons brings other substantial benefits for the student teachers' learning. Effective integration into the teacher's lesson of the part for which the student teacher is responsible depends on close collaboration between the two of them, especially but not only at the planning stage; and this kind of collaboration gives student teachers highly educational access to models of how experienced teachers set about their planning and decision-making.

It is of course essential, at later stages of their ITE programmes, for student teachers to experience extended practice in teaching whole classes on their own. Even at these later stages, school-based teacher educators, working in collaboration with their teaching colleagues, are exceptionally well placed to ensure that student teachers' practice is well judged for their learning needs. While all the time taking account also of the pupils' needs, it is possible to place student teachers with more or less challenging classes, and over time with classes providing different learning opportunities, perhaps because of their different academic levels, the diversity of their cultural backgrounds, or simply the difficulty of managing them.

Feedback

This third key element in learning any complex skilled activity is almost certainly the one that school-based teacher educators have developed most fully and most widely. The provision of critical feedback used to be primarily the task of visiting supervisors from HEIs, but it is a task that mentors and their school-based colleagues are well placed to carry out much more effectively. Their great advantage is their far greater and more intimate knowledge of all the different contextual factors that are relevant to the provision of helpful feedback. As people on the spot, they are well placed to monitor on almost a daily basis student teachers' developing skills, so that they can praise improvements, reinforce attention to neglected aspects, and move on when appropriate to new considerations. Knowing also the classes being taught and their histories, and the individuals in them, they are well placed to know how easy or difficult specific teaching tasks were, and what opportunities and problems the teaching of these pupils was likely to present. Similarly, an intimate knowledge of constraints and opportunities of space, time, course structures, assessment arrangements and available resources should allow school-based teacher educators both to recognize student teachers' achievements and to bring neglected possibilities to their attention.

In all these three ways, then, the possibilities for ITE have been enormously enhanced by it becoming largely school-based. It is not difficult to imagine how thorough flexible curricula could be developed much more fully in order to enable beginning teachers to develop their expertise in the complex skilled activity which is teaching. We believe that these opportunities should be taken. At the same time, we must recognize that teaching is much more than a complex skilled activity.

People becoming teachers

The usefulness of the analogy with learning to drive a car is limited, and not just because the task of classroom teaching is infinitely more complex. Of even greater importance is the fact that the main instrument used by teachers in teaching is not an external object but *themselves*. The human dimension of becoming a teacher is both of central importance and also multi-faceted (cf. Tabberer 2005). And here, too, new possibilities are added when ITE is school-based.

The emotional challenge of becoming a teacher

Thoughtful commentators on the teaching profession (e.g. Nias 1989; Clandinin 1993; Connelly *et al.* 1997) have noted how closely teachers' personal and professional identities tend to be intertwined. Teaching is for relatively few people a job taken on during a limited number of prescribed hours of the week but not relevant to the kind of people they see themselves otherwise to be. Those who spend many hours each week endeavouring to stimulate, to engage, to guide, to manage and, most critically, to educate young people in groups of twenty or thirty, but each with minds of their own, generally find it neither easy nor helpful to detach themselves from their work. Most teachers find that their individual humanity and the totality of their human experience are essential resources on which they draw as classroom teachers.

This being so, the process of becoming a teacher can for many be quite an emotionally demanding experience. Student teachers are generally people who have been at least reasonably successful students at school and, in most cases, at university. Some have had successful careers elsewhere and some have already experienced the responsibilities of parenthood. Furthermore, people are not generally accepted into ITE programmes unless they seem to be mature, confident and emotionally secure people. In addition, most people who are motivated to become teachers have some kind of vision of the teacher that they want to be, and many are inspired by high social and educational ideals (e.g. Edmonds *et al.* 2002; Younger *et al.* 2004). But the work of classroom teaching is very different from any that most student teachers have previously undertaken; and so the emotional demands of learning to do it are often unexpected. Young people in classrooms frequently do not respond generously to novices' eager, benevolent but unskilled attempts to teach them. It is only too easy for student teachers' high expectations for their relationships with students, and for their inspirational influence upon them, to be undermined by the brutal realities of direct experience. It is equally easy for student teachers to suffer feelings of incompetence to which they are most unaccustomed. Most, of course, learn quite quickly. But the easiest thing to learn can be to fit in with what appear to be the institutional norms of the school; and that may involve a very uncomfortable feeling for student teachers of having to appear to be what they are not. It may also mean their abandoning their ideals, or at least temporarily setting them aside, and so learning in ways that are not influenced by them. Thus student teachers who start off with a confidence in themselves grounded in past experience, and with visions and ideals that have inspired them to be teachers, can become subdued and much less enthusiastic conformists, or else be turned off teaching altogether.

That is something that need not happen, but which certainly did happen all too frequently when ITE was predominantly university-based. Encouraged as they were to debate educational ideas, student teachers in their university environments tended to develop increasingly radical, idealistic and child-centred attitudes. But, faced with the reality of working in schools, most of them responded sensibly by going into reverse, tending either to change their minds or else at least to express views strategically consistent with school norms (e.g. Morrison and McIntyre 1967; Lacey 1977; Zeichner *et al.* 1987). The problem was not just, or even mainly, that schools and universities were pulling in different directions. The much more serious problem was that student teachers were not being helped to build realistically on the educational values and high ideals that had brought many of them into teaching, nor to come to terms rationally with the complex problems of relating their roles as teachers to themselves as persons. Somehow, most muddled through; but it seems likely that much unnecessary pain was suffered and that the teaching profession was denied a great deal of idealistic energy that it could fruitfully have used.

Has making ITE more school-based automatically overcome these problems in England? To some extent, perhaps. And certainly it has changed the nature of the problems. Today there is far more realism built into ITE programmes from their beginning: it is much more difficult for student teachers to pretend to themselves about the kinds of teachers they will be and about how their students will respond to them – and that is a clear improvement. It is less obvious, however, that student teachers are helped more effectively to make sense of themselves, their values, their ideals and everything that they bring to teaching, and to work out how all that can best contribute to the task of teaching as their schools define it. How might that be done? We shall return to that question after considering some more intellectual facets of people becoming teachers.

The process of developing a teacher's craft knowledge

The importance of the human dimension of becoming a teacher does not lie only in the emotional stresses and struggles involved. At least equally important is the intellectual challenge involved in developing the expertise needed by teachers. In Chapter 2 we articulated a view of classroom teaching expertise which, we suggested, implied that the priority task of ITE must be to enable student teachers to develop fluency and practical competence in classroom teaching and also the necessary understandings, skills, attitudes and habits for systematically engaging in informed critical examination of their own developing craft knowledge. The idea of developing fluency and practical competence in classroom teaching fits well, we believe, with the idea that we have discussed of learning teaching as a complex, socially skilled activity. But systematically engaging in informed critical examination of their own developing craft knowledge goes far beyond such learning of skilled activities; it involves student teachers as individuals in accepting the intellectual responsibility for ensuring that what they do is consonant with their position as professional public educators.

It must be accepted that this is an awesome responsibility to ask student teachers (and also, of course, practising teachers) to accept; but we can see no alternative. We have not been able to find any credible theoretical understanding of classroom teaching which could allow teachers to rely, in the complex, subtle, tacit, situated judgements which they constantly need to make in their teaching, simply on the authoritative judgements of others. While teachers can of course draw heavily on the wisdom of others, it is ultimately only they themselves who can be sufficiently aware of what they are doing in their teaching for them to be able to subject their developing or established practices to anything like the necessary degree of regular critical scrutiny.

The problem is that none of the elements of any skilled teaching are merely the kinds of instrumental moves necessary in, for example, driving a car. Everything a teacher does, from her facial expressions through her choice of language to the relationships she seeks and establishes with pupils, is replete with significant value judgements and theoretical assumptions about what is educationally valuable and about how educational ideals can most effectively be realized. So, when student teachers begin developing their ideas about what they want to happen in their classrooms and about what they can do to promote such happenings, the practical ideas which they gather and select are already heavily theory- and value-laden; and it is partly the theories and values implicit in these practical ideas that will have made them attractive. So then there is the need for critical examination of all these ideas, both as ideas and, where relevant, as elements of the developing practice of the student teacher.

What is the significance of predominantly school-based ITE in relation to this need for student teachers to engage in systematic critical examination of their own developing craft knowledge? The need is certainly not a new one; but school-based ITE provides a magnificent new opportunity for the need to be effectively met. Student teachers have throughout the twentieth century been encouraged to engage both in critical evaluation of educational ideas and also in constructive development of their teaching repertoires and skills. In the twentieth century, however, these tended to be two separate activities, with the former 'theoretical' activity being mainly valued and primarily pursued in the universities, and the latter 'practical' activity being relatively more highly valued and necessarily primarily pursued in the schools. School-based ITE provides the opportunity, not for everything to be done in the schools, but for the work to be sufficiently concentrated in schools that it becomes both necessary and possible for these two activities to be integrated. Most crucially, the ideas that student teachers can and should be obliged to evaluate most critically are those same ideas that they are actively using in developing their teaching practices. 'Practical theorizing' thus becomes the core activity.

Practical theorizing as the core activity of school-based ITE

We use the term 'practical theorizing' where others might talk of 'reflective practice'. The problem with the latter term is the wide diversity of meanings which it can be given. It will be recalled from Chapter 1 that one of the central weaknesses found by Furlong *et al.* (2000) in their surveys of predominantly school-based teacher education in England was that the majority of student teachers tended to interpret reflective practice as a kind of common-sense evaluation of their own practice. Useful as that can be, it is a quite inadequate way of learning to teach. As argued, for example, by McIntyre (1993), beginning teachers need primarily to learn in their practice from other people's ideas, both those of experienced practitioners and those of educational researchers and scholars; and they need to submit all these ideas, and of course their own, to a critical examination that goes well beyond common sense. It is for this much more demanding kind of reflective practice that we use the term 'practical theorizing'.

Practical theorizing means both looking for attractive ideas for practice and subjecting these ideas to critical examination. To become competent practitioners, all beginning teachers need quickly to develop large repertoires of practical ideas to draw upon as the need arises; and they need to practise using these ideas. The usefulness of all of these ideas depends, however, upon their having been effectively evaluated against a variety of criteria. Some of these criteria are properly of a practical nature. Most obviously, are the ideas acceptable for use in the particular school context, are they practicable in terms of the time, space and resources available, and can student teachers use these ideas effectively to achieve particular educational purposes in the given context? Immediate answers to such questions may be found relatively easily, either from authoritative advice or through trial and error. Longer-term questions, however, will be more complex, partly because of the need to consider other criteria and partly because of the need for more generalized thinking. Such questions will be concerned, for example, with the values and assumptions embedded in different practices, the purposes for which they are appropriate and the circumstances in which they tend to be effective. For example, for what purposes and in what circumstances is it beneficial for school pupils to plan and conduct their own experiments, rather than carrying out exper-

iments planned by their teacher? How, if at all, and under what conditions is it possible to enable students to engage in truly authentic classroom conversations in the target foreign language? Such more complex
questions will not generally be answered quickly or readily. Answers to
them may emerge not only gradually as a result not only of quite extensive experience and very careful consideration but also through debate
with experienced colleagues and through reference to relevant research
and scholarship. During his or her initial professional education, a teacher
can expect to reach confident answers to only a few such questions, but
provisional answers to many more; but even more important than such
answers is acquiring the habit of engaging effectively in such practical
theorizing.

It is both more difficult and more important for some practical ideas to
be examined than others. Among the most difficult and most important
are those ideas to which individual student teachers are themselves most
attached and which may have been significant in attracting them to a
teaching career. For example, student teachers frequently combine high
ideals about helping others or about sharing their love of their chosen
subjects with what can be quite naïve ideas about what they will be able
to do and about how responsive their pupils will be to them. As we have
noted, such beliefs and values may be important to student teachers in
defining their own identities, so questioning them can be a highly stressful and emotional process. On one hand, therefore, the high ideals and
strong motivation that such student teachers bring to teaching are greatly
to be welcomed and should surely be carefully cherished. On the other
hand, they need to be helped to engage in demanding practical theorizing
processes to ensure that their professional commitment comes to be based
on intelligent understandings of the realities of schooling.

Other practical ideas that are equally difficult to examine, but for quite
different reasons, are those that are embedded in the practices of the
schools and teachers by whom student teachers are inducted into the profession. Here the primary problem for student teachers is a social one:
while critical examination of their school's practices is essential for
student teachers' professional education, and is often not difficult for
them intellectually or emotionally, it is socially not their place as novices
to question the well-established practices of their host institution.

At first sight, the difficulties of questioning those practical ideas to
which student teachers are themselves deeply attached and those that are
embedded in the practices of schools may seem very different. In practice,
however, they are often experienced as two sides of the same problematic
coin, rather than as separate difficulties. It is the contrasts between the
way things are done in the school and how the student teacher has imag-
ined she would do them, between the ways in which teachers are obviously expected to relate to pupils and her vision of the relationships she
would foster, between the National Curriculum and Key Stage 3 strategy
and her conception of how young people can be inspired to love her

subject, that can be most disturbing. So the delicate social problems, the stressful emotional problems, the inherently very complex intellectual problems and the fundamental practical problems about what to do and how to do it effectively can easily all get combined into overwhelming difficulties that are just too complex to be faced, especially on one's own.

The basis for a way forward

What can be done to help beginning teachers as they each struggle to come to terms with their own version of such difficulties? The answer is certainly not simple; and, even by the end of this book, we shall not be pretending to give a complete answer. Here, however, we can offer three important foundations on which we believe an answer can be built.

First, we introduced the idea of 'practical theorizing' by pointing to the crucial importance of integrating practical and theoretical agendas: as we said, the ideas that student teachers can and should be obliged to evaluate most critically are those same ideas that they are actively using in developing their teaching practices. The important practical work has always had to be done in the schools, but so long as the universities were at the centre of teacher education, the theoretical work was almost inevitably done there, detached from the practical world of schools. Even the sometimes quite frequent visits of university supervisors to their student teachers in schools tended to be seen as an extension of the theoretical perspectives of the universities into schools, clearly distinguished from the student teachers' everyday work there. Because of its separateness, the theoretical work was often very nearly useless; and for the same reason, the complex practical work of learning to teach was largely uninformed by the disciplined intellectual analysis that it crucially needs. Now, in so far as it is accepted that the main work has to be done in schools, then it is possible to begin confronting the task of how practical theorizing in schools can effectively be supported.

Second, we already have the beginnings of a solution to that problem. Practical theorizing was not facilitated in schools in the past because all the professional teacher educators were employed in and by the universities. Tutors based in universities were, and continue to be, well able to lead student teachers in their thinking about the issues in generalized terms, and also to help them to cope with many of the tensions and stresses they experience as student teachers. But, having neither detailed knowledge of school situations nor any status within schools, they have not been in a position to deal with issues as *school* issues. It is in schools, not in universities, that the most committed and idealistic of student teachers often face identity crises; and it is in schools that student teachers have needed to find ways of avoiding the social confrontations to which honest questioning of established ways of doing things could easily lead. In the past, there was nobody in schools whose task it was to recognize that these were not just private problems for individual student teachers, but systemic problems. Student teachers have not generally, therefore, been able to think through the issues that concerned them as matters of practice, because nobody else in schools seemed to be engaged in theorizing about these things. Now in England we have thousands of dedicated professional school-based teacher educators. It is true that they are generally given very little time, and perhaps true that most of them do not yet see their key role as one of ensuring that student teachers are stimulated and enabled to engage in practical theorizing. But we do have professional school-based teacher educators; and so for the first time there are people who are in a position, and do have the capacity, to plan school-based programmes that take account of the real problems and needs.

Third, however, it is true that student teachers are individuals, each attracted into teaching for their own reasons, each with their own ideals, values and preconceptions. They are first and foremost, as we noted at the start of this section, people; and it is their humanity and individuality that will be their greatest assets as schoolteachers. Inevitably, therefore, the intellectual, practical, social and emotional problems with which they have to grapple as student teachers are different for each of them. We have argued that they will grapple with these problems most fruitfully if they deal with them as serious intellectual issues, which therefore must first be articulated explicitly and examined. That is not, however, the sort of thing that many of us do readily on our own. We need someone else to ask us questions, to probe, to challenge and sometimes to support and to guide. And, given the individual nature of the issues, that needs to be someone working with us on a one-to-one basis. We are fortunate, therefore, that the system of school-based teacher education that has already been established in England is one geared to such individual support. In striking contrast to the often unavoidable mass-processing systems of higher education, we can build on foundations already in place for a school-based teacher education system that is in large measure individualized.

The roles of schools and of others in ITE partnerships

We have explained that our primary concern in this book is with school-based ITE. We are not, however, suggesting that the whole task can be done most effectively by schools; we believe that any of the routes into teaching necessarily involves three partners – government, schools and higher education. The function of this section, therefore, is to begin to clarify the part that we believe should be played by schools and how that part needs to be complemented by contributions from their partners.

The most common current patterns of ITE for graduate student teachers in England are 36-week courses, in which a minimum of 24 weeks for prospective secondary school teachers and 18 weeks for prospective primary school teachers must be spent in at least two schools (Department for Education and Skills 2002). The shorter period in primary schools does not derive from any arguments about a lesser need for school-based preparation, but rather from a recognition that even acceptable first degrees generally provide prospective teachers with a less satisfactory preparation in the content of the primary school curriculum than they do for secondary school curricula; and that university or college education departments are best placed to provide, within a period of a few weeks, the necessary minimal supplementary preparation for this aspect of teaching. It is evident that in these circumstances primary school teacher educators are faced with an especially difficult task; and that more effective preparation for primary school teaching would be possible if courses were extended to allow 24 weeks to be spent in school-based work, as in secondary schools. While the requirement for school experience in at least two schools is sensible enough, we are in no doubt that effective school-based teacher education is possible only through a student teacher's engagement in one school over a sustained period. Apart, however, from these few words, we are content for our discussion to take for granted such current organizational frameworks; our concern is with what can most fruitfully be done within them.

The idea of partnership in ITE was vigorously debated in the 1980s, by ourselves among others (e.g. McIntyre 1980, 1988, 1991; Benton 1990; Booth *et al.* 1990). At that time, we were primarily concerned about partnership between schools and HEIs; and a significant concern was to assert the importance of mutual respect and equality of esteem between the two partners. Since then, two important things have changed. One of these is the emergence of government, not initially as a partner but certainly as a very active and dominant player in teacher education. Second, we now have considerable experience of school–HEI partnerships for ITE and can learn both from their strengths and from their problems; and furthermore, both sets of partners have become sufficiently accustomed to such partnerships for there to be less concern about equality between them and more about who can do what best. We need, in the light of these two changes, to think about the general terms of partnership for the future.

The government and teacher educators

We have become accustomed in England to being told what to do in teacher education by national government, whether directly or indirectly through the Teacher Training Agency. And, although in recent years the Teacher Training Agency has been acting more like a partner, engaging readily in widespread consultation, we in schools and HEIs have on the whole acquired the habit of doing what we are told to do, sometimes grudgingly, without perhaps reflecting enough on how our own roles and that of government or Teacher Training Agency might more clearly and most appropriately be defined to complement each other. Assuming that government involvement is here to stay, we should be more active in seeking to define the parts that we should play.

There are things that governments are entitled to do and are well placed to do, and there are things that they cannot competently do. It is proper that an elected government should define broad national educational priorities and that it should determine also what priorities it has for ITE. And only government can decide how much it will spend on education and how much of that expenditure should be devoted to ITE. Schools and educational scholars should of course advise government about realities that need to be taken into account, including what is and is not possible through ITE and under what conditions, including financial conditions. Government also needs to identify, with the advice of professionals, the matters on which it is necessary to establish the best possible national consensus; and it is, in addition, well placed to co-ordinate procedures for establishing such consensus. Thus, it seems to be widely recognized that establishing consensual national standards about what beginning teachers need to be able to do competently in order to be awarded qualified teacher status, and doing so through careful processes of consultation (Department for Education and Skills 2002), was, at least in principle, a constructive government initiative. There seems, on the other hand, to be much less acceptance of the wisdom of imposing, with much less consultation and on the basis of questionably expert opinion, methods of teaching that student teachers must be taught to use. In our view, and in the light of our discussion in Chapter 2 of the nature of good practice in teaching, governments go beyond the limits of their competence when they attempt to specify *how* teachers should do what they need to be able to do.

But the less we would like government to do, the more we as the other partners in ITE have to accept responsibility for doing well ourselves. If we wish the government to stop short at specifying the professional standards for qualified teacher status, then it becomes our responsibility, as school–HEI partnerships, to plan well-conceived curricula through which student teachers will be enabled to meet these standards (and others that we ourselves believe to be important). There has, we suspect, been too much readiness simply to place student teachers in schools with mentors and to ask the mentors to create opportunities for the student teachers to practise meeting, and eventually to demonstrate their ability to meet, each of the separate standards. This list of standards is not, and could not be, anything more than a list, an unintegrated, untheorized list. Nobody could seriously argue that learning to meet each of the standards separately could be equated with learning to teach. Nor is being able to meet all the standards anything like a guarantee that anyone is well prepared for teaching. For each and all of the standards, the competent beginning teacher needs a repertoire of different ways of meeting them, suitable for different circumstances, including the need to meet at the same time different combinations of other standards. The distinctive merits of each way for meeting each standard need to have been considered by the beginning teacher in relation to various criteria of practicality, of effectiveness and of educational values, and through drawing on various sources of information. Furthermore, what is most important is the development of pedagogical ways of thinking that will enable student teachers to go on increasing their repertoires intelligently as and when necessary. And such practical theorizing will not be done most effectively by treating specific means to specific ends in isolation, but will instead view these specifics as elements of coherent overarching strategies for teaching. We as teacher educators need to generate much better curriculum frameworks for student teachers' learning than can be offered by the standards.

For example, the pedagogical implications of different ways of construing and taking account of differences among pupils in their past academic achievements (cf. Hart *et al.* 2004) would need to be considered in relation to the concerns embedded in a number of standards. There is not a lot wrong with these standards, but to be useful in ITE they need to be integrated into a coherently planned curriculum for practical theorizing as well as for the development of teaching practices and skills. Furthermore, as is obvious to anyone experienced in working with beginning teachers, it is not sufficient just to consider, practise and master each element, then to tick it off the list. All the many important facets of teaching need to be considered from different perspectives, using different approaches, and in increasing depth, within spiral curricula. And all this has to be planned to allow the flexibility that, as we have noted, is needed to take account of the individuality of each student teacher.

The task of constructing a coherent and well-conceived curriculum for ITE that takes adequate account of such specifications of standards as those for qualified teacher status currently in operation in England is thus a formidable one; and it is a task that only professional teacher educators, in schools and in universities, are equipped to undertake. One very important consideration in constructing such curricula has to be about what mutually complementary roles schools and universities are best equipped to play.

The roles of schools and of universities

The effectiveness of school–university partnerships for ITE depends on a carefully considered, realistic, shared understanding about how the contributions of the two partners can best complement each other. In considering what that division of labour might most fruitfully be, we can best start by reminding ourselves of two very obvious asymmetries of which account should be taken in the positions of the two.

First, there is a severe asymmetry in the extent to which the two types of institution were designed for educating adults. Higher education institutions are built, staffed and resourced with the specific purpose that they should be cost-effective for the education of adults, including at least part of their professional education. Schools, in contrast, generally seem to have been designed with no thought as to their suitability for the continuing professional education of the adults who work in them. Schools and the teaching profession are changing. More and more schools, for example, are enthusiastically embracing mentoring and coaching at all levels of the workforce, and engagement in continuing professional development is becoming accepted by teachers and support staff as both an entitlement and an obligation. It remains the case, however, that in many schools adults who are focusing their energies on their own professional education, rather than 'getting on with the work' of the school, generally seem to be going against the grain. For example, the organization of time and of space, the facilities that are and are not available, and the social climate of schools all tend to make such adults feel out of step. Recognition of these obvious differences was probably an important factor underlying the location of most ITE in HEIs throughout most of the twentieth century, in England as elsewhere.

Whereas that first asymmetry is a consequence of what are presumably largely alterable assumptions in the design and running of schools, the second asymmetry seems inescapable, and yet has not in our view been given the importance that it merits. It is this: whereas what student teachers learn from and for the practice of teaching in schools cannot but be a relevant part of their professional education, the relevance to their professional lives of anything that they learn in HEIs is far from certain. The significance of any seminar or workshop that they engage in at university, of any book from the university library that they read, or of any essay that they write for a university tutor is dependent on its significance to them *for their practice in schools*. Practice is the only touchstone against which relevance in initial profession education can be assessed, and practice happens only in schools. However well founded the ideas learned in a higher education context, however profound, and however potentially helpful they are, they are useless unless their usefulness for practice in schools, now or in the future, is established in the minds and in the practice of the student teachers. The failure of those of us in higher education to recognize this simple truth has led to much of the excellent thinking that we have shared with our students over the last century being wasted.

What are the implications of these two asymmetries for how schools and HEIs can best complement each others' efforts? On the one hand, it seems that it will be in schools that many crucial things can be done most effectively, because that is where the practice of teaching is. That, broadly, is the premise on which this book is based. Most fundamentally, whatever student teachers need to learn to do as teachers in schools for their future careers, it is in schools that they need to learn to do these things. That means not only that it is in schools that teaching as a complex, highly skilled activity needs to be modelled and practised; it also means that it is in schools that they most need to engage in the complementary and equally important activity of practical theorizing.

So is there any need for HEI involvement, and if so, why? The most fundamental reason for the involvement of universities, it is widely suggested, is that the access they can provide to bodies of theoretical and research-based knowledge, and even more their traditions of independent, questioning, critical inquiry, are central to the development of student teachers' thinking. Wilkin, for example, writes of 'the critical tradition of the universities' (1999: 2) and the importance of that tradition for ITE because it is 'essential for the student teacher to acquire the habit of critical thinking' (1999: 5). She also quotes Darling-Hammond (1999: 24–5), who suggests that it is the spirit of inquiry which characterizes a university education, and the knowledge and understanding that flow from this, that 'render the teacher's practice more intelligent, more flexible ... Seeing more relations, he [sic] sees more possibilities, more opportunities'.

We concur that it is the distinctive relevant kinds of knowledge that universities can offer and their traditions of critical questioning that are the most important reasons for their involvement in ITE. But we have to be very cautious here. For one thing, university-based teacher educators have not shown themselves to be at all expert at those important kinds of thinking concerned with questioning the practicality of apparently good theoretical ideas. Second, as we have emphasized, the twentieth century should have taught us the inadequacy of valuing academic knowledge and thinking when it is offered separately from practical learning in school. Far from it being enough to teach student teachers such knowledge and such critical questioning in universities, the need is to find ways of teaching them to engage in informed and disciplined practical theorizing as a part of their everyday practical learning in schools. That, quite evidently, is not something that university-based teacher educators can do on their own.

It can, however, be argued that school-based teacher educators also cannot do it on their own:

> Because of the nature of their work and the institutional context in which they are based, professional teacher educators (in universities and colleges) are able to support this sort of learning in a way that is impossible for teachers or even whole schools acting alone. Good teachers do reflect on their own experience and that is a vital part of professional learning and development. But, given that they work in schools, few teachers can have access to the range of other forms of knowledge that good (HEI-based) teacher educators can bring to bear ... if they are to learn and to move forward, teachers and schools therefore need to work in partnerships ... with those in universities and colleges, who have ready access to a wide range of other forms of knowledge.
>
> (Furlong 2000: 14–15)

The most important reason, then, for school–university partnership is that high-quality support and guidance in practical reasoning depends on both school-based and university-based teacher educators. But, as the need for both groups implies, there are two very different roles to be filled. School-based teacher educators are needed alongside student teachers in schools not only because of the importance of their own school-situated professional expertise but also because it is in schools that they need to help student teachers to learn to engage in disciplined everyday practical theorizing, and more generally because it is on a school-based curriculum that the student teachers' professional learning directly depends. The core ITE curriculum has to be a school-based curriculum. University-based teacher educators, in contrast, are needed because they have a vital *service* role to play in feeding into and supporting the core school-based curriculum. They need to help both the student teachers and the school-based teacher educators to draw on research-based and other academic kinds of knowledge, and to support them in asking critical questions, so that the school-based learning can draw strongly on university traditions of independent and disciplined thought.

What, then, in more concrete terms is this service role that HEIs should play? We need to take account of not only the central argument about universities' traditions of critical scholarship and inquiry but also the asymmetry that we noted between, on the one hand, universities as purpose-built centres for adult education and, on the other hand, schools as not generally at all geared to adult learning. Therefore, whatever can equally well be done in either place should be done in HEIs, because it is they that are set up for such adult education enterprises. Most obviously, as seems already to be widely recognized, ITE programmes can most easily be managed by HEIs; and it is also in HEIs that subject knowledge can most sensibly be taught. Second, for similar reasons, universities frequently hold relevant scarce resources, such as their libraries and scholars with specialist expertise, and appropriate advantage should be taken of these resources. For example, HEIs should act as flexible resource centres to support student teachers and school-based teacher educators in their pursuit of their school-based practical theorizing work.

The third and most fundamental role for HEI-based teacher educators is to contribute whatever can effectively be dealt with at a general or abstract level and does not depend on engaging with particular school students, circumstances and activities. One very important element of this should be a meta-role, helping student teachers to understand the nature of teaching and teaching expertise in general and also the processes through which teaching expertise is developed. This should include in particular the nature of the agreed practical theorizing agenda and its importance in developing their own expertise, and the central role that they as student teachers have to accept in their own development within the course. Equally important is the need to enable student teachers to understand in conceptual terms the theoretical and research-based knowledge that will have to be the focus of much attention in the core school-based curriculum.

A partnership can be effective, however, only when its enterprise is a joint one; and even more important than the partners' shared understanding of their different contributions is their shared understanding of the joint enterprise itself. One of the most important roles of both schools and HEIs in ITE partnerships is therefore jointly developing appropriate and realistic plans for a shared curriculum, a curriculum that they commit themselves to pursuing in a co-ordinated way in both types of location. This needs to be a very well-planned curriculum, with at its core the school-based curriculum, but with a very carefully co-ordinated university-based curriculum designed to support that core curriculum. Themes about which all student teachers need to learn should be agreed. A set of core practical ideas in relation to each of these themes should include, first, what are generally regarded as good practices in the partnership schools; second, all alternative ideas reflecting, as suggested by experience, common preconceptions of student teachers; and third, any alternative ideas for good practice favoured by the university-based teacher educators and viewed as worthy of serious consideration by most of the school-based teacher educators. It is especially crucial that this third set of ideas, stemming from academic sources, should be chosen through an active consensus, especially of school-based teacher educators, since a basic principle has to be that the university-based support curriculum should introduce only ideas that are going to be actively pursued in the school-based core curriculum.

The curriculum planning should also involve reaching agreement on a core set of questions to be pursued, appropriately and flexibly, in practical theorizing about all suggested 'good ideas'. Among these questions, some should identify practical issues to which it would be wise for student teachers always to attend, about for example the availability of, or the practicability of preparing, necessary resources; the time required to pursue a suggested practice effectively; the arrangements of space and of furniture necessary to optimize the intended learning processes, and the practicability of making such arrangements. Other questions might concern assumptions that suggested practices make about school students' thinking, attitudes, skills and interests and the understanding that they will need in order to succeed. Diverse other kinds of questions might be concerned with, for example, the clarity of the suggested ideas, the purposes for which they are proposed to be appropriate, the grounds for believing that they will be effective for these purposes, the circumstances in which they are likely to be appropriate and effective, the educational values implicit in the practices and the teaching skills necessary for their effective use.

Such joint curriculum planning seems essential both at whole-school level and also for each subject curriculum area in secondary partnerships and for each phase level in primary partnerships. It should provide the core agenda for practical theorizing and skills development, to be pursued in school by each student teacher, working with the support of the appropriate school-based teacher educator. That agenda would of course be developed and pursued in a unique way in each case, taking account of the aspirations, concerns, values and preconceptions of the student teacher, the realities and practices of the school and department, the opportunities and difficulties experienced by the student teacher in practice, and the questions, judgements and concerns of the school-based teacher educator.

This whole-school-based curriculum should be concerned with providing optimal activities for the modelling, practice and feedback of good ideas for skilful teaching and for the complementary activity of practical theorizing about these ideas. The choice and use of these activities and ideas should be directed towards attainment of the goal that student teachers should become competent beginning teachers and also of the goal that they should acquire the understandings, skills and habits to go on developing their expertise critically as practising teachers. But it is important to note that the achievement especially of that second goal will depend not only on the ideas and activities of the planned curriculum but also on the climate within which these are pursued. Unless the school-based teacher educators and other teachers with whom student teachers work themselves reflect a self-critical concern to develop their own teaching, it cannot be confidently expected that the student teachers will be inducted into such a conception of professionalism in teaching.

It may be noted that, having suggested earlier that schools have not traditionally been at all well geared to fostering the learning of the adults who work there, we are now suggesting that schools' effectiveness as ITE institutions does depend on their developing a general climate characterized by active and evident professional learning.

This issue of the school context in which student teachers are learning becomes even more important in relation to the third priority goal that we suggested for ITE, that of student teachers learning to respond constructively but critically to innovative ideas. Such learning depends on experiencing and dealing with the serious tensions that innovations always bring with them, between the uncertain rewards that new ideas might bring and the certain costs of abandoning well-learned practices in which much has been invested and of having to learn new ways. Since student teachers' own practices tend to be still far from stable and well learned, their learning about such tensions must in large measure be vicarious. A very important condition for the effective pursuit of this goal is therefore that the host school or department would need to have committed itself to exploring the merits of such innovations *for its own improvement*. Schools committed to their own improvement can indeed benefit greatly from their engagement in this aspect of ITE, both through having student teachers and through their partnerships with universities. We would envisage that a partnership planning group might agree on a menu of innovations that seemed attractive to the schools or departments involved. The HEI could appropriately take on the roles of advocate and facilitator for each of these innovations, with the task of leading both teachers and student teachers in thinking about the benefits to be looked for and about necessary conditions and changes for the realization of these benefits. The student teachers in each school or department could appropriately be the main action researchers, with responsibilities both for implementing the innovation on a small scale and for investigating its advantages and its problems. Such action research projects should offer excellent professional education for student teachers in relation to the processes and problems of innovation. But the value and indeed the practicality of such projects would depend crucially on the schools or departments having the active level of interest in them that would come only from seeing them as potentially contributing to their own improvement.

Towards a school-based approach to ITE

We have in this chapter outlined some elements of the kind of predominantly school-based approach to ITE that we believe will best prepare teachers for twenty-first-century schools. It is an approach that builds on the developments of recent years, during which thousands of school-based teacher educators in England have taken on major ITE responsibilities and have thoughtfully developed a high level of competence and considerable confidence in that role. It is, however, an approach that will depend on these teacher educators and their partners in universities taking on the task, deliberately neglected in the early 1990s by the then government, of fundamentally rethinking the ITE curriculum and how it can most effectively be pursued. It therefore both builds upon the strengths, and takes account of the weaknesses, of current ITE practice in England.

At the core of the proposed approach is our analysis of the nature of classroom teaching expertise, outlined in Chapter 2, which concludes that it is primarily from the craft of classroom teaching, embedded in the practice of experienced classroom teachers, that both student teachers and also we as analysts can derive our best understanding of such expertise. Our analysis puts emphasis on the sophisticated, contextualized decision-making in which classroom teachers have to engage, taking account of multiple and complex considerations, and necessarily doing so to a considerable extent in a tacit and intuitive way. But it also emphasizes that any claims that particular cases of such practice represent good practice must be based on searching, critical analysis, drawing on, among other things, the fullest learning possible from diverse traditions of classroom research.

Accordingly, in this chapter we have focused primarily on the kinds of learning necessary for the development of such expertise. Our concern has been to identify in general terms the kinds of learning activity that can most purposefully and effectively be directed to the fostering of such development and towards the three goals that we identified: a high level of competence as beginning teachers; ability to continue learning with experience; and ability to respond constructively and critically to innovations. We have considered the advantages of work-based learning in general, and those of school-based learning more specifically. While acknowledging the advantages of incidental learning, we have concluded that effective learning for teaching will need to be quite highly structured. More precisely, we have emphasized the need to combine a firm maintenance of a normal realistic work context with provision of the necessary structures to give student teachers effective access to that reality and especially access to the expertise used in practice by experienced teachers. For example, appropriate assessment structures are valuable in order to discipline and give shape to the learning, but they should not – as we fear they all too often do at present – distort the realities with which the learning should be concerned.

In this chapter, we have discussed in rather abstract terms the kinds of learning activities that are necessary to enable student teachers to develop the expertise that they need. On that basis, we can with confidence assert some general guiding ideas:

1 The idea of 'school experience' or 'school placement' in ITE should be replaced by that of a coherently planned, structured and comprehensive school-based curriculum which should form the core of the whole ITE curriculum, closely integrated with a supporting HEI-based curriculum.
2 The curriculum should be directed towards student teachers' acquisition of the distinctive kind of expertise required for skilled and self-critical classroom teaching and also towards the ability to develop that expertise critically from experience and the ability to respond constructively and critically to proposed innovations.
3 The school-based curriculum should be planned to take account of the distinctive opportunities offered by school contexts for professional learning:
   • It should place a very high value on the professional craft knowledge of experienced teachers.
   • It should be structured as much as is necessary to maximize learners' cognitive access to the realities of schooling, including especially teachers' craft knowledge, but not in ways that distort those realities.
   • It should provide time and appropriate opportunities for diverse kinds of learning, including incidental learning, implicit learning and deliberative learning.
   • It should give particular attention to the modelling, practice and feedback processes necessary for developing skilled teaching and to the practical theorizing processes necessary for critically evaluating ideas for practice.

4 It should enable learners to deal effectively with the considerable emotional, cognitive, practical and social difficulties involved in finding and critically examining good ideas for practice and developing the skilled use of these practices.
5 It should treat student teachers as key players in their own professional education, with their own values, beliefs and agendas being accepted as highly significant for shaping the content and activities of the curriculum.
6 Theorizing and practical learning need to be closely integrated as practical theorizing in schools, with each student teacher being challenged and supported on an individual basis by school-based teacher educators.
7 While ITE curricula must be planned in the light of the current realities of school life and organization, it is also the case that their effectiveness will depend on the general school climate being evidently supportive of ongoing professional learning.

Very little is known, however, about what such coherent and comprehensive school-based curricula would look like in practice, far less how we can best move towards them from the basic school-based activities in which student teachers are commonly asked to engage at present. We need, therefore, to explore both questions about the content and structure of such curricula and also questions about what may be involved in the development of such curricula. Some of the questions which seem to arise from our reflections in this chapter are the following:

• How can student teachers effectively gain access to experienced teachers' professional craft knowledge? How is this possible given the tacit and intuitive nature of teachers' craft knowledge? How can the problem of teachers taking their own expertise for granted be overcome? How can the need for student teachers to think critically about all practices of teaching be made compatible with the need for them to be respectful to experienced teachers? What factors facilitate or constrain such desirable processes?
• How can effective account be taken of student teachers' ideas in a school-based curriculum? How is it possible to respond positively and constructively to student teachers' agendas? How is it possible to prevent student teachers' preconceptions from interfering with necessary learning? How can curricula take account of the wide diversity in student teachers' values and preconceptions? How can the curriculum take account of student teachers' cognitive and affective development without making false assumptions about common patterns in their development? What factors facilitate or constrain such desirable processes?
• How can a structured curriculum for student teachers be made compatible with the realities of schooling, when these realities are both the context and the content for learning? How can the quality of model-

ling, practice and feedback for student teachers be optimized in ways that support and do not distort the normal work of schools? How can a systematic curriculum for practical theorizing about agreed themes and ideas be effectively fitted into the ordinary work of schools? How can the curriculum be structured to help beginning teachers cope with the emotional, social, intellectual and practical difficulties of learning to teach through practical theorizing? How can universities most usefully support such desirable processes? What factors facilitate or constrain such desirable processes?

• What kinds of processes of curriculum development seem to be necessary in order to establish acceptable, viable and effective ITE curricula in schools?

In Part B of this book, we give an account of an experimental initiative undertaken in order to develop one possible element of a school-based ITE curriculum. Our aim is to use that experimental initiative to test out some of the ideas we have outlined, and especially to begin to answer some of the above questions. We shall also expect, of course, to discover new guiding ideas, new problems and new questions.

Part B

Tapping into Teachers' Professional Craft Knowledge

4 An experiment in the modelling of teachers' professional craft knowledge

In Chapter 3, we pointed to the need to develop, to test and to learn to use new methods for school-based teacher education. We argued that a largely school-based approach offered exciting new opportunities for ITE, opportunities which have as yet remained largely unexplored. But, while we were able to articulate in generalized and abstract terms the considerable potential advantages of a planned school-based ITE curriculum, we had to admit that we knew very little about what such a curriculum might look like in concrete terms. Furthermore, we knew equally little about what might be involved in practice in the planning of such a curriculum. We suggested therefore that there was a need for experimental projects to explore these issues.

Accordingly, this chapter and the next are devoted to an account of such an experimental project. The project is concerned with a new method for school-based ITE, one aimed at enabling student teachers to tap into experienced teachers' professional craft knowledge. This project was carried out within the framework of the secondary Postgraduate Certificate of Education (PGCE) course at Oxford University, more commonly known as the Oxford Internship Scheme.

We need to be careful not to exaggerate, but also not to underestimate, the importance of the method with which the project is concerned. It was, from the beginning, viewed as only one small experimental part of the whole programme, although a very significant part. Its significance stems from the fact that student teachers do not generally seem to gain access to very much of experienced teachers' professional craft knowledge. This enormous potentially available and highly relevant knowledge resource was not effectively tapped during the twentieth century simply because it was not sufficiently valued. It is more highly valued now, but lack of careful thought about school-based ITE has meant that it is still far from adequately accessed. Traditional school-based ITE methods do not provide such access. Observation of experienced teachers has been common but, for the various reasons discussed in Chapter 3, it has not been used effectively for this purpose. Novices do not know what there is to be learned, nor how they can learn it; experienced teachers take their tacit, intuitive expertise for granted and are not therefore motivated to reveal and explain it; and schools are busy *workplaces*, in which time is not generally scheduled for such professional learning. In so far as, in recent years, time has been scheduled for student teachers to learn from their mentors, the focus has very largely been on the *student teachers' teaching*, and therefore on what mentors see as directly and immediately relevant to that. So the method explored in this project is significant because it is one possible method for redressing this major previous failure to find ways for student teachers to gain access to, and so to learn from, the professional craft knowledge of experienced teachers. It was for that reason that the project was undertaken.

In the context of this book, however, the project that we are about to report has an additional significance: it exemplifies both the new methods that are needed for school-based ITE and the kinds of investigation of these methods that are needed. Furthermore, it exemplifies in its findings the kinds of opportunities and problems of which curriculum planning for school-based ITE will have to take account. There are three main reasons for its appropriateness for exemplifying these things. First, as we have noted, it is concerned with what should be one of the core purposes of school-based ITE, the sharing of experienced teachers' expertise with novices. Second, it involved, as all new such methods will, facing up to the tensions between wanting student teachers to learn about schools as they are but needing to plan systematically so that they could gain access to the complex knowledge available. Third, it took as its starting point, as we believe all such new methods should, the best research-based theoretical understandings of which we were aware both about what we wanted the student teachers to learn and about how this learning might be facilitated.

This part of the book, reporting this specific project, consists of two chapters. This chapter explains first what we were trying to do, how we set about it, and what we learned from our first two years of exploratory studies, especially about necessary conditions for the proposed ITE procedure to be feasible. It then goes on to report our testing in the third year of the investigation of the core hypotheses by which our action research was driven, using our most fully developed version of the procedure. Could we persuade and enable the student teachers to do what we believed they needed to do? And would such actions on their part lead to their getting access to teachers' professional craft knowledge? Then, in

Chapter 5, we report on our evidence, from interviews in that third year, of the reflections of the teachers and the student teachers on their experience of the method in use and of its advantages and limitations.

The initial rationale

Given our commitment to helping student teachers to gain access to the rich and expert professional craft knowledge of experienced teachers with whom they were working in schools, how were we going to try to do that? Our starting point was some research on teachers' professional craft knowledge in which one of us had been involved, research reported in Brown and McIntyre (1993).

Brown and McIntyre's study is important in two respects. First, it offers an empirically grounded model of the nature of the knowledge that teachers use in their everyday classroom practice. Second, and of equal importance, their study suggests that it is possible to gain access to teachers' professional craft knowledge. This led to the question that was fundamental in shaping the research and development project in Oxford: if researchers can gain access to and describe teachers' professional craft knowledge, is it not possible to learn from their approach in order to give guidance to student teachers? The question facing us then was: in order to access the knowledge embedded in the practice of the teachers with whom they work in schools, could student teachers use the same general approach as had been successfully used by Brown and McIntyre?

They summarize that approach as:

- emphasizing what was good about the teaching, in the eyes of the teachers and pupils;
- focusing on specific classroom events which occurred when both teacher and researcher were present;
- determinedly avoiding the imposition of any researcher preconceptions about good teaching or about how to make sense of teaching;
- helping teachers to remember what was involved in doing the things they did well, the most important element in this being to interview the teachers very soon after the observed lessons (1993: 48).

It could not be assumed that by employing such an approach student teachers would be equally successful in tapping into that knowledge which is not generally made explicit and which teachers are not necessarily always conscious of using. The summary above does not do justice to the detailed preparation, extensive preliminary negotiations with schools, teachers and pupils, and the high level of interviewing expertise that characterized Brown and McIntyre's research approach. Moreover, even if the student teachers were able – and indeed willing – to adopt key features of the approach, there was no guarantee that experienced teachers would respond at all in the same way to trainees as they had done to respected academics.

At a broad level, the concern of this project was then with the possibilities and the implications of student teachers gaining access to the professional craft knowledge of experienced practitioners, and more specifically with exploring the possibilities of building on the work of Brown and McIntyre for that purpose. The questions to be investigated were about the procedures for gaining access to teachers' craft knowledge as an integral part of an ITE programme.

A number of studies were conducted over a three-year period in order to collect evidence, and thereby acquire understandings which in turn led to successive developments in the procedures to be used, and in the choice of contexts within which they were used. This series of studies can be seen, therefore, as following a classical action research pattern.

The research carried out in the third year represented the culmination of the three-year programme, with procedures and contexts for their use having been chosen and shaped in the light of considerable evidence and experience acquired over the first two years of the project. Our first task therefore is to explain what was learned from these first two years.

Getting started

Our interest in whether teachers could articulate their professional craft knowledge to student teachers within the constraints of everyday life in school found expression in the following question:

- Given how busy the practising teacher normally is, how can student teachers get access to practitioners' professional craft knowledge?

In addition to this central question were the following three subsidiary questions:

- What are the environmental and organizational conditions that encourage articulation of professional craft knowledge?
- How is it possible to get teachers to talk about their teaching in a non-defensive way that genuinely reflects the ways in which they do things?
- Are there particular problems and/or possibilities associated with teachers articulating their professional craft knowledge to student teachers?

While the research depended very heavily on the work of Brown and McIntyre (1993), it was a project of a very different kind to the one they had carried out. The main concern of this study was with student teachers and their professional learning. We were interested in the interactions between experienced teachers and student teachers, not those between teachers and their pupils.

Before embarking on any preliminary trials or pilot studies, we set about sensitizing ourselves to issues revolving around student teachers learning from the teaching of experienced teachers. To this end we interviewed two teachers who were generally acknowledged to be good practitioners and effective mentors. The focus of these lengthy but informal interviews was on how the teachers worked with student teachers, their suggestions for improving the ways in which teachers and student teachers worked together, and their views on our thinking about how to enable student teachers to access teachers' professional craft knowledge. In addition, in the context of the student teachers' programme of general professional studies, a session on observation was set up in which four groups of them were asked to write about the most interesting things they had learned from observation and the advice they would give other student teachers to enable them to get the most from observation.

The interviews and the written responses of the student teachers served to reinforce the view that if student teachers were to access teachers' craft knowledge they would need considerable help. That such help would be valuable and necessary seemed clear on a number of grounds:

1 There was a widespread view apparent among student teachers and their mentors that observation of the latter by the former, while of some value in the first few weeks of the PGCE year, was of limited value overall and was therefore rarely undertaken in the middle and later stages of the year.
2 Available evidence suggested that, even when observation was undertaken, little time if any was given to teachers' explanations of what they had been doing and why; teachers seemed widely to believe that what happened in their lessons was 'obvious' and generally not very interesting.
3 From Brown and McIntyre's study it was apparent, from the pleasure shown by teachers who had been helped to talk about the knowledge and expertise they had used in observed lessons, that despite their experience in supervising student teachers, the articulation of such knowledge was a new experience for them.
4 The complexity, sensitivity and incisiveness of teachers' accounts of their use of knowledge in specific observed situations contrasted with a tendency towards simplicity and overgeneralization in their decontextualized talk about teaching.

Designing the study: preliminary trials

It was one thing to know that student teachers would need help if they were to tap into teachers' professional craft knowledge, but it was quite another to know what form that help might take. In order to work that out, we carried out a series of preliminary trials.

Before involving any of the student teachers in the trials, we needed to know more about how to facilitate teachers' readiness and ability to reveal their professional craft knowledge in a way that took account of time constraints in a 'normal' school week and was not dependent on a video or audio recording of the lesson. In a school where one of us had at one time been professional tutor, three teachers were observed, each on four occasions, and within 24 hours of each lesson were interviewed about the observed teaching. Following the main principles of the strategy used by Brown and McIntyre (1993) in helping teachers talk about how they made sense of their teaching, the emphasis in the interview was on what was good about the teaching, as seen by the teacher, and the focus was on specific events of the observed lesson.

As in the studies carried out by Brown and McIntyre, teachers' talk of particular classroom situations and actions revealed a richness of knowledge use which went well beyond what the observer had surmised from observation, and which pleased and excited the teachers themselves. These early attempts held out the promise, then, of gaining access to teachers' craft knowledge through the relatively simple procedure adopted. However, a question to be considered was whether the teachers would talk in this way when they were being interviewed by student teachers. The readiness of teachers to reveal their thinking seemed in this case to flow from their sense of security with a trusted ex-colleague and from their knowledge that the interviewer would understand and sympathize with what they had been doing. The trials had also indicated that access to teachers' craft knowledge would depend on skilful, disciplined and thoughtful behaviour on the part of the observer/interviewer: from our own experience we were acutely aware of the temptation to ask generalized questions such as 'Is this a feature of your teaching?', and of the difficulty for the interviewer in refraining from offering one's own preconceptions about how to make sense of teaching. If these were problems for us, it was anticipated that they might also be problems for the student teachers.

This indeed proved to be the case when the same three teachers were each observed and interviewed by the two student teachers attached to them. From the audio recordings of the discussion following observation, it became clear that the student teachers' questions – most of which did not conform to the guidelines they had been given – had not enabled the teachers to talk about the observed teaching and the thinking underlying that teaching as they had done with their ex-colleague or in a way that was helpful to beginning teachers. There was, however, a great deal to be learned from this failed first attempt, not least about the student teachers' concerns and preconceptions. It was now possible to draw up revised guidelines – partly through the use of telling examples – that were more relevant to the distinctive position and problems of the student teachers. Among the points which emerged and the consequent actions taken were the following.

Types of conversation. The student teachers were eager to acquire generally helpful information and ideas – for example, about the differences among pupils, about the qualities that a good teacher needs, about how to motivate pupils, or about how to make lessons interesting. They therefore tended to seek the kinds of conversations in which they could learn such things and in which the talk was not tied to specific contexts. The indication was that they did not recognize that the kind of conversation they could most usefully have about a teacher's teaching following observation of that teaching would be different from the other kinds of conversations that as student teachers they were likely to have with experienced practitioners. To value this kind of conversation does not imply any devaluing of the other kinds of conversations, but it does imply a recognition of its distinctiveness and of the necessity of it not getting mixed up with the other kinds. This was one of the more important insights gained, and arguably the most difficult one to act on, because it suggested that success was dependent on student teachers understanding the differences among types of conversation, and also valuing teachers' professional craft knowledge to the extent that they would be prepared to restrict themselves on given occasions to the appropriate context-bound kind of conversation.

Revised guidelines included commentary on the notion of different kinds of conversations with experienced teachers. In addition, in discussion with both the student teachers and the teachers, it was pointed out that as the post-observation conversation would be much more useful if confined to this distinctive context-bound kind of talk, it might well be more formal in tone than other kinds of conversations.

It was also recognized that any future plans should take account of the need for more time to be given to helping the student teachers to gain a fuller understanding of, and to place greater value on, the idea of professional craft knowledge.

Sticking to specifics. The student teachers had found it very difficult to relate all of their questions to the particular observed lesson.

To address this, the general rule was formulated that all the questions asked of teachers should be in the simple past tense. Second, examples were given of the kinds of questions to be avoided, such as 'Do you think lots of gestures are important for teachers?' or 'Do you always arrange pupils in groups like that?'. It was also pointed out that, in answer to a question about a specific event in the observed lesson, the teacher might very revealingly move away from the starting point in the lesson under discussion by talking about how they might have acted differently had the topic, or time of day, or phase of the lesson, or the pupils involved, been different; but that such talk, in response to a specific question, was very different from the talk that would be prompted by the question being posed in general terms.

Student teachers' own agendas. The student teachers found it difficult to accept that experienced teachers might formulate and think about issues in ways quite different from their own. Such was their concern with the issues as they saw them that they had great difficulty in avoiding closed either/or kinds of questions, and in asking instead the open kinds of questions to which teachers can more easily respond. A pervasive concern of the student teachers in this trial was with planning as opposed to spontaneity. Questions such as 'Did you decide to do that on the spur of the moment?' and 'Is that what you planned to do?' were frequent, and the teachers generally seemed to find such questions confusing and unproductive.

Since access to craft knowledge seemed clearly to depend on the avoidance of closed questions of this kind, attempts were made to explain more fully to the student teachers why this was so, and relevant examples of open and closed questions were added to the guidelines.

Teachers' defensiveness. It was not difficult for the teachers, who had been working amicably with their student teachers for several months, to be put on the defensive by the substance and tone of the student teachers' questions. The student teachers, themselves very sensitive to criticism of their teaching, seemed to have little understanding of the vulnerability to such criticism of their supervising teachers. Not only did they ask teachers to justify their teaching, but also their general demeanour and way of asking questions meant that even innocent questions seeking explanations could be experienced as demands for justification. In these situations, teachers could quickly become prickly, and switch from revealing the thinking behind their practice to standing on the dignity of their status and experience.

It was evident that earlier attempts to explain the importance of the part played by student teachers in helping teachers to talk about their observed teaching had failed. This time the discussion about the importance of their contribution to the exercise focused on extracts from the audiotapes of their conversations with the teachers. In addition, the difficulty for teachers in unpicking the practices that are normally taken for granted, and the ease with which they could feel threatened, were underlined. More specifically, an additional rule was added to the guidelines: a favourite question of the student teachers – 'Why didn't you … ?' – was banned.

As part of the attempt to overcome this problem of teacher defensiveness, the teachers themselves were reminded of the great value that the University placed on their professional craft knowledge, and they were urged not to undervalue it themselves. Finally, it was suggested to them that it was not unusual for student teachers to give the appearance of being critical when in fact they were simply eager to understand.

The complexity of teaching. As in Brown and McIntyre's study, it had been noted that teachers' initial response to questions about what they had done in the observed lesson tended to be brief, but that with patient probing they had a great deal more to say. In their conversations with the student teachers, however, this initial reticence was not so easily overcome. The student teachers tended either to join in with suggestions of their own about the teaching or to accept the first response as representing the totality of the teachers' use of their craft knowledge.

Efforts were made, therefore, to persuade them to pursue most issues further, and not be shy of probing for explanations or more extensive responses. 'Could you tell me what made you decide to do that?' and 'Could you say a little more about that?' were offered as examples of questions that could be helpful in getting the teachers to elaborate on initial responses.

The revised and extended guidelines were then tried out with 12 student teachers, some of whom worked with teachers who had been involved in earlier trials, while others observed and interviewed teachers who had no previous experience of the procedure.

Although results were mixed and, with small numbers involved, the effects of different factors could not be disentangled, the revised guidelines certainly seemed to have offered effective guidance. Several of the student teachers had learned to use the procedure skilfully and productively, making it relatively easy for teachers to share their craft knowledge with them. It was also noted that some of the teachers, having become fully convinced of the value of the enterprise, became less dependent on the student teachers' questions. For example, they would convert closed questions into open ones which they could more usefully answer, suggest questions which they thought might be asked, or ignore the aggressiveness which might have seemed implicit in a question.

The one entirely unproductive follow-up conversation suggested that, even with clear guidelines, the attitude of the student teacher when interviewing the teacher was of crucial importance: a judgemental stance could undermine the possibility of teachers being able to articulate their craft knowledge. In this particular case the student teacher made it clear that he had no interest in knowing how the teacher went about maintaining the kind of working classroom atmosphere she saw as desirable, as he did not 'approve' of it.

At a theoretical level, these preliminary trials had highlighted the fundamental difficulty of the task of enabling student teachers to gain access to the craft knowledge of experienced practitioners. Why was it so difficult? There appeared to be three reasons:

- It is not only easier for student teachers and teachers to concern themselves with more generalized kinds of knowledge about teaching, it can also superficially seem more useful; so, for both these reasons, it can be considerably more attractive.
- Experienced teachers take for granted the expertise and thinking embedded in their day-to-day teaching, do not easily or 'naturally' recognize its complexity or importance, and often find it difficult to unpick it in any detail.
- Student teachers are primarily concerned with their own very differently structured problems, seek general solutions to these problems, and tend to be unaware of the sophistication, subtlety and importance of teachers' professional craft knowledge. In their innocence and at this stage in their learning, the questions they want to ask are not generally related to the craft knowledge of teachers.

To sum up: the trials involving the student teachers had served to remind us of the multi-faceted complexity of the problem. They had also indicated that it was both possible and useful to enable student teachers to gain access to the craft knowledge of experienced teachers. We had learned the following:

- It was possible for student teachers to gain access to the craft knowledge of experienced practitioners within the constraints of everyday life in schools.
- In so far as student teachers could recognize that they do not know what they need to know, their very ignorance could help experienced teachers to talk about those things they usually take for granted.
- By revealing their professional craft knowledge teachers could help student teachers to learn from them.
- Both teachers and student teachers could come to see engaging in the procedure as a valuable use of their time, and to welcome it as a valuable way of learning about effective teaching.
- Both teachers and student teachers recognized the process as something they had not experienced before. This newness was important, indicating as it did that both teachers and student teachers would not only have to learn how to engage in this kind of conversation, but also have to be persuaded that it was a valuable and perhaps the only source for a particular kind of learning.

The culmination of this first stage of the study was the production of a package of training materials, including a training videotape showing negative and positive models, intended both to be persuasive and to give practical guidance to student teachers about how to engage in observation with follow-up discussion.

Institutionalizing the proposed procedures: first attempts and initial evidence

The next step was to move, in the second year of the project, from working with small groups of student teachers and teachers to institutionalizing the procedure. That student teachers should gain access to the craft knowledge of experienced practitioners was an agreed element of the PGCE programme, which meant that all the student teachers on the course and their mentors within the partnership scheme were being encouraged to engage in the procedure.

In testing the adequacy and usefulness of the preparation of student teachers and mentors, we were seeking answers to the following questions:

- Do mentors and student teachers understand what they are being encouraged to do? If not, why not?
- Do those student teachers who do understand get the opportunity to engage in the procedure?
- Are the student teachers willing and able to translate that understanding into action?
- If they are willing and able to do so, does such action lead to the kind of mentor talk deemed desirable by the researchers and recognized as useful by the student teachers and mentors?

To prepare them for this particular kind of observation and interview, the procedure was introduced to the student teachers in the university during the two-week period of induction to the PGCE course. In the initial oral presentation the following three key points were emphasized:

- the contrast between student teachers' conscious and deliberate planning for teaching and teachers' routine and largely hidden use of craft knowledge, and the importance and difficulty of getting access to the craft knowledge;
- the complexity and skilfulness of the teaching which would usually underlie an apparently straightforward lesson;
- the pitfalls of learning to teach through trial and error, and the value of learning from the teaching of experienced practitioners.

The presentation was followed by a showing of the training video. Written materials were distributed and the session ended with discussion of the procedure and its purpose.

Mentors and university tutors had been introduced to the procedure and to the thinking behind it at a series of seminars held as part of a two-day conference during the previous summer. Copies of the materials given to the student teachers were now sent to the mentors who were encouraged to engage in the procedure on a regular basis, perhaps once a fortnight. University tutors were also reminded of this element of the PGCE programme and were asked to encourage the mentors and the student teachers in their subject areas to use the procedure on a regular basis.

One further point was important about the initial guidance given: the student teachers were strongly encouraged to audiotape the post-lesson interviews with mentors or other teachers. Although it was mentioned that the tutors (the researchers) who had introduced the procedure would value the opportunity to listen to the tapes in order to asses the adequacy of the advice given, this was not offered as the major reason for audiotaping. Earlier experience had suggested that a good deal of student teachers' talk during such interviews was aimed at checking that their understandings of what the teacher had said were correct; so the suggestion that the interviews should be recorded was aimed primarily at giving the student teachers the opportunity to listen to what had been said and to reflect on it, and it was in these terms that the suggestion was explained.

The initial response of the student teachers and of the university tutors to the meetings about gaining access to teachers' craft knowledge seemed very positive. Furthermore, reactions from the schools were encouraging. A number of schools asked for an opportunity to view the training videotape, while others invited the researchers to talk to mentors about teachers' professional craft knowledge and ways in which it might be accessed by their student teachers. It was therefore with a growing sense of disappointment that we came to realize that the suggested procedure was being used very rarely. We now had to find out why this was so.

Unsystematic evidence derived from participant observation suggested that we had grossly underestimated the pressures on time for student teachers and mentors. The initial suggestion that they engage in the procedure on a fortnightly basis now seemed naïve in the extreme. Furthermore, this initiative was jostling with many others in the PGCE course for the attention of student teachers and mentors; a feature of two of the curriculum programmes, for example, was the need for student teachers to carry out audiotaped interviews with their mentors.

The first structured attempt at gathering evidence to help us to understand what was going wrong was the distribution of a brief questionnaire to the PGCE students early in the second term. This was also seen as an opportunity to encourage them to engage in the procedure during the coming weeks: the letter accompanying the questionnaire reminded them of the presentation during the induction period, was sympathetic to their not having engaged in the procedure, and suggested they observe and interview a teacher – and audiotape the interview – on two occasions before the end of the term.

Of the cohort of 143 PGCE students, 120 returned completed questionnaires. The first question invited them to choose from among five options the statement that best described what they had done following the presentation in October. The results are presented in Table 4.1. To begin with,

Table 4.1   PGCE students' reported activities following the October presentation

	Frequency (%)
1 I have a tape of an interview with my mentor (or other teacher) following an observed lesson.	12
2 I have attempted to follow the procedure outlined, but I have not taped an interview.	23
3 I observed my mentor (or other teacher) and talked with him/her afterwards, but did not restrict myself to the kind of interview suggested.	59
4 I have not attempted to observe and interview my mentor (or other teacher), but the way in which I have approached teachers has been influenced by what was said in the presentation about the professional craft knowledge of teachers.	7
5 I do not think I have been influenced in any way by the presentation in October.	0

it was encouraging that none of the respondents chose the fifth and most negative option, 'I do not think I have been influenced in any way by the lecture in October'. However, the dominant response, from 59 per cent of respondents – 'I observed my mentor (or other teacher) and talked with him/her afterwards, but did not restrict myself to the kind of interview suggested', sent out a clear message: two-thirds of the PGCE students had not been successfully persuaded to try and adopt the kind of procedure that had been developed.

Ninety per cent of the respondents accepted the invitation to comment on their reasons for doing what they had done. Fifteen per cent of the comments indicated that the guidelines or at least the ideas behind them had been useful, for example:

After some initial embarrassment, the interview proved to be honest, illuminating and very helpful in terms of understanding the methodology and management techniques of an experienced teacher. I also found that the questions asked were directed in such a way (because of the formal setting) that they would not have been asked in our normal exchanges with our mentor.

A useful exercise and the lecture was helpful in stressing the need for the student not to seem antagonistic during the interview.

Almost all the other comments fell into three clear clusters, of roughly equal size, concerned with time, taping and formality.

It was felt simply that there was not enough *time* to use the procedure. While some pointed out that 'teachers don't have time to talk after lessons' or that 'We have so many other things to observe and think about in the first term that we just haven't had time to organise the interview', in most cases it was not clear whether the perceived problem was with the mentor's or the PGCE student's lack of time.

Three main kinds of problems with the *taping* were mentioned, all with more or less equal frequency. First, the student teachers themselves considered taping unnecessary or inappropriate, and preferred taking notes:

> It would be a rather artificial kind of interview which would be altered fundamentally by the 'silent presence' of the tape recorder. I get all I need from notes and they don't get in the way.

> I'm not happy about this taping business.

Second, mentors were reported as not liking to be taped:

> They don't like being taped, it makes them react unnaturally – they try and give us the answers they think the University would like them to give us ...

Finally, there were practical problems such as the need for a quiet room, the lack of a tape recorder, or technical problems when recording was tried:

> It seemed unduly intimidating to actually tape the interview – I was quite relieved when we couldn't find a power point in the room.

In addition, several of the student teachers who had been set specific tasks in relation to their curriculum programmes which involved taping conversations with their mentors, commented that it would be unreasonable to ask for any more taped conversations.

Turning to the issue of *formality*, student teachers reported that they found it easier, preferable and more useful to talk with their mentors informally. In their view the formality of the suggested procedure was artificial and contrived, mentors did not see the need for it, and the guidelines could be followed roughly in an informal way:

> I feel that any useful information can usually be picked up in a casual 5–10 min. chat after the lesson, and so I haven't bothered with the more structured and formal approach.

> My mentor does not seem to be the kind of person who would enjoy this type of close analysis after a lesson. Also I feel it would be a rather artificial kind of interview.

These problems of time, taping and formality were closely interrelated. In schools, teachers' time – other than that timetabled with pupils – is rarely available in clear, structured units. The tendency is for time to be found when doing something else – having coffee, walking to the next lesson, preparing apparatus, marking books; talking 'on the hoof' is commonplace. Given such a situation it is not surprising that structured and disciplined conversations among adults are the exception rather than the norm. It was clear that the kind of formalized interviews that PGCE students had been encouraged to engage in with their mentors was alien to the culture of school life. And the taping of those interviews had served to exacerbate their alien formality.

Digging deeper: interviews with student teachers and mentors

As the PGCE year progressed, it continued to be clear that the recommended procedures were rarely being followed. A lot had been learned from the questionnaire survey, but we needed to get a fuller and broader picture. We needed to understand more about, for example, how mentors and student teachers construed teachers' expertise and learning about teaching; and how they saw access to teachers' craft knowledge – whether by the proposed procedure or in other ways – fitting into the totality of what there was to be learned from teachers and how it could be learned. After two years of trying to work out how to enable student teachers to gain access to experienced teachers' professional craft knowledge, we needed as full an understanding as possible of what was happening. To that end, a stratified random sample of 24 students and 24 mentors, representing four students and four mentors from each of the six subject areas, were interviewed in the final month of the course.

Since one of the purposes of the interviews was to find out how the student teachers and the mentors saw teaching expertise, learning to teach and learning about teaching, the interview questions were very open. This meant that the only basis for the analysis of the interviews was the data itself, from which understandings were inductively generated.

The views of the student teachers

Emerging from an examination of the transcripts of the interviews with the student teachers were seven propositions that offered some insights about the factors on which student teachers' access to experienced teachers' professional craft knowledge might depend.

- *Ideas about alternative methods of learning.* If student teachers believe that experienced teachers' teaching can be understood through observation alone, or that experienced teachers can pass on all their valuable knowledge through giving advice to student teachers, then discussion of observed teaching will be seen as superfluous.

- *Conceptions of how the knowledge accessed could be used.* If student teachers see useful knowledge as that which they can use immediately in their teaching rather than that which adds to their understanding of teaching or is such that it can be stored for future use, then the motivation to gain access to experienced teachers' craft knowledge is not high.
- *Conceptions of good teaching.* The tendency to see teaching in 'holistic' terms and to think in terms of overall teaching styles leads easily to the belief that it is only possible to learn from the kind of teacher of whose style one approves.
- *Recognition of the complexity of teaching.* Only when student teachers recognize that 'rules of thumb' are of limited value, and that skilled teaching depends on taking account of the many conditions impacting on each situation, can they appreciate the kinds of things it is possible to learn from the teaching of experienced practitioners.
- *Own experience of teaching.* The capacity and motivation of some student teachers to learn from observation and the follow-up discussion of the observed teaching appears to increase in so far as they can relate experienced teachers' observed actions or remembered actions to situations they have faced in their own teaching.
- *Suspension of one's perceptions.* It is only in so far as student teachers can set aside their own ways of formulating the issues of concern to them, and listen to the ways in which experienced teachers construe situations, that they can learn from those teachers' craft knowledge.
- *Good relationships with experienced teachers.* As student teachers are anxious to get on well with and be accepted by the teachers with whom they work, they tend not to press teachers to engage in the suggested procedure if the teachers themselves do not seem keen to do so.

The views of the mentors

There were some interesting differences between the talk of the mentors and that of the student teachers. Whereas, for example, the students had focused exclusively on classroom teaching, the mentors talked of the teacher's wider role; and for the mentors the starting point in thinking about teachers' expertise and student teacher learning was *what* there was to be learned, rather than *how* such things are learned. It was also interesting to note that although they had not been asked to, virtually all of the mentors talked of the professional benefits they saw accruing to them through working with student teachers. The most striking feature of these interviews, however, was the distinctiveness of the concerns and logic of each mentor. This meant that only a small number of propositions could be formulated and sustained as reflecting the thinking of mentors generally, as revealed in the interviews:

- *Recognition of one's own craft knowledge.* Teachers' motivation to make their professional craft knowledge available to student teachers depends on their recognition of the expertise used in their daily teaching and the realization that it is embedded in their teaching rather than readily available as prescriptive generalizations.
- *Recognition of the importance of long-term learning.* Teachers are less likely to take time and trouble to make their professional craft knowledge available if they are overwhelmingly concerned with student teachers' capacity to cope adequately with their immediate teaching responsibilities.
- *Recognition that understanding can lead to autonomy.* Teachers are frequently sceptical of the merits of student teachers observing them or other teachers because they reject any idea of student teachers learning by imitation. They are more likely to be motivated to make their craft knowledge available through observation followed by discussion if they recognize that student teachers are better placed to develop their own autonomous practice through understanding how experienced teachers engage in their teaching.

Preparing for the third year of the project

The results of the questionnaire, and the insights from the interview data, together led to modified plans being made for the forthcoming academic year and a fresh cohort of PGCE students. It was clearly necessary to create the conditions which would make it relatively easy for the PGCE students to engage in the suggested procedure, to persuade them to take the time to do it, and to help them to use in a productive way the expertise that they might get hold of. It seemed necessary, therefore, to effect change in three areas.

First, the procedure should become an integral part of the subject curriculum programmes. In this way it would not have to compete with all the other demands on students and mentors, as it would have its place in a programme jointly planned by curriculum tutors and mentors. Furthermore, the 'artificiality' of the procedure would be something that had been negotiated at a general level and would not have to depend on personal initiatives from them.

Second, there was a good deal of evidence to suggest that the kind of questions that student teachers were being encouraged to ask following observation were more meaningful for them in the second half of the PGCE year when they were engaged in learning how to evaluate their teaching. Moreover, it was much more likely that in the second half of the year they would be in a position to appreciate the complexity of teaching.

Third, it seemed that student teachers were more likely to be motivated to gain access to teachers' craft knowledge in relation to an aspect of teaching that was of particular concern to them, rather than to teachers' craft knowledge in general. It was, therefore, important to take much more account of the agenda of the individual student teacher.

It was for these reasons that we worked in the following year through curriculum tutors. It was not difficult to enlist the support of the curriculum tutors in history, maths and English in making this aspect of the PGCE course – the accessing of teachers' craft knowledge – part of the programmes that were jointly planned by curriculum tutors and mentors. It was also agreed that the students in these three areas should engage in the procedure as part of the self-evaluation task that was set and assessed by the university. The co-operation of the mentors in these three subject areas was sought, and it was explained to them that the student teachers were being asked to carry out this procedure as part of both the self-evaluation process and assignment, and that the audiotaping of the conversations following observation would not only help the student teachers to reflect on what they had learned, but would also assist the researchers who would use the taped conversations as data.

In the lecture about learning from experienced teachers delivered at the beginning of the academic year, we put far greater emphasis on the use to which student teachers might put the accessed craft knowledge, using concrete and authentic examples from the questionnaire and interviews with PGCE students from the previous year. Following the lecture, the student teachers watched the training video, had follow-up questions to discuss in seminar groups, and were given revised guidelines. Then, towards the end of their second term, and as part of the preparation for the self-evaluation assignment, the students in the three areas were given a much more elaborated explanation of the rationale and the procedures for getting access to teachers' professional craft knowledge.

Having thus, in the light of the preliminary studies, been able to structure the context for the use of the suggested procedure in a way that seemed as optimal as was realistically possible, we planned the research strategy for the following year.

Testing our hypotheses about the procedure

During the first two years, we had identified quite a lot of difficulties to be resolved in using our proposed procedure for helping student teachers to gain access to experienced teachers' professional craft knowledge. As a result we made new arrangements in the third year, designed to overcome these problems. By then, the time had come to put our procedure to the test: was it going to be effective for the purpose for which we had designed it? The emphasis now was less on developing the procedure and more on research into its strengths and limitations.

We still had two main kinds of research questions. There were crucial questions about *how far the procedure worked*. That is, how far had we managed to establish conditions in which the student teachers did what we thought was necessary? And, if they did, to what extent did that lead the experienced teachers to share their professional craft knowledge with the student teachers? These were quantitative questions, about the extent to which the actors did what we hoped they would do. So answering them was a matter of categorizing what the student teachers and the experienced teachers did, as revealed by tape recordings of their conversations, and then of working out how much they had done of different kinds of things. As tends to be the case for such quantitative research, a good deal of quite technical work was involved, both in the development and use of valid categorization systems and in the statistical analyses. Guessing that most readers will not be interested in these technical details, we have in the remainder of this chapter provided a non-technical account of our investigation of these questions. For those who are interested, a full technical account may be found in Hagger (1997).

But whether or not the procedure was found to work effectively, there were other important research questions about *why* this was so. These questions were about the ways in which the student teachers and the experienced teachers perceived the tasks they were set, and how they thought about and approached these tasks. Answering these questions therefore depended on qualitative research, mainly involving interviews with those involved. In Chapter 5 we report the findings from that qualitative research.

All 56 PGCE history, maths and English student teachers were involved in the study. As part of their school-based curriculum work during the final term of their three-term postgraduate course, they were each asked to observe lessons by two teachers, selected by the student teacher on the grounds that the teachers had expertise of interest to them. As soon as possible after each observed lesson, the student was to interview the teacher in order to gain access to the craft knowledge used in the lesson, and the interview was to be audiotaped.

Although nearly all of the student teachers claimed to have taped at least one conversation with a teacher following an observed lesson, some of these tapes were not delivered to the researchers, and some of those delivered were blank and others inaudible. However, 28 of the student teachers produced audible tapes of their conversations with at least one teacher, and the quantitative analysis included one such conversation for each of these student teachers. The analysis was aimed at answering the following three research questions:

- To what extent do the student teachers use the various suggested kinds of questions and actions that were suggested to them?
- To what extent do the teachers appear to articulate craft knowledge that they have used in the observed lessons?
- To what extent does the student teachers' use of the various suggested kinds of questions and actions correlate with the teachers' apparent articulation of the craft knowledge they have used in the observed lessons?

The investigation and findings for each of these questions are discussed in turn below. However, to set the scene, we can first look at the overall structure of the conversations. The intention was that the conversations should be about the student teachers exploring the teachers' professional craft knowledge, and so it was anticipated that they would be dominated by questions from the students and responses from the teachers, with follow-up questions and reactions from the students figuring prominently. That is exactly what happened: of the total number of 'moves' in all the conversations, 21 per cent were questions, with a further 12 per cent of follow-up questions, from the student teachers; 34 per cent of the moves were responses from the teachers; and 12 per cent were reactions from the student teachers. There were no questions from the teachers nor responses from the student teachers. The student teachers, furthermore, made very few statements, and hardly any of these were about their own teaching. So the general shape of the conversations was as we had wanted.

To what extent do the students use the various suggested kinds of questions and actions that were suggested to them?

Although this is a descriptive question, there is an implicit hypothesis that, if our suggestions were sensible, if we had introduced the student teachers appropriately to the procedure and if we had made appropriate arrangements, they would generally act in the ways that had been suggested. We needed to develop reliable ways of describing the extent to which their actions matched the suggestions made to them.

The student teachers had been advised to ask open questions, to probe for elaboration and to focus their attention on the specific lessons observed. They had also been encouraged to ask questions about the teacher's successes or achievements in the lessons, the actions taken to bring about any such achievements, and the reasons for the actions taken. From this advice, we developed a content analysis system to categorize the student teachers' talk as outlined in Table 4.2. To what extent did the student teachers follow the guidance they had been given?

Openness

The student teachers had been encouraged to ask open questions, so that the teachers could respond to them in their own terms. However, only 42 per cent of their questions were classified as open, while 53 per cent of their questions were closed. In most of the 28 conversations, about half the questions were open or partially open. Either the student teachers found it quite difficult to ask mostly open questions, or they had not been persuaded of the merits of doing so.

Table 4.2   Outline of content analysis system for student teachers' talk

Dimension	Categories
Openness The extent to which student teachers followed the advice to ask open questions	3 categories of degrees of openness
Nature of questions The extent to which student teachers followed the advice to seek explanations of why or how teachers had done or achieved things	3 categories: 'why', 'how', 'other'
Specificity The extent to which student teachers' questions were related to the specific observed lesson	4 categories of degree of specificity
Evaluation The extent to which student teachers followed advice to focus on what had gone well in the lesson	3 categories: positive, negative, qualified
Probing The extent to which student teachers followed advice to probe teachers' responses asking for elaboration	8 categories differentiating various kinds of reaction, including two categories for probing questions seeking elaboration and those seeking justification

Nature of questions

It had consistently been stressed that observation with follow-up discussion was an opportunity to learn how an experienced teacher made sense of a lesson. To this end student teachers had been encouraged to get the teachers to talk about how they had done or achieved things in the lesson or why they had done things. Only modest success was achieved here: on average, 25 per cent of the questions sought causal or purposive explanations, most of them framed as 'why' questions; 16 per cent of the questions sought procedural explanations, most of them being 'how' questions; and 59 per cent fell into the residual category, typically 'what' questions.

Specificity

One important concern was with the extent to which the student teachers had focused their questions on the particular observed lesson, as they had been advised to do. In 13 of the 28 conversations, there were no questions that were not related in some way to an aspect of the observed lesson and, of all the questions asked, only 19 per cent fell into this category. In this respect, then, the student teachers seemed to have followed the guidelines.

Evaluation

The student teachers had been advised to focus on what had gone well in the lessons. So were their questions positive? We found that, while there were no questions containing negative evaluations, only 10 per cent were positive. In the great majority of questions, there were no embedded evaluations, either positive or negative.

In the conversations more generally, the student teachers were equally sparing in the evaluations, but similarly positive when they did express a view. Thus, while there were expressions of 'positive affect' in only 5 per cent of their reactions to what teachers said, there was virtually no 'negative affect'.

Probing

Since experience had suggested that most teachers can with encouragement say much more about their use of their craft knowledge than they initially tend to say, the student teachers had been advised to use probing to encourage the teachers to elaborate on their initial responses. It was emphasized that such probing should be clearly concerned with elaboration, not with justification, of what the teachers had said. The student teachers generally followed this advice, in that 38 per cent of their reactions included probes for clarification or elaboration, while only 2 per cent included probes for justification. The success that this implied was, however, severely qualified by the fact that the student teachers tended to formulate these follow-up questions in more closed terms, and to ask even fewer 'how' or 'why' questions, than they did in their questioning generally.

In summary, the student teachers generally seemed to understand and to accept a good deal of what they had been advised to do. In line with the guidance given to them, they tended to:

- take on the questioning role;
- refrain from talking about their own teaching;
- focus on the teacher's observed teaching;
- be far more positive than negative;
- ask follow-up questions (probes).

On the other hand, they tended only to a limited extent to heed the advice to:

- ask predominantly open questions;
- ask predominantly questions seeking explanations ('how' or 'why' questions).

Furthermore, they generally did not follow the advice to:

- ask follow-up questions that probed initial responses more deeply and fully.

We may speculate that the student teachers generally understood very well the task and the opportunity that they had been given and were well motivated, but that they were also motivated by a concern to seem sensible and knowledgeable and to assure the teachers that they understood. So they found it difficult to ask open questions, to seek explanations and to probe for deeper explanations, any of which might in their eyes have made them look like ignorant student teachers. It is important to note, however, that the apparent tendency for the student teachers not to have fully accepted the advice given reflects considerable variations among them, variations on which we shall focus later.

To what extent do the teachers appear to articulate craft knowledge that they have used in the observed lessons?

How were we to recognize the articulation by teachers of the craft knowledge they had used in the observed lessons? As for the student teachers' questions, one key characteristic was that the teachers' talk should be about the specific observed lesson. For the rest, we depended on Brown and McIntyre's (1993) model, according to which teachers' professional craft knowledge typically involved pedagogical actions directed towards the attainment of several types of short-term classroom or pupil outcomes. Teachers' professional craft knowledge was described as also involving consideration of a wide range of factors both in the choice of actions and in judging the adequacy with which outcomes were achieved. The content analysis system for analysing the teachers' talk is outlined in Table 4.3.

To what extent did the teachers appear to articulate their craft knowledge? We have already noted that, as intended, the role played by the teachers in the conversations was overwhelmingly that of responding to the student teachers' questions. Our interest therefore is in the nature of these teacher responses. As we had hoped, the responses were concerned with the teachers' teaching; and, like the student teachers' questions, the responses predominantly related to specific aspects of teaching in the observed lessons. So what precisely did the teachers talk about in the observed lessons?

Pedagogical actions

In 69 per cent of the teacher 'moves' in the conversations (most of which were responses) teachers mentioned pedagogical actions they had taken. Such actions were therefore clearly a primary focus of their talk.

Table 4.3 Outline of content analysis system for teachers' talk

Dimension	*Categories*
Specificity The extent to which the teachers' responses were related to the observed lesson	4 categories in relation to degree of specificity
Pedagogical actions Actions taken by teachers or decisions about how to act	A single category
Types of outcomes The kinds of outcomes identified by Brown and McIntyre as characteristic of craft knowledge, distinguished from other kinds of outcome (e.g. longer-term outcomes)	5 categories, 3 characteristic of craft knowledge and 2 other categories
Factors of which account is taken Factors of which account is taken either in deciding what action to take or in evaluating outcomes	9 types of factor distinguished and, for the 'pupils' category, a further nine subcategories
Explicit links Explicit links made between actions, outcomes and/or factors	A single category

Types of outcomes

Overall, teachers mentioned on average at least one outcome in each move. Of these, 65 per cent were outcomes of the craft knowledge kinds identified by Brown and McIntyre (1993), concerned with pupils' short-term progress and with classroom activities, atmospheres and relationships. This aspect of professional craft knowledge was therefore also a primary focus of the teachers' talk.

Factors taken into account

Like the teachers studied by Brown and McIntyre (1993), the teachers mentioned many factors, and many kinds of actions, with those concerning pupils being much the most frequently mentioned as shown in Table 4.4. Again, this seems clearly to suggest that the teachers were indeed articulating their craft knowledge.

Links between actions, outcomes and factors

Teachers' craft knowledge consists of course not only of the different actions, outcomes and factors which they consider but also crucially of the

Table 4.4 Factors taken into account in teacher talk moves

Factor	Proportion of total number of factors (%)
Pupils	69
Time	4
Resources	3
Content	14
Phase	3
Social acceptability	0.3
Teacher state	5
Classroom circumstances	1
Average number per conversation	45
Average number per move	1.69

connections they make between these. So an important test of whether teachers were articulating their craft knowledge lay in how far they revealed such connections. It was found that, on average, teachers made 28 such links per conversation.

In general, then, the teachers responded to the student teachers' questions by revealing what seemed to be a substantial amount of their craft knowledge. But just as we noted that there were considerable variations among the student teachers, so there were even wider variations among the teachers. We go on next to ask about how far such variations among teachers might have been due to variations in the student teachers' questioning.

To what extent does the student teachers' use of the various suggested kinds of questions and actions correlate with the teachers' apparent articulation of the craft knowledge they have used in the observed lessons?

The central hypothesis underlying this action research, it will be remembered, was that the teachers would be more likely to articulate their craft knowledge if the student teachers acted in accordance with the advice they had been given. We tested this hypothesis by asking whether or not there were positive correlations between our measures of how far the different student teachers followed the advice given and our measures of the extent to which the teachers had articulated their craft knowledge. A certain amount of caution is needed here. First, we cannot be certain about how well our variables have operationalized the abstract ideas with which we were concerned. This is especially the case in relation to how far our simple quantitative measures have captured the complex idea of teachers' articulation of their professional craft knowledge. Second, correlations between variables do not, of course, tell one anything about patterns of causation or influence. It might be the case, for example, that the student teachers' questioning was influenced by the way that teachers acted, rather than (or as well as) the other way round. We were, however, somewhat reassured by the strong finding that the conversations were dominated by questions from the student teachers, responses from the teachers and reactions from the students. As intended, it was the students who took the initiative, and it is plausible to assume that the ways they acted had a dominant influence on the ways in which the teachers responded. More generally, we were sufficiently confident about the adequacy of our operationalization of the hypothesis to at least explore what it could show us.

So, were there positive correlations between our measures of how far the student teachers followed the advice given and our measures of the extent to which the teachers had articulated their craft knowledge? Since we had all these measures for each of the 28 conversations, it was easy to calculate all the correlation coefficients. It was much less easy, however, to inspect the resulting large array of correlation coefficients intelligently. While we could see that many of the correlations were highly positive, it was also clear that some were not, and it was difficult to reach a balanced view simply by inspecting the whole array. We were able, however, to solve this problem by using principal components analysis, a form of factor analysis and the standard statistical technique for summarizing large arrays of correlation coefficients. It does this by inventing new variables – 'principal components' – to represent sets of variables that all correlate with each other.

For the student teacher variables, there was one dominant principal component which suggested a tendency among the student teachers to adopt the advice *in a generalized way* to greater or lesser degrees. It summarized the fact that those student teachers who focused their questions on the specific lessons also tended to ask questions seeking explanations and to be positive in their reactions to what teachers said. These positive connections did not, however, extend to asking open questions or to the use of probing.

For the teacher variables, there was one dominant principal component which very clearly was a general craft knowledge factor. Those teachers who tended most or least to articulate one aspect of their craft knowledge also tended correspondingly to articulate other aspects most or least; specificity, pedagogical actions, short-term outcomes, number of factors mentioned, and number of links made were all positively connected.

The principal components analyses had thus very helpfully generated for us two new overarching variables, a student teacher variable which we could interpret, with some qualifications, as measuring students' tendencies to follow the advice of the guidelines, and a teacher variable which seemed unambiguously to measure how far the teachers had articulated their craft knowledge. We could therefore use these two newly defined variables to test our hypothesis: what kind of relationship was there between these two new overaching variables?

The relationship between the two variables is shown graphically in

Figure 4.1. This shows that there is a strong linear relationship between 'students following advice' and 'teachers articulating craft knowledge': the more student teachers tended to follow the given advice, the more teachers tended to articulate their professional craft knowledge. The correlation between the two factors was 0.73. We conclude, therefore, that the evidence strongly supports the central hypothesis.

Figure 4.1 Relationship between factor scores for the variables 'teachers articulating craft knowledge' and 'students following advice'

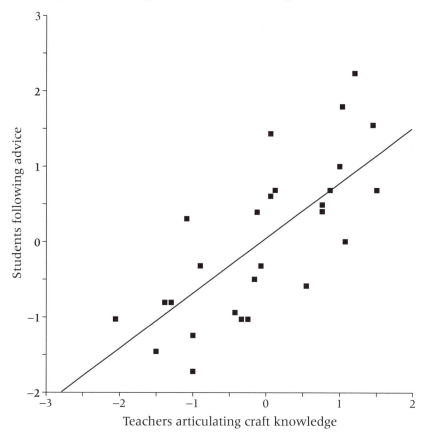

We are left, however, with some loose ends to which we must attend. The general tendency to follow the advice given, reflected in the 'students following advice' factor, included neither openness in student teachers' questions nor the use of probing. We needed to look more closely at these variables. And sure enough, the original correlation coefficients show no significant positive connections between these student variables and any of the measures of teachers' articulation of their craft knowledge. There were even negative correlations between probing and measures of the specificity of teachers' responses. So the conclusion that our hypothesis is strongly supported by the evidence has to be qualified in that it does not extend to those aspects of the advice we gave to the students. It is perhaps significant that these were two aspects of the suggested pattern of questioning which student teachers seemed least inclined to follow.

For Brown and McIntyre (1993: 36), openness was 'a crucial strand' of their research strategy: 'Openness on our part was seen as essential if the teachers were to be encouraged to bring to consciousness their own perceptions, concepts and decision-making processes'. Nor had we, in our preliminary studies, found any reason to doubt the importance of such openness. The lack of correlation between the openness of questions and the accessing of craft knowledge is therefore puzzling. The problem may be that the simple number of open questions is not in itself an important influence. From the transcripts of the conversations, it appears that the context of the questions is very important: the open questions that worked well tended to be asked when the teacher had already been helped to paint quite a full picture of the lesson, often through responding to more closed questions. This is clearly something that needs further exploration.

Probing is the second area of the procedure that calls for further work. The results show that the student teachers, while successful in avoiding follow-up questions that put teachers in the position of having to justify their teaching, tended to use probing in order to clarify or confirm their understanding of responses to earlier questions, in effect saying 'Have I understood you properly?'. Moreover, the negative correlations between student teachers' use of probing and the specificity of teachers' responses suggest that the probes were frequently seeking wider generalizations, encouraging the teachers to talk in decontextualized terms. Clearer and more persuasive guidance about the kinds of probing that will not appear negative but can give access to richer information about teachers' craft knowledge seems to be needed.

Conclusions

In this chapter we have described the extensive investigations carried out over a two-year period in order to develop this new element of the school-based curriculum, and then the findings of our quantitative research through which, in the third year, we tested the effectiveness of the new procedure.

From the developmental studies, we came to recognize that, to make it possible for such a new element of the curriculum to be effective, we needed to take very serious account of the preconceptions, attitudes and concerns of both the student teachers and their mentors. The student teachers especially, working from very strong agendas of their own, could, for example:

- find it difficult to suspend their own ways of thinking to listen to teachers;
- look for generalized solutions to the problems of teaching;
- ask questions that sometimes made teachers defensive;
- reject 'formal' or 'artificial' kinds of conversations with teachers;
- be very concerned about the lack of time available for innovative procedures;
- see useful knowledge as that which they could use immediately;
- take considerable time to learn to recognize the complexity of teaching;
- be most motivated to learn from teaching that they connect with their own;
- be anxious above all to get on well with, and be accepted by, teachers.

To take account of such student teacher preconceptions and agendas, we judged it necessary and found it practical to make important changes in the third year of the study in the arrangements for this element of the curriculum:

- integration of the new element into the formal assessed curriculum;
- timing of this element in the second half of the PGCE year;
- linking this element to student teachers' individual agendas;
- much fuller attention to student teachers' understanding of the rationale;
- emphasis on the distinctive nature of the conversations involved.

The main conclusions that we can draw from the quantitative research findings can be summarized in four propositions:

1 The parts played by the student teachers in the conversations corresponded with varying degrees of closeness to the guidance they had been given. In general, they tended to:
   - adopt a questioning role;
   - be positive (or at least avoid being negative) about the observed teaching;
   - ask follow-up questions;
   - focus on the specific issues.
   On the other hand, their activities corresponded less consistently with the advice to:
   - ask open questions;
   - ask questions seeking explanations;
   - ask follow-up questions of the kind that probed more deeply and fully the teachers' initial responses.
2 In many respects, and especially in the kinds of outcomes they emphasized, the multiplicity of factors and links they discussed, and the concentration on pupil factors, the teachers' talk tended to be similar to teachers' articulation of their craft knowledge as described by Brown and McIntyre (1993).

3 A strong linear relationship was revealed between the extent to which the student teachers tended broadly to follow the guidance offered and the extent to which the teachers with whom they engaged in the exercise appeared to articulate their craft knowledge.
4 The readiness of the student teachers to follow certain aspects of the guidance offered – in particular, on openness and probing – was not positively correlated with teachers' apparent articulation of their craft knowledge. Further investigation is needed of these aspects of the procedure.

This quantitative part of the study therefore indicates that we were able to develop an element of the school-based curriculum, based on procedures broadly similar to those used by Brown and McIntyre (1993), through which student teachers could access experienced teachers' craft knowledge. It is also, however, important that we should take account of the reactions of the people involved. In Chapter 5, we go on to explore the student teachers' and teachers' own reflections on the procedure.

5 The experience of the student teachers and teachers

The focus of this chapter is on the findings from the semi-structured interviews carried out with the student teachers and teachers. The interviews were undertaken in an attempt to find out about their experience of the procedure, and their understanding and perception of the place of the procedure in relation to other ways of student teachers learning from experienced teachers.

Within each of the three curriculum areas – English, history and maths – seven student teachers from among those who claimed to have engaged in the procedure and audiotaped the conversation were randomly selected for interview. In addition, one of the two teachers with whom each of the 21 student teachers had carried out the suggested procedure was interviewed, selection determined by the toss of a coin.

The potential problems attendant on interviewing as a means of collecting data – for example, interviewer bias and the desire of interviewees to please the interviewer – are compounded in an action research study in which the actor is the research instrument used to collect evidence from other actors about the impact of his or her actions. There was no escaping the fact that the interviewer was an enthusiastic advocate of the procedure about which the student teachers and teachers were being interviewed; so the normal problem confronting interviewers of respondents telling them what it is assumed they want to hear was magnified. We addressed this problem in two ways. First, the interviews took place at a time when student teachers and teachers were less likely to be concerned about how the interviewer reacted to their accounts: the student teachers were interviewed after all their work had been assessed and they knew they had 'passed' the course, and interviews with the teachers took place after the student teachers had left and the PGCE year was over.

Second, we decided to be transparent both about the researcher's agenda and the potential problems for interviewees of giving honest answers to questions put by someone they knew was not a disinterested observer. The teachers and student teachers were explicitly asked, recognizing this situation, to be honest in telling us of limitations or weaknesses of the procedure, and they were constantly assured that it was their experience and their perspective that were of interest.

For student teachers and teachers alike, the interview opened with straightforward questions about the observed lesson and follow-up conversation – including, for example, the making of arrangements – as it was assumed that inviting them to talk in descriptive terms about their experience made it more likely that subsequent responses would be rooted in what had happened. The second sequence of questions focused on the place of the procedure in relation to other ways in which student teachers learned from teachers. The final sequence of questions for the teachers revolved around the practicability of the procedure. In the final part of the interview with the student teachers, they were presented with some ideas which the previous year's study had suggested could be barriers to the success of the procedure, ideas which were couched in terms of statements to which they were asked to respond.

The interviews, each of which lasted for 35–90 minutes, were audio-taped and subsequently transcribed. The interview data was qualitatively analysed: within a broad and explicit framework of the research questions and the interview agenda, the shape, structure and texture of the themes and categories were determined by what the respondents had to say.

Student teacher interviews

Effects and adequacy of the steps taken to improve the procedure

The student teachers' understanding of the procedure

The student teachers, as well as being clear that they were being asked to carry out a focused observation of a teacher with whom they would have a follow-up conversation about the observed teaching as soon as possible after the lesson, showed that they were familiar with the guidelines suggesting how the follow-up conversation might be conducted. They were also conscious that the conversation they were expected to engage in was different from other conversations with teachers, as is illustrated in Neil's comments:

> What we'd been told was that this was a different way of talking with teachers, and they'd have different things to say ... I knew we'd been advised to stick to a particular lesson to get more out of it, and that it was important to let the teacher do most of the talking.

While as a group they had a shared view of what they were being asked to do, their accounts of what they actually did reveal the differences among them. The variation in practice makes it possible to group them in the following four ways:

- those who understood the guidelines and were apparently successful in following them;
- those who understood and attempted to follow the guidelines but with a limited degree of success;
- those who misunderstood the guidelines;
- those who consciously rejected all or some of the guidelines, and modified the procedure to suit their individual purposes.

To judge by their own accounts, some of the student teachers managed to use the guidelines in an exemplary way and reaped the appropriate rewards. Georgina, for example, had as her focus discussion lessons, describing her own attempts at them as 'total disasters', but knowing her mentor to be particularly skilful at them. In accordance with the guidelines, the observed lesson was followed by a lengthy discussion held in a private office. According to Georgina, her mentor, in responding to her questions about his actions during the observed lesson, was able to explain 'what he had done and why he had done things, so that I could understand', with the result that her 'whole discussion lessons changed'.

Those students falling into the second group encountered the kinds of difficulties discussed later in this chapter, the unnaturalness of the procedure and their perceived inadequacies as interviewers.

There were a number of students who talked confidently of having 'found the guidelines very helpful' and then in reporting what they had done revealed that they had misunderstood them. Ingrid, for example, explained that 'the conversation was of a general type and took place two weeks after the lesson', while Hakim commented that 'it was a two-way conversation because it ended up with us discussing my own frustrations about classroom management'.

The largest group comprised those who modified the procedure, the two most common reasons for such modifications being a desire to have a more natural conversation with the teacher, and an interest in broad concerns such as the teacher's overall philosophy:

> a lot of what you gave us as a formalized way of presenting something and actually getting concrete answers is there for you to use, but if you actually get a teacher who you actually get on very well with, those kinds of things tend to come quite naturally and you don't tend to have to use such a formal thing ... so with Paul [teacher] there was none of this 'Can you tell me a little more about?' He knew what to focus on. The important, the useful point

is actually telling them what you want to focus on so that they're ready to talk to you about that.

(David)

Within each of the four broad categories outlined above there is, of course, more subtle variation, not least because a number of students, while remaining true to their respective category, made changes to the way in which they conducted the interview with the second teacher. In virtually every case, changes were made to accommodate the teacher's personality, as did Maria, for example:

> obviously it's judging the person you're talking to – it's important to make them feel at ease. With Kate [mentor] I find she's very relaxed and I could ask her anything, and I didn't have to worry what I said, whereas when I did the other one, with Sarah, I was much more sort of polite and careful because she's different, much more cold …

Reasons for engaging in the procedure

It is clear that the students engaged in the procedure because it was part of the self-evaluation process which in turn was an important and assessed component of the PGCE course. Thus, even those who did not follow the suggested guidelines – either through lack of understanding or because they found them unhelpful – did observe two lessons and have follow-up conversations with the respective observed teachers. That they took seriously the self-evaluation is shown by the extent to which their chosen foci for observation emanated from their appraisal of their teaching, in particular on one or more aspects of their practice that they wished to improve. Adrian's comment is typical:

> I was focusing on … pupil–pupil discussion, and what I've been trying to do – because I feel that my own teaching is not right, I'm still not using this style of teaching that will maximize learning, and I would say pupils could learn so much more than when we're investigating mathematics. Or I'm using discussion at the wrong point of the day … so I was looking at, basically styles of teaching – how can I maximize the learning process? This is what is going on in my mind – what is appropriate in particular circumstances and particular learning situations?

For some of the students the choice of teacher to observe was straightforwardly governed by the nature of their chosen focus; they approached a teacher whom they regarded as especially skilful at that aspect of teaching on which they were focusing. Deborah, for whom this was the case, explains her choice of teacher in the light of her concern with classroom control and discipline:

She's got very good classroom control. She can get absolute silence in the class. She's always got her eye on everything that's happening ... I'd seen her with her Year 9 before displaying that kind of strength.

Virtually all of the students chose to observe teachers within their respective host departments. Such decisions were taken for a variety of reasons. To begin with it was easier to arrange to carry out what they saw as a 'demanding and elaborate' procedure with teachers whom they both knew and knew to be approachable, and for most of them here was the opportunity to delve further into the expertise of a teacher with whom they were familiar. Generally, then, the choice of teacher came from a mixture of expediency and sincere interest in, and admiration for, aspects of the teacher's expertise. Their reasons for engaging in the procedure as a whole are less complicated, and are best summed up by Elaine who explained that they 'had to do it'.

Setting up the procedure

In the student teachers' talk about setting up the observation and discussion – which for most of them was anything but straightforward – two topics recur: time constraints in school and teacher co-operation.

As well as being very conscious of how busy teachers are, the students were mindful of their own busy schedules, and in their description of the time it took to make arrangements a certain amount of resentment can be sensed. Normal time constraints were exacerbated by the elaborate nature of the procedure, demanding as it did discussion with the teacher both before and after the observed lesson. Not only was what they were being asked to do time-consuming, it was also complicated since it necessitated finding a time when both student teacher and teacher could be free of all other commitments.

The extent to which the students saw the success of the arrangements as dependent on teacher co-operation is very marked in their responses; indeed, for a number of them one of the criteria in deciding which teachers to observe was the teachers' 'approachability'. Most students found the teachers 'genuinely wanted to help', even to the extent of taking account of the students' concerns when planning the lesson to be observed.

Difficulties experienced

There were difficulties, too, in carrying out the observation and discussion in accordance with the guidelines. A number of students attributed what they saw as disappointing outcomes to their own inadequacies as interviewers, but most of the difficulties experienced stemmed from the procedure itself.

All of the students were conscious of what they saw as the unnaturalness of the procedure. It was planned; observation was carried out with a specific, agreed focus; there were detailed suggestions about the way to conduct the follow-up conversation with the teacher; and the conversation was to be audiotaped. All these ingredients gave to this particular way of engaging with teachers a much greater degree of formality than was usually the case. One or two of them welcomed what they saw as 'formalized learning', arguing as Helen did that in 'casual chats after lessons' not only was there no time in which to think of questions one might want to put to the teacher, but also 'you're not going to take special note of what was said and take it in'. For most of them, however, far from giving rise to 'a deeper level of concentration' the formal nature of the procedure was a source of great discomfort. A number admitted that they found it 'difficult' because they were 'unsure actually how to approach it', while for others the problem was that they were not used to doing it. Their attempts to follow the guidelines led to a situation that was negatively described as 'stage-managed', 'contrived', 'artificial', 'unnatural', 'too restrictive', and 'too ritualized'. More than anything else, the perceived unnaturalness came from the fact that this was a new experience for most students who during the year had not had opportunities to have extended conversations with teachers following observation; the procedure simply did not fit in with the relationships that had developed over the time they had been in school.

For most of the students who talked of the difficulties they experienced, their perceived inadequacies as interviewers and the unnaturalness of the situation were mitigated by the teachers' attitude and behaviour. In their talk of the importance of the part played by the teachers in the success of the conversation, they tended to highlight one or more of the following features: the teacher's personality; their capacity for reflection on their own teaching; and their familiarity with, and interest in, working with student teachers. Teachers who 'made it easy' are variously described as 'a great person who produced open arms even when the questions weren't good', or 'very secure in his teaching ... chatty and talkative', or as Georgina commented:

> He was out to analyse his own teaching anyway ... he thought this was a brilliant idea ... The questions, he didn't find them difficult. There are some who would say, 'I don't know why I did that sort of thing', but he wasn't like that at all. He generally very quickly understands what you're talking about and he talks right to the kernel of the issue and he doesn't need a lot of probing.

Matching styles of teaching

In the discussion of the preliminary trials in Chapter 4, it was pointed out that one of the obstacles to the students engaging in the procedure was their generally held belief that they could only learn from teachers whose overall style was similar to their own. This time, the students' unanimous rejection of this notion was very striking. A small minority argued that although they each had their own style of teaching, it was possible to learn from teachers with different styles, but for most of the students, the notion was untenable because they questioned the concept of overall teaching style. For these students, there was an important difference between, on the one hand, the skills and strategies used by teachers and, on the other, the overall 'attitude', 'philosophy' or 'teaching personality' of individual teachers. Jane and Chris are typical of the students who claimed that it was possible to select what one wanted to learn from teachers:

> there are always things that you can pick up and either incorporate in your teaching wholesale or in adapted form. Things that you can see are really effective and clearly make sense in the classroom, that you can learn from, although you might not want to buy the whole package.
>
> (Jane)

> I've found with most teachers that even if I've thought 'I don't want to teach like that' there is something in their teaching that I really like, or I realize they do very well. There's millions of things I respect about Claire [mentor] but I don't want to teach like her – though there are lots and lots of things I can learn from her.
>
> (Chris)

Reactions to the experience

Perceptions of the observed lessons

In talking about the observed lessons, the students focused, as we had hoped, on the teachers, referring to the pupils only in so far as their activities illustrated the teachers' achievements. Barbara, for example, in recalling a maths lesson she observed, comments:

> She [the teacher] pitched it just slightly above their heads all the time so that they were having to think to be able to answer her all the time. And she must have used about ten different activities throughout the lesson, things like the weather, counting, things like that. And she moved from one activity to the next beautifully smoothly, as if there was no transition really ... They were all so keen to get it right, and really enthusiastic.

The second noteworthy feature of their reports of the lessons is the extent to which they evaluated them. Most such evaluations were positive; comments such as 'a bit boring after a bit' and 'I thought it wasn't a

very good lesson' were rare. Far more typical of the judgements passed
are the following:

> the children were really involved – an exciting lesson
>
> (Simon)

> they are usually difficult children, but they just sat there, they did
> their work, they joined in. It was just a kind of perfect classroom
> atmosphere.
>
> (Ray)

Reactions to what the teachers had to say

For every student the starting point in making judgements about what
the teacher said was to ask themselves the simple question:

- Did I get what I wanted?

Since there was variation among them as to what constituted a successful
conversation, it follows that what was frustrating for one might well be
welcomed by another. So, for example, conversations in which the
teacher talked about specific aspects of the observed lesson – a feature of
a successful conversation according to the guidelines – were seen as
unhelpful by those students who were seeking more generalized talk.

The other questions posed by the students when deciding on the value
of the teachers' talk were:

- Could I have accessed this knowledge by engaging with teachers in
  other more straightforward, less time-consuming ways?
- Am I learning about the reasons behind the teachers' actions, and getting access to their theories about their teaching?

For some the talk of teachers with whom they had worked very closely
left them with what Ingrid called 'a feeling of rehearsal' as they felt they
had already heard what the teacher had to say, and they were thus disappointed that the time invested in the procedure did not pay dividends. In
addition, there were those who found that what the teachers had to say
added nothing to their understanding of the teaching acquired through
observing the lesson, and the discussion was therefore 'a waste of pre-
cious time', in direct contrast with those students who in talking about
what they had learned from the conversation made explicit mention of
the fact that they 'wouldn't have known that just from observation'.

The other yardstick by which teacher talk was evaluated was the perceived capacity of the teacher to go beyond a narrative account of the
specific lesson: the students wanted the teachers to reveal their thinking
behind the observed lesson, and when appropriate to call on their

experience of other lessons. This point is exemplified in the comments of Paula, an English student, comparing the talk of the two teachers with whom she carried out the procedure:

> She [the first teacher] was able to articulate that development, how she had got to the point where she could work with the class in that way ... What came out in the conversation was the way in which she had thought everything through – it didn't just happen – she'd thought very carefully how to set it up so she could get those particular elements in the lesson ... [The second teacher] didn't know how to articulate, how to theorize about what he'd done very much, it was all very superficial. I didn't think I actually learned anything from the conversation that I hadn't worked out watching.

Claimed benefits from engaging in the procedure

While a small minority got little or nothing from engaging in this procedure with teachers, most students claimed to have gained something from at least one of their attempts at observation and follow-up discussion. These claimed benefits were in three broad areas:

- feeling reassured and more confident;
- developing an understanding of teachers and teaching;
- developing one's repertoire of teaching strategies and skills.

Feeling reassured and more confident

In talking of affective benefits the students distinguished between the feeling of well-being they experienced when, for example, the teacher's attitude or educational aspirations and concerns resonated with their own, feeling reassured, and feeling encouraged that, given time, they would be able to teach in ways to which they aspired.

Jane's comments are typical of those from students who saw in the teacher talk endorsement of their own ideas:

> [Although] a lot of the things they were coming up with were things that I had also thought of independently and put into practice ... it was very important for me to have other people telling me that they do these things – without any prompting from me – and to know that other people are obviously recognizing them as quite a useful thing to do, and in a way it makes you feel a bit more confident about the educational purpose of doing that sort of thing.

Reassurance came chiefly from teacher talk about the realities of teaching and their acknowledging that even for experienced practitioners 'not all lessons work out as you want', which was welcomed by Nassem as 'proof not to panic'. Deborah, one of the maths students, concerned that as a novice teacher 'you never know whether what you feel you ought to be aiming for is totally realistic', was reassured by the teacher's remarks that 'you accept that at any one time two or three might not be concentrating, as long as it's not the same two or three pupils throughout the lesson'.

For those students who were conscious of a large gap between their own practice and that of the teacher observed, it was encouraging to hear the teachers talk about the ways in which they had worked while striving to achieve fluency in their teaching. Barbara, for example, who had 'felt completely inadequate' when observing a teacher of modern languages, because 'she was handling everything so well and very smoothly', found the follow-up conversation very helpful:

> It was a real encouragement to know that when she started she used to write everything down in a handbook, and that she used to practise things, because it was like I could get to that stage.

Developing understanding of teachers and teaching

A significant feature of the students' accounts of the benefits of engaging in the procedure is the number of references to developing their understanding of teachers and of teaching. Adrian described this as 'filling in the picture of the teacher's teaching', adding that from the conversation he got 'a broader view of what, as an experienced teacher, he thought was acceptable in the classroom, and which led to a good atmosphere'. In some cases it was a question of having misunderstandings and misconceptions challenged by what the teacher said. Neil, for example, firmly believing that there was a simple correlation between the teacher's personality and generating enthusiasm in the classroom, came to realize that 'it's not just how they come across, it's what activities they had planned and things like that'.

Notable in the reports is an awareness that it is possible to learn from a teacher's thinking behind actions taken in the classroom while neither wishing or being able to emulate those actions. As Paula explains:

> You're not just going to be able to walk in there and do it the same way because you're not at the same stage, but ... you can see a route through so you know where you're going or where you want to go. I thought it was really useful, not because I was picking up any particular tricks of the trade, but because I realized that if you thought in that way you could with care eventually reach that outcome.

For others, the teacher talk served both to remind them of the complexity of teaching and to illuminate aspects of it. Helen, one of the history students, put it this way:

> Through these discussions you do learn that good teaching is not mysterious, that it can be broken down, there is more than one reason for doing something and often very complex reasons ... it broad-

ens your knowledge of what particular reasons there might be ... [and that's] very useful for us as beginning teachers because you tend to see things very much in a one-dimensional way and in an obvious way.

Extending one's repertoire of teaching skills and strategies

That few of the students incorporated into their own teaching what they had learned from the teachers through observation and follow-up discussion is not to suggest that for the majority the procedure proved unhelpful. In addition to those who were not looking to acquire specific skills, there were those who argued that they did not have the opportunity to try out their theoretical understanding of specific aspects of teaching gleaned from observation and discussion, as they did not have a teaching timetable which made such attempts appropriate, or they felt that, as Maria put it, 'a lot of that depends on having established the right kind of relationship with the class'. This latter group intended to put any such newly acquired skills to the test when they were established in their first teaching posts.

The students who did incorporate what they learned into their own array of teaching skills and strategies were very excited by their success. Adrian, for example, claimed to have learned about the importance of 'being absolutely clear about what you're going to do', in addition to finding out how to run an oral lesson:

> I'd really thought about it, there was no half-heartedness about it – it was going to be an oral lesson and I decided I wanted them to work in groups, and I did the same as Anne [the teacher] ... It was brilliant! For the first time we were doing group work, we weren't just talking in groups.

As well as adding to their repertoires, these students were reminded that teaching skills and strategies are learnable, which as learner teachers they found very encouraging. As Georgina commented:

> My whole discussion lessons changed. I did one after that [the observation and discussion] and the way it went was totally different from the way I had been doing it because I was taking all those things I had learned from him in my mind and trying to put them into practice ... Every single thing he told me was of use ... I saw it happening before my eyes ... I did the same topic and started off the lesson in just the same way because I wanted to see whether it was me as a person that was getting it wrong or the questions I was using at the beginning were wrong ... It wasn't me as a person that couldn't do discussion, it was the way the questions were phrased and how you went about it.

Other ways of learning from experienced teachers

The students talked at length – and with some passion – about the ways in which they had learned from experienced teachers during the year. They had a lot to say about their experiences of:

- observing teachers;
- being observed and given feedback on their own teaching;
- teaching alongside teachers;
- going over lesson plans.

Observing teachers

Most students, while acknowledging the potential usefulness of observation, were dismissive of their own experiences of it, describing it as 'boring', 'pathetic', 'tiring', 'a waste of time', and 'a bit like being at school'. The most commonly offered explanation of such judgements was that the period of observation had been concentrated at the beginning of the PGCE year when they felt they were ill-equipped to learn about teaching through observation. As Chris commented:

> At the beginning you go in there and you have no idea what's going on. It completely washed over me. Without having actually had any teaching experience I don't think you fully appreciate what's going on.

Added to this was their sense of frustration at being held back from engaging with the pupils in the classroom. 'I wanted to get in there and do it', said Paula, adding that observation 'marked [her] off from the mechanics of the classroom'. This image of the bored, frustrated and puzzled student teacher sitting in the classroom is captured in Simon's comment that:

> I couldn't see what they were doing. Generally at the beginning you're just waiting for the bit where they say 'Would you like to help? Go round?' And it didn't always come.

In contrast with their generally negative appraisal of their experiences of classroom observation at the beginning of their time in school, such was their eagerness to observe teachers once they themselves had had some experience of teaching that they expressed regret that there were not more opportunities for observation in the second half of the course. They were adamant that to benefit from observation you have to be aware of what is happening and such awareness only comes with some experience of teaching. This argument, summed up by Paula who asserted that 'observation has no validity until you've done some teaching yourself', is far from straightforward. First, and most important, they felt that with experience they had acquired sufficient knowledge and understanding of teaching to make sense of what they saw going on in classrooms:

> Now you're aware of what you're looking for and you're aware of what the craft of teaching is, and I think at the beginning of the course it was all a complete marvel to me. I was in complete awe of the teachers and what they were doing and felt 'How am I ever going to do these things?'. Because they seemed to happen so naturally and automatically to teachers and I didn't think they would to me at the time … [now] you know what you're looking for and you know what you need to improve rather than just looking at it all and thinking 'Gosh, what the hell do I make of this? What do I take away from it?'.
>
> (Helen)

Second, for observation to be valued it has to be seen as relevant to perceived learning needs: beginning teachers are quite properly concerned overwhelmingly with developing their expertise as classroom practitioners, and it is when they are able to focus on what they and/or others see as their individual needs as learning teachers that observation assumes a relevance hitherto missing and is therefore valued.

In addition to suggestions that observation was of far greater value at the end of the year than at the beginning – a view shared by all those interviewed – a number of students pointed out the limitations and dangers of observation, at any time of the year, without some discussion with the observed teacher. As Jane, for example, commented:

> It's easy to get the wrong end of the stick about why teachers do certain things in the classroom, what their ultimate aims and objectives are … you just can't get that from observing the lesson, you have to talk to them independently afterwards.

Being observed and given feedback

Broadly speaking, the students were disappointed with their experience of being observed and given feedback on their teaching. The most commonly voiced complaint was that teachers were over-critical of the teaching they observed, such teachers being seen as insufficiently sensitive to the feelings and learning needs of student teachers. The comments of Chris, a maths student, illustrate the impact such an approach can have:

> I've learned very little from the people who were very critical of my lessons because I would go on the defensive very quickly, and that part of me that wanted to learn would shut itself off and I'd just be wanting to defend my teaching … And it would be people sort of

saying 'this went wrong, and this went wrong', and I knew they'd gone wrong and I didn't want somebody sitting there straightaway after the lesson telling me yet again what had gone wrong.

While those teachers who had little to say after observing a lesson did not undermine confidence as much as did those seen as over-critical, the students found them equally unhelpful in relation to their developing practice. Their frustration with such feedback – variously described as 'bland', 'elusive', 'vague' and 'unfocused' – is illustrated in Barbara's comments:

She [the teacher] just said 'Oh, everything's fine, I've no worries, that's all fine' when it's patently obvious that everything hasn't been fine, where there are certain things I could have learned, and there's been no discussion.

The kind of feedback they found most helpful and from which they felt they could best learn, was one in which the teacher adopted 'a constructive stance'. On such occasions, while highlighting those areas of the student's practice that needed to be improved, the teacher would also make specific suggestions as to how that improvement might be brought about. In commenting on feedback from his mentor, Mahmoud also underlines the importance of the teacher's manner and the way in which feedback is given:

Her comments were always of good balance in that she would tell me what went wrong, and she would also talk about the kinds of things I could do to put it right. She was always very clear, had a nice tone of voice and you could tell she wanted to help me improve.

Teaching alongside teachers

For the students who had been involved in co-teaching it was a very positive experience. First, since the teacher retained overall responsibility for the lesson, it enabled them to build up their confidence within a protected environment. Second, they were able to make adjustments to their teaching in the light of interjections from the teacher actively engaged in the lesson with them. Laura explains how this worked in practice, and why she valued it so highly:

[The teacher did] a sort of running commentary, of not criticisms but often questions to find out what I thought and things like 'Well, do you think this might help?' or 'Maybe it's gone on a bit too long'. I've had the benefit of her experience actually at the moment of teaching that thing, so I've been able to weigh up what I thought of the situation, plus what the experienced teacher thought of the situation at the same time.

It should come as no surprise that those students who did have the opportunity to teach alongside a teacher found it such a satisfying experience, as it enabled them to draw on the teacher's knowledge and understanding in a way that was directly relevant, and of immediate benefit, to their own teaching.

Discussing lesson plans

The students saw discussion of their lesson plans, especially early on in the PGCE year, as a potentially valuable way of learning from teachers whose expertise could help them transform 'some vague ideas' into 'something that was like a real lesson' (Tom). The perceived value of the experience, however, appears to be dependent on the stage in the planning process at which the teacher becomes involved. Those teachers, for example, who did not comment on the plans until they had been finalized by the students, were seen as unhelpful irrespective of whether the plans were approved or criticized. On the other hand, there were teachers who regularly contributed to the students' planning, and their input was appreciated, as is illustrated in Stuart's comments:

> you learn what won't work, because ... often there's a massive gap between what your ideas are and how it's actually going to work. They [the pupils] might not actually do what you've asked them to do, or be able to ... and you get the benefit of their knowledge which really bridges that gap, especially in the early stages.

The suggested procedure and other possible ways of learning from teachers

Almost without exception, the students saw the suggested procedure as more elaborate, more time-consuming and more formal than other possible ways of learning from teachers, and for some of them it was worth neither the time nor the trouble. Simon, a maths student, gives an account of his preferred way of talking with teachers:

> I find it easier to talk about things informally. I find teachers come out with more useful remarks when they are not sitting down specifically discussing something ... If it's in the context of a natural conversation, people are much more likely to say what they think ... they might have an instinctive reaction which is their real reaction – when they start thinking about things they give you a different answer from what they had instinctively thought.

David was one of a small number of students who felt that classroom teaching experience made redundant any discussion following observation of teachers:

> Things I wanted to look for came out in the observation ... I find it easier to look at a lesson than to try and unfold what the teacher's

thought of because it's a very unconscious thing. ... in the classroom situation you're much more aware and you're learning much more than when it's just talking about it afterwards.

For others, it was the elaborate and formal nature of the process that led to both students and teachers 'taking it seriously' and to 'more focused and concentrated learning'. These were the students who saw the procedure – with its two related components of observation and discussion – as more valuable than either component on its own. The importance of the observation (and even those who were eager to 'get on to more general topics' found 'it useful as a starting point to the conversation'), lay in the authenticity it gave to the teachers' talk, as Deborah, for example, explains:

It's not as convincing if you don't see them doing it ... I would need to actually see them in the classroom and see what's good for what I'm prepared to take on board and what she says works and what doesn't.

The most striking feature of their talk about the ways in which the suggested procedure related to other ways of learning from teachers is the emphasis given to opportunities to access the teachers' reasons behind the actions observed. Jane was one of a number who pointed out that this can only be 'guessed at' from observation alone:

Why did the teacher say so and so to the class at that point? If you haven't got the chance to stay behind after the lesson to ask that teacher you automatically assume that it must be the reason you think.

This history student also asserted that knowing there will be an opportunity to discuss the observed lesson affects the quality of the observation itself because 'you're not putting your assumptions onto the actions of the teacher in any way'.

For most students, then, the procedure was an elaborated, formalized version of observation which enabled them to get at the teachers' thinking both in and beyond the lessons observed.

Teacher interviews

Reactions to the experience

For the overwhelming majority of teachers interviewed, the procedure represented a new experience. The teachers were used to being observed, and conversations with student teachers were commonplace; this was different in that the observation and conversation was planned as a single operation, and the conversation was led by the student and focused on the teacher's teaching.

All but three of the teachers claimed that the experience had been broadly worthwhile and enjoyable. As Ken commented:

> I remember the conversation being full and I felt at the end of it that I'd got across the things I would have liked to have done about the things she was asking. I felt it was quite rewarding both ways.

The overall positive reaction of the teachers can also be gauged by their response to a question seeking their views on how the experience of the procedure might have been more satisfactory. Far from detailing what had gone wrong and what changes needed to be made, they tended rather to focus on the reasons for it having worked. Three broad topics dominated their explanations: the procedure itself; the student teachers; and the stage of the PGCE year.

The procedure itself

Widespread among the teachers was approval of the observation and follow-up conversation because it was 'planned' and 'precise' rather than 'spontaneous' and 'vague'. The planning meant that the observation was followed very quickly by the discussion, thus ensuring the lesson was still fresh in the teacher's mind. There was also the suggestion by a number of teachers that it meant that the conversation 'wasn't just a casual one', as can be seen in Donald's comments:

> my schedule tends to be fairly hectic anyway, and by having that 'we must sit down and talk about it for half an hour' made us sit down and concentrate for half an hour – whereas the informal discussion would be over a cup of coffee in the staffroom and there would be other people demanding my time and whatever – so that was useful to sit down and concentrate on it …

The other element of the procedure seen as being a salient factor in its effectiveness was the specificity of the student's focus and subsequent questions. For a number of teachers this got the conversation off to a good start as it ensured not only that there was plenty to talk about but also that the talk was pertinent.

Many of the teachers commented on the preparedness of the students and the guidance they had been given. Typical of the approval of the advice given to them on how to conduct the interview with the teacher are the comments first of Ian, a history mentor, and of Ros, one of the English mentors:

the questions were good and if you have a student that was not very forthcoming and couldn't think of questions themselves that were useful then this [the procedure] would focus them in a direction that would be useful and give them ideas to get them going.

(Ian)

her [the student's] manner wasn't threatening. I think it's important that the young teacher doesn't say things like 'Why didn't you do this?'.

(Ros)

The student teachers

Alongside their approval of the formal procedure, the teachers tended to attribute its success, as they saw it, to the qualities of the individual student teachers. A number of teachers claimed that they were 'fortunate' or 'lucky' to find themselves working with such 'good' students.

The picture of the 'good' student that emerges from their comments is of someone who in addition to being 'perceptive', is keen to learn, is capable of taking the initiative, and has well-developed interpersonal skills. The teachers' perception of the students' sincerity as learners as a key factor in the effectiveness of the procedure can be seen in the following extracts:

she [the student] was prepared to learn and I felt that by talking to her she was actually going to pick up on some of the things, and I was impressed by her.

(Donald)

I am not saying that you should have people that you like all the time, it doesn't need that, but people who want to learn make you as a teacher … quite happy to expose your weaknesses because you don't feel threatened. If the students are far more critical in a destructive way you would close up – their attitude has to be one of wanting to learn and to be humble. … she [the student] was sufficiently questioning and sufficiently humble to keep asking questions, and she made me think about things that I might not have thought about before.

(Paul)

The clearest message coming from the teachers was that the procedure depended on quite a demanding range of qualities in the students. In their comments, there was also the suggestion that ultimately it is not the system that matters so long as the people with whom one is dealing have the right attitudes, skills and understandings.

Stage of the year

In talking of the factors that had led to the perceived success of the observation and follow-up conversation, virtually all of the teachers made reference to the stage in the PGCE year at which it had been undertaken. In their view, students were 'ready' for this procedure when their understanding of classroom teaching was such as to allow them to focus

> really sensibly on what was happening ... to delve and understand what was going on, and make more sense of it.
>
> (Kate)

They were also clear that such necessary understanding came from the students' own teaching, as two of the mentors explain:

> in the early stage they really don't know how to focus on what to ask you, but they have to actually get a feel of things and when they try them out themselves then they know how to ask you.
>
> (Ian)

> they've got to do some by themselves first or else they're not going to find the questions to ask ... we all function better finding what we want to know.
>
> (Sara)

A number of teachers also argued that the relationship between the student and the teacher needed time in which to develop before the procedure was attempted. For Peter, one of the English mentors, this meant being able to rely on a body of shared understandings:

> both Paula and I had got to a stage almost naturally when ... she was more able to ask the kind of questions that were meaningful, and I was more ready, able to respond to the kind of stuff that she was asking.

For others it was more a question of affective development:

> [The student is] able to relax with me and vice versa ... it needs to be done when you have reached a certain stage in a relationship, not too early.
>
> (Jenny)

> we'd worked together for a while, so I felt at that stage I was willing to admit my errors to him.
>
> (Jo)

It is worth noting the relationship between these three factors emerging from their comments as the perceived necessary conditions for observation with follow-up discussion. In commenting on the procedure itself, the fact that the students took the lead at all stages was seen as important: the teachers highlighted the students' perception and sensitivity as observers and more especially as interviewers; and the main focus of comments about the timing of the procedure was the development of the students to the point where they wanted to find out more about the teacher's teaching and were likely to respect what was revealed to them.

The procedure compared with other ways of working with student teachers

In contrast to other ways of working with student teachers, two features of the procedure seemed to stand out in the teachers' minds: it was driven by the agenda of the individual student; and the focus was the teacher's account of his or her teaching. It was the combination of these two factors that made the procedure singular in their eyes.

It is not that teachers were unused to talking about their teaching: in whatever way they worked with student teachers, a central point of reference for them was their experience and knowledge. For a number of teachers, however, the procedure gave them an opportunity to talk about their teaching in their own terms and without conscious concern for the student's learning. It was the teacher and the teacher's teaching that took centre-stage, and it was having the spotlight on them rather than on the student that made this a different experience. The comments of one of the history mentors aptly illustrate this point:

> I think the difference was that it was me, I felt that he [the student] was asking me questions rather than I was giving him the opportunity to express his ideas ... in the past we'd always been talking about him, and we hadn't been talking about me. And even if I said something like, 'Well, one of the ways in which I get round a problem is by being very well planned', it was still giving him help and advice. And I didn't see this session that we were trying to find ways necessarily to help him, but rather we were talking about how I felt and how I operate, and that was quite different.
>
> (Nevine)

The features of the procedure that made it distinctive for the teachers also point perhaps to its attraction for them: it was the complementarity of the students deciding what they wanted to know and the teachers being therefore licensed, within these limits, to talk about their teaching in their own terms.

All save one of the teachers argued that students could learn far more from observation with a follow-up conversation than from observation alone. From their comments it appears that for many of them observation was often undertaken without a specific focus and with no discussion of the observed teaching; for these teachers one of the procedure's novel features was that the observation was focused.

Even the small group of teachers who made a case for observation were mindful of what they saw as its limitations, as can be clearly seen in the following comments:

> if you go and observe a lesson, even if you are concentrating on something in particular, if you don't get the opportunity to talk about it, then in a way, that's wasted because you may have thought things – 'Oh, the teacher did this because of so and so'. But you haven't clarified it with the teacher, perhaps they didn't do it for that reason … it helps to actually talk about it.
>
> (Anne)

One of the three teachers referred to earlier as having reservations about the procedure was alone in arguing that

> if you sit in the staffroom talking generally … a student learns more.
>
> (Claire)

All the other respondents spoke with approval of the conversation following observation, seeing it as serving a different purpose from the more informal conversations. The latter conversations, invariably referred to as taking place 'in the staffroom', were variously described as 'spontaneous', 'much more sort of incidental', and 'an ongoing stream of consciousness'. The key perceived difference between a conversation of this kind and the conversation as part of the procedure was that the latter was linked to an observed lesson, which resulted in the post-lesson discussion being of 'a different quality'. The observed lesson was seen as important, not only because it made possible a more detailed and more precise discussion, but also because it enabled the teacher to reveal her thinking through the use of concrete examples:

> whatever you are talking about, or explaining or anything, you need an example, as an example would help to learn something new.
>
> (Anne)

For some of the teachers the conversation was both broader and deeper than those they were accustomed to having with students, as exemplified in the comments of a maths mentor:

> it went a stage further than most of our conversations had gone. With the normal running of the school the time that is available is really limited to reviewing a plan … making sure that you've got

something that is going to work ... Because we had set time aside to do it, we were able to go deeper and begin to think about the children's understanding of what was going on ... the children's pleasure in learning, issues that do go below skin deep, which we would love to give more time to but you seldom have the time.

(Jo)

The features of the procedure highlighted by the teachers – the interdependence of the observation and discussion, questions from the student seeking answers from the teacher, the specific nature of the questions – together with the factor of protected time in which to engage in it, led to the conversation not only being seen as different from other conversations with student teachers, but also as distinctively valuable.

Claims about what the student teachers accessed

As suggested earlier, the teachers were in no doubt that their talk in the discussion following the observation of their teaching was different from their talk on other occasions; they were also clear that this was due in no small measure to the fact that the discussion was led by the student. In response to student teachers' questions, the teachers had talked about matters that they might otherwise, in the words of teacher Kathy, 'take for granted', a point endorsed by Jill, a teacher of modern languages, who explained that the questions from a maths student made her

sit back and think what was it that I was doing, because I do it automatically and don't really think about it ... it's things that tend to be second nature.

Echoes of this notion of the knowledge accessed by the students being automatic, taken for granted by the teachers, and not usually put into words can be found in many of the reports.

It is interesting to note the similarities in the teachers' descriptions of the knowledge accessed by the students as part of the procedure, especially in the light of their accounts of the substance of the discussions. While it would appear that for all of them the discussions began with talk about the specific observed lesson, such commonality was dissipated once the discussions were under way: some teacher–student pairs focused on specific aspects of the observed lesson throughout the discussion, while others had conversations that went 'backwards and forwards'. In a number of discussions the teacher soon moved on to more generalized talk, as the following example indicates:

The lesson was certainly our starting point, but we very quickly drifted off from that to the main thing about how can we get over the idea of being enthusiastic ... the lesson gave us something to keep coming back to, but it wasn't all pervasive.

(Nevine)

The teacher goes on to explain that in this 'far more general' conversation she had an opportunity to talk about 'how I see myself in the school'.

Irrespective of the scope of the discussion in which they were engaged, there was general agreement that it enabled the students to access the teachers' reasons behind actions observed or referred to:

I was explaining my actions. And although she could observe my actions perhaps she didn't understand the reasons for me doing that.

(Donald)

A number of teachers also claimed that the discussion served to help the students to get 'behind' or 'underneath' the lesson. In the quotation that follows, an English mentor gives an indication of the detailed planning that went into the observed lesson:

something like that looked quite easy, and what ... was made accessible was the way in which it wasn't arbitrary, the way in which before that lesson I'd actually worked out exactly who was doing what and when. Not only that – because there are some difficult children in there – the way in which I'd actually chosen who was going to work with each other ... Certainly that became accessible, the way in which a lesson like that doesn't just happen.

(Peter)

There was, then, a broad consensus among the teachers that the conversations with the students had enabled them to make accessible what they generally took for granted in their teaching and the planning and reasoning that underlay their observable teaching. The conversations had differed, by the teachers' own accounts, in that elucidating the observed lessons had been the primary and most valued achievement for the majority while using the observed lesson as a springboard for discussing more general concerns was what had been valued most by a minority.

Claims of the value of the procedure to the student teachers

With the exception of Harry, an English teacher, who explained that while he had 'thoroughly enjoyed the conversation' he was not sure whether the student 'had got anything out of it', all the teachers claimed that it had been a valuable exercise for the students. The three broad areas in which they claimed students benefited were:

- developing understanding of teaching and teachers;
- extending their repertoire of teaching strategies and skills;
- the process of pursuing through their questions the thinking underlying the teachers' observed teaching.

Developing understanding of teaching and teachers

There were many references to students developing their understanding of teaching. In some cases the emphasis was on helping the students avoid potential future mishaps through reducing their naïvety. A maths mentor highlights the need for caution in some circumstances:

> maybe you have been working on a line of approach for a long time in order to reach a particular performance – and I'm thinking there particularly of pair work where I could in that lesson [the observed lesson] slot them into working and asking each other lots of questions. Somebody who thought 'I would like to do that' might go in and have a total disaster because they didn't realize you had to train a class to work in a particular way.
>
> (Jill)

For others, the value was in student teachers becoming more aware of aspects of classroom teaching that were regarded as relatively sophisticated; and there is a suggestion in these accounts that it was a combination of the procedure and of its timing – coming as it did in the second half of the course – that made possible the claimed learning. In one case the observed lesson was an introductory lesson to a module and in the follow-up discussion the teacher was able to explain 'how that fits in with the scheme of things', which she saw as useful for the student because:

> as teachers we have to have a longer view of what's going on in a classroom. However much we are forced to go from day to day, you are inevitably ... thinking ahead and seeing how this fits in with the wider scheme of things, and it's important, particularly at the end of the teaching practice, to see that.
>
> (Lynn)

A significant feature of the teachers' comments is their insistence that student teachers, rather than trying to adopt observed teaching behaviours, should 'develop their own style': accessing a teacher's thinking behind observed actions was seen as enabling them to do just that, a point exemplified by the following extract:

> it helps him identify the different processes that were at work there and ... it was a way to develop his own lesson of that nature. Of course it's not exactly the same, but it's geared towards his own per-

sonality, his own way of working. ... it gave him a good insight into what I was thinking ... how my thoughts had been going ... and it gave, as it were, a toe-hold on how he was going to get into it.

(Jo)

In this second example, a history teacher argues that an understanding of the observed teaching is an essential prerequisite to 'real learning':

It's not just watching somebody and copying, it's looking, questioning, making decisions about what they've done, really understanding what they've done, and then deciding 'Well, I agree wholeheartedly with that and I'm going to try and do this', or 'I see why he's done this, but it's not me and I'm not going to do it anyhow, but it works. So perhaps there's something else that I can do that will achieve the same sort of thing.'

(Matthew)

The teachers were quick to refute the suggestion that an understanding of teaching in a single specific lesson might be of limited value to a learner teacher. One of the maths teachers, for example, while conceding that the kind of knowledge accessed by the student was likely to be very context-dependent – 'local knowledge', as she put it – asserted that

they can translate it to their situation, their classroom situation.

(Anne)

A second example comes from a history teacher:

although the set up of a class on one instance may be unique ... , there is your concrete example and from that you can extrapolate your abstractions. So I might never see that class again, but you could learn from it.

(Jackie)

A number of teachers pointed out that in getting access to the thinking of an individual teacher, the student teacher was learning not only what was important to that particular teacher, but also that every teacher has a set of beliefs and preferred ways of working, a point illustrated by the following quotation:

One of the things they need to be aware of is there's a lot of different ways to a common end, and they need to be very tolerant in their relations with staff. If they realize ... everybody has to have their own style and that styles can be equally effective even if it's not your style, that would be useful to them in the long run.

(Ian)

Extending repertoire of teaching skills and strategies

Only two of the teachers talked of students incorporating into their teaching repertoire a specific skill or strategy learned through the procedure. This is not altogether surprising since, according to many of the reports, students were looking to develop a greater understanding of a particular teacher's teaching, or of an aspect of teaching that cannot be narrowly classified as a single skill or strategy: for example, Laura was reported as being interested in how to be more relaxed in the classroom, Maria in differentiation, and Jane in 'how to motivate unmotivated students'.

Both teachers who claimed that their respective students did try out the specific skill or strategy on which they had focused, spoke of the procedure not only helping students to understand how a particular desired outcome is achieved, but in the process giving them the confidence to make the skill or strategy part of their own classroom practice. In the words of the two teachers:

> I did try to answer the question each time because I didn't want her to think 'I wouldn't be able to do that because I'm not experienced enough', and trying to give her reasons for my actions as often as possible it meant that she could do that. ... she saw my discussion lesson and she performed the same way with another class and it worked very well and she was pleased that she could do it ... that was instant feedback on whether she could do it, and it boosted her morale and confidence.
>
> (Geoff)

> I hope it sort of gave him some practical ideas about how to approach open-ended lessons, things like writing their suggestions on the board, so you give them worth, you can address them with the class ... A few simple techniques which I then saw him do, and very successfully ... And basically the confidence in him as well. I think he thought 'I've seen it done ... now I can do it, no maybe not for so long ... maybe not in so much depth, but I can start'.
>
> (Jo)

The process

Comments on ways in which the student teachers benefited from the process of engagement in observation with follow-up discussion were plentiful. Lynn was one of many who saw it as generally stimulating the students' thinking about their own teaching:

> It is making them ... think about their own teaching. 'How come she does it that way? Maybe I'll adopt it. Why does that work for her, but it hasn't for me? Why does that not work for her and it did for me?

For another teacher there was a direct link between student questions of the teacher and questions about their own teaching. In his words:

> [the process] enables them to begin to ask the right questions of their own teaching, their own preparation, of their own relationships with kids in the classroom ... Once they begin to ask the right questions, they'll begin to find their own answers.
>
> (Matthew)

This teacher was in no doubt that engaging in the procedure would 'help them to learn much more quickly'. For another, the process of pursuing in detail how the experienced teacher worked out what to do, and how, was ideally suited to helping the student teachers to learn to think like teachers themselves:

> it's really getting to the heart of why people do things in the way they do them ... it would be easy to say, here's a subject, here's a topic, teach it. And you could do that. The student could be given all sorts of tips on how to teach it, but unless they actually see somebody doing it and are able to ask questions about and observe and notice why I do things in a certain way it becomes just a topic, they haven't really made it their own, they haven't got themselves into it.
>
> (Jenny)

Claimed benefits for the teachers

A significant feature of these reports is the teachers' unsolicited references to the way in which the procedure impacted on them. All save one – who attributed her disappointment to the circumstances of the particular occasion, namely a 'half-hearted' student who 'geared the conversation to how she was going to teach next year' (Claire) – claimed to have found it a positive, enjoyable experience.

That so many of them described it as 'interesting' and 'unusual' suggests that there were few opportunities for them in the normal course of their working lives to talk about their teaching. As Paul, one of the English mentors, explained:

> the whole thing about teaching is that you work on your own with the door shut and you have your own ideas of what you want to achieve, but don't talk about them with anybody else in the school because at break time you don't want to talk about teaching. You never have a chance ever to talk about what you want to do in teaching ... this is the only opportunity you get to talk about what you are trying to do.

A more straightforward explanation of why, in his opinion, 'most teachers like doing it' came from one of the history teachers:

> Teachers are generally interested in teaching, and they're interested in their teaching too.
>
> (Matthew)

Many of the teachers also welcomed the experience because it was seen as making them think about their own teaching:

> How good it is for the teacher to be asked those questions, because it makes the teacher think, too. We often don't think about what we do in that way ... we actually haven't much time to think about why we do what we do.
>
> (Lynn)

In a small number of cases teachers claimed that they made adjustments to their teaching in the light of their thinking articulated in the conversation. One of the English teachers, for example, was 'grateful' that talking about her lesson – an 'ambitious one' in which she was trying to equip pupils with language with which to discuss language – made her aware of areas in which she might not have achieved her purposes, but which could be put right in future lessons. In her words:

> he [the student] said he was impressed with the lesson, but I actually felt that I could have done it better, I thought ... I'm still making mistakes here, I haven't got it right ... and at the end, after talking about it with Simon, I was concerned that I hadn't got everything across to them that I wanted to. I'd talked about, you've got to carry things through, so in the next couple of lessons I consolidated it and it was alright.
>
> (Sara)

The wistful note struck by one of the teachers in his account of the importance for teachers of the procedure may help to explain why so many of the respondents claimed to have benefitted from engaging in it:

> I think that sort of conversation used to take place at the end of the school day and I don't think it does any more ... a lot of people are so busy that they are doing, doing, doing, and not doing enough of the reflecting and thinking about why am I doing this, why am I here anyway.
>
> (Jack)

Although in their talk of claimed benefits there are few explicit references to the value to them as teacher educators of engaging in the procedure, from their overwhelmingly positive reaction to the procedure and their claims about its value for the students it is reasonable to infer that they felt the time invested in it was worth it from their perspective as school-based teacher educators. One of the three teachers who did make explicit the benefits to them as teacher educators explains the pleasure she felt when her student had a successful lesson with open-ended discussion along the lines of the lesson that had been observed and discussed:

> he copied it and for me it was very gratifying, because I felt 'he's actually taken on some of the things and worked on them' … it was thrilling. I sat there thinking 'he's doing it, he's doing it'.
>
> (Jo)

Suggestions for future use

When invited to comment on the usefulness of the procedure and on the desirability and feasibility of it taking place on more than one occasion during the PGCE year, all of the teachers argued for its inclusion in the course. There was also agreement as to what constituted essential elements of the procedure:

- focused observation of a teacher's lesson, the focus determined by the student teacher;
- a follow-up discussion to take place as soon as possible after the lesson;
- the discussion should not be disturbed by extraneous interruptions;
- the procedure should take place after the student has had some experience of teaching.

When talking of possible future use the teachers said little about the perceived formality of the procedure, from which one can assume that they accepted the level of formality that a planned, structured procedure would necessarily entail. Only one teacher suggested that the procedure would benefit from being less formal, arguing that the 'atmosphere needs to be more relaxed' so that the follow-up discussion could become 'a case of sharing ideas' (Claire).

The mentor who felt that carrying out the procedure with each of her two students was 'enough' and that more 'would be quite draining' (Jo) was alone in arguing against increasing the frequency of the procedure; all the other teachers claimed that in the future they wanted observation with follow-up discussion to take place more often. As might be expected, there was a wide variety of views about the number of times it could or should take place. The real differences, however, lay in attitudes to time constraints, with the teachers' comments falling broadly into two categories. The more common view was that the procedure should happen more frequently and that there was sufficient time for this to happen. Those whose views come within the second category were equally enthusiastic about the procedure, but felt that without more time it would not be possible to do it on a more frequent basis. As Michelle, one of the teachers who was not a mentor, commented:

> I'd be willing to do it – I'm sure most teachers would be ... most people would like to be observed and then interviewed. Time is the only thing.

The final words in this section come from a history teacher who scornfully dismissed the suggestions that the procedure was too complicated and time-consuming and that, whatever the students had accessed through engaging in it, there might be easier ways of so doing:

> I cannot think of a more efficient method. Teachers are under pressure at times and training new teachers is something that you must make time for, I don't think there is any way round this problem. Training teachers takes time, though.
>
> (Jackie)

Conclusion

This chapter has been concerned with what the student teachers and teachers had to say about engaging in the procedure, and their views of its place in relation to other ways in which student teachers learn from experienced practitioners.

The student teachers' perspective

An important element in the success of the procedure was that it gave a central place to the student teachers' individual agendas. Although the conversations were about the teachers' craft knowledge, the areas of the teachers' craft knowledge on which the conversation focused, and the choice of teachers, depended on the student teachers' particular agendas, related to the wider self-evaluation exercise in which they were engaged.

Coupled with this proper self-centredness was the students' concern for, and appreciation of, the teachers. An expression of this concern can be seen in the students' readiness to take account of the teachers' personalities in modifying the procedure to suit them. And the positive appreciation by most of the observed teaching, and of the insights revealed in the conversations, clearly extend beyond the formal procedure.

Most, but not all, of the student teachers generally saw the procedure as having distinct advantages, in enhancing their confidence, in developing their teaching repertoires and especially in developing their understanding of teachers and teaching. In striking contrast to this were the negative comments about observation and to a lesser extent about being observed and given feedback, the two most commonly experienced other ways of learning from teachers. Much of the criticism of being observed and given feedback was couched in terms of the insensitivity of teachers in undermining their confidence. They had a great deal to say about confidence, in terms not only of the importance of not being undermined, but also of the benefits gained from engaging in the procedure. And when talking about the teachers, the teachers' affective characteristics and their own dependence on teacher approval were common concerns. The interviews are, therefore, an important reminder that the success of any school-based strategy for student teachers' learning is likely to depend on taking account of the importance to them, and of the quality, of their relationship with teachers.

A dominant concern of the student teachers was with the formality of the procedure, or its 'artificiality'. Many felt uncomfortable because they were obliged to try to behave in a way that was inconsistent with the normal pattern of doing things in school. The strength of their feeling suggests that very few of them would have been sufficiently persuaded of the merits of this 'unnatural' exercise to engage in it had it not been a required part of their programme.

As we discussed in Chapter 4, the preliminary studies carried out in the previous year had enabled us to identify a number of widely held beliefs among the student teachers that acted as barriers to their valuing the procedure. These concerned *what* was worth learning (knowledge had to be of immediate practical relevance to their teaching), *whose* craft knowledge it was worth accessing (only teachers with a style that the student aspired to), and *how* useful teacher knowledge could be accessed (observation on its own and feedback from teachers on the student teachers' teaching seemed adequate). In this third year, in contrast, evidence of such beliefs was negligible which would suggest that the steps taken to overcome them had been successful. These included efforts to explain more fully to them the nature of teachers' craft knowledge, making the exercise an integral part of their programmes, and locating the exercise in the latter stages of the one-year course.

The students were as concerned with the relevance of activities and tasks to their own perceived needs at this stage of the year as at any earlier stages, but their boundaries of relevance had changed. It seems that by this late stage they see developing their practice as going beyond being able to do certain things in the classroom. By this stage their understanding of teaching, and its hidden complexity, has developed to the point that they are able to recognize both the value and difficulty of increasing their understanding. And perhaps they have also acquired sufficient confidence and fluency in the classroom for help of immediately practical relevance to have become less essential.

The teachers' perspective

For most of the teachers, the procedure was new and different. They contrasted it primarily with being observed but not having the opportunity then to discuss what had been happening, and with having conversations with student teachers which were not rooted in any shared concrete examples of their own teaching. They were generally enthusiastic about the merits of this unusual combination, and correspondingly negative in most cases about observation on its own. They appreciated the care with which the observation and the student teachers' questions had been planned, the fact that the questions were focused on specific aspects of the observed teaching, and the demanding, interesting and intelligent nature of these questions.

The value of the procedure as experienced was variously attributed to its inherent characteristics as a procedure, to the qualities of the individual student teachers with whom they had worked, or to the stage of the year. With regard to the latter, teachers emphasized the student teachers' *readiness* to engage in such a procedure by that stage, especially because the students had sufficient experience of teaching by then to understand enough to be able to ask intelligent questions. Perhaps most important was the way the procedure combined the student teachers' agendas, ensuring that they were eager to learn from the experienced teachers, with the focus on the teachers' own teaching and thinking, something that was unusual in their conversations with student teachers or indeed with colleagues.

With one exception, the teachers were unaware of problems for the student teachers in finding the opportunity to engage in the procedure, since it was the latter who had taken the lead and had made all the necessary arrangements. In making suggestions for the future use of observation and follow-up interview, however, while all save one of the teachers argued that it should take place more frequently, there was less agreement about the possibility of that happening within existing time constraints. It would seem, then, that although teacher attitudes to the procedure would not create problems for student teachers in finding the opportunity to engage in it, the concern of some with time constraints might well do so.

Remarkable by their absence were concerns expressed by the teachers about the formality of the procedure, either from the point of view of the arrangements made for time and privacy for the conversation, or in relation to the stylized conduct of the conversation. Perhaps the student teachers, who had been much concerned about such issues, managed to soften and adjust the formality so that it was not much noticed by the teachers. However, the evidence of enthusiasm on the part of the teachers for the careful planning of the conversation, together with the sharply focused nature of the questions, suggests that they welcomed much of what the student teachers experienced as 'artificial'.

Two of the teachers claimed that their respective student teachers were successful in adding to their repertoires the teaching strategies on which they had focused in the procedure. While, then, the overwhelmingly majority of teachers made no claims about the ways in which the student teachers made use of the knowledge and expertise they accessed through engaging in the procedure, all save one had no doubts about the usefulness of the exercise for them, not least because the knowledge accessed – variously described as natural, taken for granted and automatic – was not usually articulated. In addition to the distinctiveness of such knowledge, the teachers also contended that it was especially useful in helping beginning teachers to understand the complexity of teaching and the sophisticated nature of teachers' classroom thinking. The potential practical benefits of enhanced understanding of teaching and of teachers were seen as the avoidance of experiencing failure in the classroom through being naïvely ambitious, and the increased likelihood of student teachers developing their own styles of teaching rather than aping the teachers with whom they worked. Many teachers were also mindful of the benefits for the student teachers inherent in the process of pursuing through their questions the thinking underlying the teachers' observed teaching, arguing that it encouraged them to question their own developing practice and helped them to learn to think as experienced teachers.

With one exception, the teachers were also conscious of the benefits accruing to themselves from engaging in the procedure. Their expressed delight and satisfaction at having the opportunity to talk about their actual practice in their own terms suggests that in their normal encounters with student teachers their craft knowledge remained tacit; and their claim that talking about their teaching in this way acted as a stimulus to their reflecting on it hints at the possible professional development benefits for them of working with student teachers.

Part C

The Way Forward

6 Constructing a school-based ITE curriculum

In this third and final part of the book, we consider the kind of school-based curriculum that is needed, and that could realistically be developed, for twenty-first-century schools. We shall be drawing on evidence from around the world and, although thinking primarily of the English context within which we have been working, aiming to develop ideas for school-based ITE that could be put into practice in any national context. Our aim is not to provide a blueprint. School-based teacher educators in different contexts, working with their university-based partners, need to develop for themselves the particular curricula through which they can most effectively help student teachers to become intelligently constructive members of the profession.

Our aim is to offer a co-ordinated set of ideas that can point the way towards the creation of a high-quality school-based ITE curriculum. There are two sorts of ideas: general guiding ideas and particular contributing ideas. The ideas on which this chapter will focus are the general organizing ideas that we argue are key to the construction of such a curriculum. For this, we shall bring together the ideas and research that we have discussed in Parts A and B of this book, together with ideas from other sources.

What can be learned from the experimental initiative described in Part B? Valuable as we believe that initiative was in its own terms, it was intended also to be helpful in more general terms. What answers does it give us to questions about the nature of a school-based ITE curriculum that could achieve the goals we have suggested, about the viability of such a curriculum, and about what would be involved in its development?

Having looked in depth at what can be learned from our efforts to develop one possible element of the kind of curriculum needed, we shall go on to look at relevant initiatives elsewhere, to explore ways in which our own vision might be enriched and broadened as a result of what can be learned from them. Taking account of these different elements, and of the ideas discussed in Chapter 3, this chapter will conclude with a general overview of the kind of school-based ITE curriculum that is needed.

What have we learned?

At the end of Chapter 3, we formulated some core guiding ideas for a school-based ITE curriculum and also some questions to which we needed answers. How far has the initiative described in Part B supported our ideas? And how far has it answered our questions?

The study reported was concerned with questions about whether and how student teachers could gain access to experienced teachers' craft knowledge. Reassuringly, it gave positive answers and also new insights into what was involved. As can be seen from the account of the preliminary trials in the first part of Chapter 4, developing a procedure that worked was far from straightforward. Student teachers do not tap into the knowledge, skills and understanding embedded in experienced teachers' classroom practice as a matter of course; they need planned structured support. Equally, however, it became clear that they can be quite resistant to such structured support. Being responsive to the needs and agendas of the student teachers proved complex and difficult. A good place to start our consideration of the wider implications of the study is therefore with the ways in which student teachers' individual concerns, preconceptions and needs can impinge on the development of an effective school-based curriculum.

The impact of student teachers' agendas

The importance of student teachers' agendas and beliefs

The study reveals that many student teachers are strongly attached to unhelpful preconceptions about both what they need to learn and how they can best learn. In particular, many are very reluctant to abandon their assumptions that teaching should be quite simple and that *generalized* solutions are possible and appropriate for all kinds of problems. They tend also to have strong opinions about what can and cannot help their learning – many, for example, believing that they have little to learn except from teachers with whose overall teaching style they feel they can identify. It takes time for them to learn that the skills they need are complex and can only slowly be acquired.

The very strength of student teachers' preconceptions means that the success of ITE curricula is likely to depend in large measure on finding ways of 'going with the flow', using student teachers' agendas rather than opposing them. An important element in the procedure we developed was that it gave a central place to the student teachers' individual agendas, embedded as it was in an exercise about what kind of teacher each of them wanted to be and about ways of becoming that teacher. As with all learners, student teachers have to see the activities they engage in as relevant to the needs they believe themselves to have.

To persuade student teachers of the value of an activity, the timing has to be right. We needed, in this case, to learn the importance of their being asked to use the procedure only in the later stages of their course. During their one-year programme, the student teachers' ideas of relevance changed substantially. It was only when they had achieved a basic competence as classroom practitioners and were correspondingly confident, that they were ready in school contexts to think beyond their more immediate practical concerns. So it seems vitally important, in developing structured curricula and procedures for school-based teacher education, to take account of student teachers' development and to match the learning activities we set up for them and the kinds of things we ask them to learn with their readiness for such learning. The changing relationships between student teachers and teachers also need to be considered. It would, for example, be counter-productive to expect student teachers to take the initiative in their learning in the early days in school. On the other hand, there comes a stage when they have the confidence to take the lead, and when that is likely to be accepted and even welcomed by teachers.

This emphasis on student teachers' developing ideas and agendas and their readiness for certain tasks does not imply that there is much uniformity in the development of their thinking. Despite common developments in their confidence, competence and openness to less immediate issues, differences among them in their agendas and beliefs seem to be as great as ever; and the strength of their personal agendas means that they still need a good deal of rational persuasion about the value of any proposed learning activity. So helping our student teachers to develop their theoretical understanding of what was needed, through a fuller discussion with them of the nature of teachers' craft knowledge, seems to have been quite important. And it was certainly also important – given the limited time available – to give them authoritative help in the form of a set of clear, carefully justified, highly structured guidelines. They could be relied upon to adapt and modify these guidelines to suit their distinctive contexts and purposes.

The importance of 'fitting in'

Of immense importance to student teachers as adults learning to become members of a profession is being inducted into the culture of the workplace so that they can very quickly be accepted as workers on the same terms as established members of the culture. In the study reported, it was such student teacher concerns that, on one hand, led to the strongest resistance to the structured procedures promoted by us and, on the other, confirmed to us the need for such procedures. These concerns to fit in and be accepted were most apparent in two particular ways.

First, while most of the student teachers were ready to follow most of the suggested procedure in its final version, there were some aspects of the procedure to which they were generally resistant. In particular, they widely resisted our advice to ask predominantly open questions, to concentrate on seeking explanations for what teachers did or achieved, and especially to probe for fuller explanations. We cannot be sure why they did this, but one likely explanation is that they believed such actions would make them look ignorant and naïve, when what they wanted above all was *not* to stand out as people who had a lot to learn about teaching.

Second, the student teachers were consistently concerned about what they saw as the formality and artificiality of the procedure. In expressing a desire to be 'natural', they were asking to be left alone to fit in with what they saw teachers doing: *informally* discussing problems, negotiating arrangements and sharing ideas, as they walked along corridors or grabbed a quick cup of tea in the staffroom. For the most part, learning opportunities for student teachers in schools at present tend generally to be governed by the busyness of schools and teachers, and especially by their own anxiety not to be out of step with the rhythms of school life.

Such 'natural' learning opportunities, however, do not lead to student teacher learning of the depth and the quality that is needed; instead, they lead to the kind of learning for which, in present circumstances, student teachers feel the greatest need, learning to 'fit in'. It is partly in order to avoid such felt needs that we need to move away from notions of school experience and placement schools and towards a planned school-based curriculum for ITE.

The influence of formal requirements

Alongside student teachers' individual but developing agendas and their strong motivation to fit in and be accepted by teachers, a third powerful factor was evident in shaping the way they responded to our initiative: the formal requirements of the course. Simply because student teachers want to complete their courses successfully, they give priority to meeting these requirements. Most strikingly in this case, the student teachers found their course a demanding one, especially in terms of the time that was required for assignments and activities that were assessed; so their attitude to the use of time was very strongly influenced by concerns about what would contribute to their success. While a structured curriculum is far from sufficient in itself to guarantee productive school-based learning, it is probably a necessary condition, helping student teachers to allocate their time and energy to useful learning activities.

The needs and concerns of teachers

Our experiment also exemplifies how teachers' needs will have to be taken into account in developing a school-based ITE curriculum. As we had anticipated, teachers commonly find it a difficult task to articulate their normally tacit craft knowledge, and difficult also to recognize that particular things that are obvious to them are far from obvious to others, especially beginning teachers. Furthermore, they too are under constant pressure, with more to do than there is ever time for. So teachers need a lot of support and encouragement if they are to engage effectively in the kind of school-based ITE that we are proposing.

The need for respect

Student teachers themselves can do a great deal to motivate experienced teachers to help them to learn, most significantly through showing evident respect for their expertise. The complex, intuitive and personalized nature of their expertise means that teachers are, and generally feel, vulnerable to misunderstanding and to implied criticism. As became clear in this experiment, it was only too easy for student teachers to ask questions which, in their substance or style, undermined teachers' confidence and so their motivation to engage in such conversations with the students. In contrast, student teachers who in the informed thoughtfulness of their questions showed a sincere interest in wanting to learn to become teachers, and a wish to understand the experienced teachers' expertise, encouraged teachers to accept the challenge of explaining their craft.

The need to understand

Teachers also need support from school colleagues and from university-based teacher educators. Most crucially, such support is needed to help teachers think through the work that they are doing with student teachers. School-based teacher educators can use procedures effectively only if they are able to do so actively and intelligently, having understood and been persuaded by the rationale for these procedures. For example, many teachers, suspicious that our proposed procedure might be encouraging beginning teachers to copy their ways of doing things, used it enthusiastically and intelligently only after first being helped to think through the benefits of student teachers *understanding* their craft knowledge rather than imitating it. Given such an understanding, the teachers involved in the experiment were motivated by the high value placed on their professional craft knowledge. As teacher educators, they appreciated the opportunity to talk about teaching as they themselves engaged in it, a very different framework from the usual one of responding to the student teachers' strengths and limitations, and a framework which offered different advantages for the student teachers' education. They appreciated too the equally novel fact, with its own complementary advantages, that the student teachers had the responsibility for formulating the questions to be explored. The teachers' enthusiasm for these kinds of broadening of the normal narrow scope of school-based ITE is most encouraging.

The need to be businesslike

Also very encouraging were the teachers' responses to the formal planning of the procedure, so much disliked by the student teachers because it was not the 'natural' way of doing things in schools. Teachers generally welcomed the planning of clearly designated and protected times and spaces for the conversations, and also the carefully structured nature of the conversations. To them these aspects of the procedure, far from being unnatural, were instead 'businesslike'. Similarly, their attitude to the amount of time needed for the procedure reflected just the kind of professionalism that we believe is needed in relation to school-based ITE: while all of them were highly conscious of the pressures of time, and while some took the view that the procedure could not be regularly pursued in existing circumstances, the majority view was that time can be, and needs to be, found for activities which are of sufficient educational value.

The need for professional development

The teachers were conscious of the benefits of this kind of procedure for themselves as teachers, asserting that focusing on their own craft knowledge and talking about it in their own terms led to their reflecting on their practice. In making plans for student teachers' learning, it is worth bearing in mind the enormous advantage of any arrangements from which experienced teachers might feel they benefit.

Designing a school-based ITE curriculum

We identify five main lessons to be drawn from this experiment about designing a school-based curriculum.

The need for preliminary exploration

Although the basic idea from which we started proved in the end to be fruitful, and although we ourselves were quite knowledgeable from the start about schools and ITE, we needed to do a great deal of learning in order to develop the basic idea into a workable procedure. For example, we initially grossly overestimated how frequently it could be used, severely underestimated how much guidance and education the student teachers would need, and had to learn how important it was for this work to be incorporated into the formal assessed curriculum.

The general very important point is that it would be both easy and foolish to underestimate the amount of learning that will be necessary in order to develop a high-quality school-based ITE curriculum. There is of course a lot of highly relevant knowledge, both from experience and from research, on which teacher educators can build; but a systematic approach to school-based ITE is something new, and extensive creative thinking, exploration, development and evaluation will be needed to realize its potential.

The importance of a structured and assessed curriculum

We argued in principle in Chapter 3 for a structured curriculum, but one that would not interfere with the normal everyday work of schools and that would indeed enable student teachers to gain access to and to understand that work. The study reported in Part B surprised us, however, in how important it showed such a structured curriculum to be. There are, it is now clear, at least seven reasons for the importance of a formal structured school-based curriculum:

- The normal rhythm of school life provides very little of the necessary time, space or encouragement for thoughtful, sustained reflection and conversation.
- Incidental learning, although important, is very far from being adequate.
- Much of the school-based learning that student teachers need to do requires hard disciplined thinking and therefore both protected time and planned professional support.
- The enormous pressure student teachers feel themselves under to prioritize 'fitting in' has to be counterbalanced by other strong pressures.
- Other things being equal, student teachers sensibly give priority in allocating their time to those things that are unambiguously necessary for the successful completion of their courses.
- Experienced teachers engaged in teacher education value professional and businesslike approaches to it, including diversified and structured approaches for different purposes and explicit formal allocation of the necessary times and spaces for specific activities.
- To be effective, a school-based curriculum needs very careful planning in order to take account of, for example, the timing across the school year of different learning activities, the crucial need to be responsive to differences among student teachers, teachers and schools, and the considerable logistical problems of ensuring that teachers can meet with student teachers at appropriate times.

The need to balance considerations of content, context and process

In Chapter 3 we suggested that, while work-based learning needs to be structured as much as is necessary to maximize learners' cognitive access to the full normal realities of the work of teaching, it must not distort those realities. And we also suggested that schools' effectiveness as sites for ITE depends on their developing a general climate characterized by active and evident professional learning. Student teachers need to learn how to engage in the normal work of schools, but that need has to be balanced with the needs both for a structured curriculum and for a cultural context in which professional learning is accepted as normal and important. Unless it is clear that 'real' teachers too are learners, student teachers will resist anything that makes it obvious that they are learners and so seems to set them apart from 'real' teachers.

The importance of a university contribution

While university-based teacher educators were clearly not at centre-stage in an exercise that was school-based and was concerned with student teachers accessing the craft knowledge of experienced teachers, their contribution was nonetheless significant. The university had a key role to play in framing the ways in which student teachers should go about their learning – through, for example, developing student teachers' generalized understandings of the nature of classroom teaching expertise, the necessary differences between novice and experienced teachers, and the rationale for and nature of different kinds of learning activities. And, while there is no reason why innovative initiatives should come from universities, it does seem likely that there will be a general need for university-based teacher educators to play something of the role they played in this case in supporting school-based teacher educators in managing, developing and evaluating the initiative.

The need to question established practices

The reported study is also a reminder that we should be prepared at least to question the usefulness of some well-established ways of working with beginning teachers in schools. Classroom observation, for example, is most commonly carried out by student teachers at the beginning of their programmes of preparation before they have had any experience of teaching. From both the student teachers and the teachers in this study came the suggestion that the former would be much better placed to learn through observation later in the programme. With more developed knowledge and understanding of classrooms and with some experience of teaching, student teachers are better able to make sense of what they observe. Moreover, given their overwhelming concern with developing their own classroom practice, student teachers are much more likely to see observation as relevant when they are able to focus on their own perceived needs as beginning teachers.

Learning from initiatives elsewhere

In this section we shall explore ways in which we might be able to learn from other current attempts at ITE reform. In Chapter 1, we explained our thinking in relation to a broad historical context, including especially the strengths and limitations of the government-imposed move towards school-based ITE in England in the early 1990s. And in Chapter 3, we made use of helpful ideas from many other writers. Our concern here is to explain how what we have argued for in this book relates to other specific initiatives for ITE reform and also how our purpose is different from that of other major initiatives. Given this limited objective, we shall be both selective and brief in our treatment of other initiatives.

The truth is that we have been disappointed not to find more in the literature of ITE reform that we could use in developing our own ideas. We have wondered why this was so, and we have concluded that most other initiatives have been directed towards different purposes from our own. None of these purposes seem to us at all unworthy, but they have been sufficiently different from our own for the strategies proposed for achieving them not to seem helpful for improving the quality of school-based ITE. We shall consider several of these other purposes in turn.

Teacher recruitment

In many countries, perhaps most notably the USA and England, there has in recent years been an opening up of diverse routes into teaching, many of the new routes being employment-based. We wondered whether we might have something to learn about school-based ITE from such alternative programmes.

Stoddart and Floden (1996) examine the differences between traditional and alternative routes in the USA. Although they point out that 'even a cursory examination of alternate certification programmes would show that they vary widely in purpose, content and structure' (1996: 90), they also point out that 'a key difference between alternate and university-based programs is the context and focus of the training ... alternate certification programs provide in-service professional education while candidates are engaged in full-time teaching responsibilities' (1996: 91), and that 'alternate-route programs tend to focus on the pragmatic aspects of teaching' (1996: 92).

In England, the Graduate Teacher Programme (GTP) is the most recent and appears to be the most successful of successive alternative schemes promoted by the government since the early 1990s. It is an employment-based route into teaching, designed primarily for trainees who are additional to school staffing, but with schools training them on the job and the government paying a grant towards both salary and training costs. Ofsted (2005: 2), the government-appointed inspectorate, found that 'the GTP attracts good candidates with the potential to be effective teachers and makes a strong contribution to recruitment in secondary shortage subjects and from under-represented groups'. However, while 'an important strength of GTP training is the range of opportunities for trainees to become more fully immersed in school life and gain a breadth of whole-school professional experiences' (Ofsted 2005: 7), it is disappointing that the Ofsted report does not mention any interesting new developments in school-based ITE.

While it would be naïve to suggest that improved recruitment has been the only motivation for the opening up of alternative routes into teaching, it certainly has been one major motive and the primary rationale for it, both in the USA and in England. The schools' major concerns have been to attract reasonably qualified new teachers. The new teachers' major concerns have been to be able to cope with the demands upon them, and to be paid even while they struggle to learn the job. And, as is clearly reflected in the Ofsted (2005) report, however much the authorities have been concerned to maintain basic standards, they have not been looking to these alternative programmes for improvements in the quality of ITE. Given recruitment as their priority purpose, we should not expect to find anything to build on there.

Reforming university-based ITE

Many thoughtful teacher educators in many different countries have in recent years reflected on their experiences and on the now extensive research literature on teacher education, and have developed and tried out plans for reform. Many of these initiatives have been based on understandings quite similar to our own, but the reforms have not tended to involve a move away from university-based schemes. We can exemplify this tendency by reference to one of the most thoughtful and ambitious of these reforms, by a group at the University of Utrecht in the Netherlands, led by Fred Korthagen (2001).

Korthagen and his colleagues have developed an approach to ITE which they describe as 'realistic teacher education'. Like us, they have rejected the theory-into-practice approach to ITE because it is 'unrealistic'. Instead, they take very seriously the thinking and concerns of individual student teachers and plan their programme on the basis of

> three basic principles in professional learning: ... A teacher's professional learning will be more effective when:
> 1. directed by an internal need in the learner ...
> 2. rooted in the learner's own experiences ...
> 3. the learner reflects in detail on his or her own experiences.
> (Korthagen 2001: 71)

It follows from these three principles that the teacher educator should give priority to helping student teachers to become aware of their individual learning needs, to find useful experiences, and to reflect on these experiences in detail. Useful experiences will be challenging, but will not be too threatening, at each stage in the individual's development. Teacher educators must give a great deal of attention to student teachers' emotions, and must not 'push' student teachers prematurely to recognition of their learning needs.

The teacher education curriculum should be planned, it is suggested, so that practical experiences and reflection upon them are part of a long-term development process. Experienced teacher educators should be able to predict what types of problems and concerns are generated by different kinds of practical experiences, as well as what kinds of theory can fruitfully be connected to these problems and concerns. The fundamental principle, however, is that skills or theories should only be introduced when student teachers have felt the need for them, perhaps as a result of experiences deliberately planned for them.

As Korthagen emphasizes, such a programme depends for its success on a close integration of school-based and university-based elements; and we hope that the very summary account that we have given of the Utrecht group's thinking is nonetheless recognizable as echoing many of the ideas in this book. But, admirable as we find much of that thinking, it is not something on which we have felt able to build, and that is because Korthagen's teacher educator unambiguously inhabits a university. There is no place in his model for teachers' expertise, nor for the agency of school-based teacher educators, nor even for schools as sites where practical theorizing needs to be engaged in. While there is much in his model that might usefully complement the work of school-based teacher education, his enterprise – and others concerned with the reform of university-based teacher education – is a very different one from ours.

School–university partnerships

> The idea of partnerships between various groups interested in improving the quality of education is not new. There is a burgeoning literature that extols the virtues of school–university partnerships and the contribution they make to teacher professional development at the school and system levels, to reforming schools and universities' practices and procedures, and finally bringing relevance to educational research.
>
> (Sachs 2003: 65)

Writing in the context of 'reconceptualizing teacher education programmes', Sachs explains that her interest is in the operation of such partnerships. She emphasizes the different possible terms of partnership and expresses a strong preference for those where there is 'a two-way model of reciprocity' and where the power relationships are 'more collaborative and equal'. Extrapolating from an important Australian project of the 1990s, the Innovative Links between Schools and Universities Project for Teacher Professional Development, she argues that partnerships between university-based and school-based staff should aspire to being 'communities of practice', and goes on to elaborate on how a partnership for ITE would work.

Sachs seems to be far from alone in Australia in taking the nature of school–university partnerships as her starting point and in extrapolating from partnerships for teachers' professional development and for research to partnerships for ITE, as is apparent from the review of Australian partnerships for ITE by Brisard *et al.* (2005). They quote Chapman *et al.* (2003) as describing a number of 'practice-based partnerships' offering innovative ITE programmes considered by the Australian Council of Deans of Education to 'highlight the positive impact of greater institutional links and emphasize how innovation within teacher education is clearly linked to building a culture of innovation in schools' (ACDE 2003: 7).

> These innovative programmes of initial teacher education all display the following common features:
> * The primary focus of the school–university relationship is the enhancement of pupils' learning.
> * The program centres on the formation of a learning community made up of student teachers, mentor teachers and teacher educators working together as 'learning partners' in the authentic context of schools, to better understand and enhance teaching and learning.
> * Opportunities are provided for student teachers and schools to pursue collaborative curriculum inquiry, curriculum development and teaching practice investigations.
> * The program places professional practice at the centre of the student's learning and theory and practice are not treated separately but are connected through collaborative reflective inquiry and/or collaborative problem-solving.
> – Schools and Faculties collaborate on program design and delivery.
> (Brisard *et al.* 2005: 88)

Although as yet we have limited information about them, these innovative programmes do indeed seem very interesting. More generally, we cannot but applaud the strong emphasis in Australian debate on equality and reciprocity in school–university partnerships. Whether or not they are right in their apparent concern to give priority to the creation of multi-purpose partnerships and then to develop ITE programmes as one element of these partnerships, we cannot tell. Our own concern has been to focus on what is needed for high-quality ITE, including what kind of partnership is required. When, in other contexts, we have been concerned with school–university partnerships for research, for school improvement, or for professional development, rather different issues seem to have arisen. But all that can be said at this stage is that the Australian approach seems to be very different.

Distinctive as the Australian approach certainly is, it does seem to have some similarities to the Professional Development School movement in the United States, to which we now turn.

Reforming America's schools

Several major reports in the USA in the 1980s sought to address two broadly similar problems. The central perceived problem was the alarmingly bad state of the USA's public schools, of student achievements in these schools and of the teaching these students received. A second problem, contributing to the first, was claimed to be the inadequate and unrealistic ITE provided by the country's colleges of education and universities. Solutions to these problems were similarly seen as closely linked. Goodlad (1990), for example, coined the phrase *simultaneous renewal* to capture his vision of how radical reform in teacher education could also be a key to solving the problems of public schools. The phrase *Professional Development Schools* (PDS) was that chosen by probably the most influential series of reports, those of the Holmes Group (1986, 1990, 1995), to describe an institution that was central to its thinking about such simultaneous renewal.

As Darling-Hammond (1994) describes them, PDSs are schools, working in close partnership with universities, in which student teachers enter professional practice by working with expert practitioners, and where they learn under intensive supervision about state-of-the-art practice. They are schools, too, where veteran teachers not only have exceptional opportunities for their own professional development but also assume new roles as mentors, university adjuncts and teacher leaders. They are also, ideally, 'schools in which practice-based and practice-sensitive research can be carried out collaboratively by teachers, teacher-educators and researchers' (Darling-Hammond 1994: 102). These schools were therefore to be in the vanguard of the 'simultaneous renewal' through which both the quality of teaching in schools and the preparation of beginning teachers were to be transformed.

The idea of PDSs clearly captured the imagination of many people in American university schools of education and led them, during the 1990s, to develop hundreds of PDS schemes in partnership with local groups of schools. This has led in turn to an extensive literature describing, celebrating, evaluating or investigating these initiatives. One is struck most of all, in studying this literature, by the extraordinary ambition of this university-led reform movement, both in the variety of elements it involves and in its aspiration to reform the country's schools. Both these characteristics are apparent, for example, from Valli *et al.*'s (1997) excellent review of research on PDSs. These reviewers found that researchers had focused on a considerable variety of themes, with collaborative relations – an intended means towards other reforms – being the only focus common to most studies. They concluded also that 'Tomorrow's Schools offers an ambitious and compelling vision of reform. Partners are, however, having great difficulty in carrying out that vision. In many instances, the vision has become so narrowed as to be almost unrecognisable' (Valli *et al.* 1997: 298).

Valli *et al.* (1997) suggest that, however attractive the vision, the rhetoric may be counter-productive if, as it seems, it is unrealistically ambitious. Other evaluators have also questioned the realism of the Holmes vision of what PDSs could do. Ross (1995), for example, notes the fragility of PDS schemes which, although numerous, have characteristically been very small-scale initiatives, dependent on inspirational individual leaders and on *ad hoc* financial support, and which have had to deal with formidable obstacles, such as barely compatible state policies.

It seems likely to us, then, that much more has been expected of PDSs than they could credibly hope to deliver. Attempting too much with too few resources, it was easy in practice for them to fall prey to inconsistencies between the assumptions implicit in different strands of their enterprise . In particular, the idea of collaboration between school teachers and university staff is regularly highlighted, but inconsistencies regularly appear with regard to the nature of that collaboration. Principles of equity and mutual respect are asserted, and there is occasional mention of the complex and distinctive nature of teachers' practical knowledge. In practice, however, the university staff's greater confidence in their own knowledge and its value for school renewal, together with experienced school teachers' eagerness to learn new ideas, seems to have meant that PDSs have generally been used to strengthen the old theory-into-practice version of ITE rather than to offer anything fundamentally new.

The published literature shows this tendency with differing degrees of awareness. Many studies (e.g. Allexsaht-Snider *et al.* 1995; Stanulis 1995; Grisham *et al.* 1999) describe the work of PDSs with enthusiasm and little apparent awareness of the lack of respect revealed for practising teachers' expertise. Other studies adopt a more consciously critical role in reporting what they see as a failure to move beyond the traditional ways of thinking about student teachers' learning. Bullough *et al.* (2004), for example, report a study of the perceived and experienced roles of clinical faculty associates (CFAs), teachers who, as proposed by the Holmes Group (1995), would come from 'the ranks of distinguished school practitioners' and would 'form a living bridge between campus and practice' (Bullough *et al.* 2004: 505–6). They found, however, that the CFAs and most permanent university staff saw the primary CFA role as being to ensure that student teacher practice is congruent with what is taught on campus.

The enormous scale and the internal diversity of what has been done within the PDS movement in the USA mean that any generalized judgement of it would be rash. We have, however, found very little indeed within that movement that seems relevant to the kind of school-based ITE for which we have been arguing. Developing the quality of ITE seems to us to be too demanding a task to be successfully undertaken as a side-issue – but that seems to be what has been attempted.

The development of good practice in school-based ITE in England

In England, selected schools have been funded as Training Schools by government since 2000 'to develop and disseminate good practice in initial teacher training, train mentors and undertake relevant research' (Ofsted 2003: 1). Ofsted claim that 'the Training School programme represents good value for money' and that 'the programme has had a very positive effect on ITT' (2003: 2). This positive effect is reported to be primarily in the numbers of trainees taken on by the schools, the greater number of teachers trained for and involved in mentoring, and claimed improvements in the quality of mentoring. Some developments in training procedures are mentioned such as 'cross-phase work in modern foreign languages; the use of interactive whiteboards; teaching citizenship; and supporting pupils with English as an additional language' (Ofsted 2003: 8–9); but little information is provided about such developments. We have been disappointed not to find reports of more imaginative developments in school-based ITE practice in Training Schools.

Nonetheless, the Training Schools initiative is the one reform initiative that we have identified that shares our own purpose of developing good practice in school-based ITE. In that it is essential that there should be a body of selected schools committed to treating ITE as a priority concern, accustomed to receiving substantial numbers of student teachers, with staff who recognize their need to develop specialist expertise as school-based teacher educators, and with adequate resources to undertake this work, it is an excellent initiative. There is some evidence, too, from the Ofsted report and from our own direct contacts, that Training Schools are beginning to consolidate a degree of good practice. What they have yet to do, in our judgement, is to develop a guiding vision of what they might do. We hope that his book will help them.

A summary of our general organizing ideas

As indicated in the previous section, we were disappointed when we explored the international literature for other initiatives that might complement and enhance our own general ideas for developing school-based ITE. It is not that there has been a lack of related thinking elsewhere. But as yet we have not found well-developed ideas elsewhere for thoughtful, serious school-based approaches to ITE. So for the moment we are dependent on the general thinking developed in Part A of this book, and especially in Chapter 3, and on the more generalized conclusions we were able to draw from the initiative reported in Part B, as outlined in the first section of this chapter. It is appropriate here simply to summarize these ideas.

There have been three central themes. One is that the theory-into-practice conception of ITE that dominated the twentieth century is fundamentally flawed and needs to be replaced. The notion that student teachers should learn good theoretical ideas in universities, and then put them into practice in schools, is flawed in many ways but most obviously in that it is based on quite false conceptions of the nature of teaching expertise and of how such expertise is developed. It is a conception of ITE, furthermore, that has scandalously neglected the expertise of experienced teachers.

The second central theme has been that the highly pragmatic but bureaucratic conception of ITE that has largely replaced theory-into-practice in England in recent years is equally flawed, again most obviously in that it is based on quite false conceptions of the nature of teaching expertise and of how such expertise is developed. And again it is a conception of ITE that has scandalously, if less obviously, neglected the expertise of experienced teachers. Furthermore, it has in large measure neglected the relevant knowledge that can be derived from the academic study of teaching and learning.

The third and most important theme is that it is possible and would be highly fruitful to develop planned and structured school-based ITE curricula realistically designed to enable beginning teachers to develop the expertise and the understandings that they will need as classroom teachers. These curricula could use, for example, the organizational frameworks that are current in England, but would be based on our best understandings of the nature of classroom teaching expertise and how it can be learned; and it would treat the expertise of experienced teachers as a major resource. It would emphasize 'practical theorizing' as a means through which student teachers would be asked to draw critically on diverse kinds of knowledge in order to develop valid teaching expertise; and as a means through which they should continue to learn and improve throughout their careers as teachers.

It is almost as important to emphasize what has not been offered in this book as what has been offered. Our discussion of issues in teacher education has been far from comprehensive. For example, we have completely ignored the fundamental issue of how subject knowledge has to be transformed for effective pedagogy, and therefore of how beginning teachers have to relearn subjects as they learn to teach them. That massive omission exemplifies very clearly how we have in this book only made a start, pointed a direction, for the work that is needed. We hope that others will take up the challenge of exploring what would be involved in the subject-specific component of a school-based ITE curriculum for student teachers of, for example, science or geography. How would a practical theorizing curriculum help them to transform their substantial academic knowledge of their subjects into subject pedagogical expertise, drawing on the expertise of subject teachers in their schools, on research and professional literature, and on their carefully planned experiences of subject teaching?

There are other major issues that we have not dealt with. For example, if practical theorizing is to play such a central part, how should student teachers' efforts at practical theorizing be assessed? University-based teacher educators are of course well used to assessing student teachers' thinking, as expressed in written essays. Should they continue to do so, even for *practical* theorizing in the context of *school-based* curricula? Or should school-based teacher educators take on the responsibility for both formative and summative assessment, drawing on their distinctive contextualized practical expertise? Or, since it is important for student teachers to develop practical theorizing expertise for use throughout their careers as teachers, should the emphasis shift from assessment of *written* practical theorizing towards other forms of assessment? There are many such questions to be considered.

Our purpose here, however, is to summarize what we have already written in this book, not to raise new issues. We can perhaps best summarize our ideas by comparing key elements of the three conceptions of ITE that we have contrasted. That is what we attempt to do in Table 6.1.

Table 6.1 Three contrasting models of initial teacher education

	Theory-into-practice	Current English model	School-based curriculum model
Assumed nature of teaching expertise	Practices derived from abstract theoretical knowledge	Competences specified by government	Professional craft knowledge of experienced practitioners, critically evaluated
Other expertise to be acquired by student teachers	Untheorized practices found pragmatically useful in particular schools	Untheorized practices found pragmatically useful in particular schools	Practical theorizing expertise
Attention to student teacher's agenda and preconceptions	None	None	A focus of practical theorizing
Nature of student teacher's presumed learning	Learning of propositional knowledge – translating into practice – practice	Practice of competences, with feedback	Planned school-based curriculum for practical theorizing, including multiple sources of ideas, types of practice and sources of feedback
Support for student teacher's developing identity as teacher	None	Socialization into school	Identity issues explicitly included in practical theorizing
Primary function of schools	Providing practice opportunities	Providing practice opportunities	Providing core curriculum
Primary teacher role	Optional adviser	Mentor	(a) School-based teacher educator (b) Embodiment of teaching expertise
Primary university role	Main source of professional knowledge	Programme co-ordinator	Joint curriculum planner and provider of curriculum support services
Subsidiary university role	Programme co-ordinator	Source of basic professional knowledge	Programme co-ordinator

7 Elements of a school-based ITE curriculum

In Chapter 6, we discussed the general organizing ideas that should guide the construction of a school-based ITE curriculum. In this final chapter we shall focus on more particular ideas that appear to us to be among the useful elements from which an appropriate curriculum might be constructed.

At present, by far the greatest part of student teachers' time in school, especially in the last two-thirds of their courses, is spent teaching classes that would otherwise be taught by members of the school staff, in preparation for that teaching and in discussing lessons they have taught. How far do we envisage changes to this pattern?

The first thing to be said is that extensive practice in classroom teaching and in preparing for that teaching is vitally necessary for student teachers: they do need to engage over and over again in these complex tasks if they are to attain the necessary wide-ranging competence, fluency and confidence to be properly employed as classroom teachers. But the second thing to be said is that this practice could surely be more efficiently used for student teachers' learning. Indeed, both student teachers themselves and the teachers with whom they work tend to view the greater part of this practice not primarily as an opportunity for student teachers' learning but rather as a contribution by them to the work of teaching school pupils. There is nothing wrong with that: most teachers are so overworked that any help for them is to be welcomed; and, as we recognized in Chapter 3, student teachers' coming to see themselves as real teachers – doing the work of the school – is an important part of their professional learning. Nonetheless, without questioning either of these important benefits, we believe that more thought should be given to maximizing the learning benefits to be gained from student teachers' extensive practice; and one element of that rethinking might involve consideration of some limited reduction in the amount of that practice, to make space for other things.

In asking about the efficiency with which student teachers' practice in whole-class teaching is used for learning to teach, we need, among other things, to consider whether the practice is sufficiently differentiated, and focused on the variety of tasks in which they need to develop expertise. For example, is there appropriate progression throughout their course, with tasks in which they have achieved adequate competence being replaced by new and more demanding tasks? Another consideration should be whether the practice is appropriately combined with modelling and feedback opportunities of sufficient quantity and quality. A further concern is that as much of the guidance from experienced teachers as possible should not be restricted to giving practical advice but should be deliberately structured to foster practical theorizing.

The ten particular ideas that we shall discuss here would contribute in different ways to a planned school-based curriculum. Some of them are about social processes that could contribute to student teachers' learning. Others are more concerned with the content of parts of the curriculum or with the pursuit of particular purposes. They are, we believe, useful ideas; but how they would relate in practice to each other or to the whole curriculum are issues that we have left open.

Specific suggestions for social processes contributing to student teachers' learning

This section focuses on ideas concerned with making fuller use of different sources and processes for student teachers' learning about classroom teaching. The initiative we described in Part B of this book concerned a new approach to modelling, as part of a larger task that included both practice and feedback and was appropriate for the later part of ITE courses. One of the specific elements that we suggest in this section – collaborative planning and teaching – is an approach to practice, modelling and feedback that is worthy of much fuller and more deliberate use in the earlier part of courses. Another of these elements focuses on progression in approaches to feedback and evaluation. A third focuses on a much neglected but immensely valuable perspective, that of the pupils taught by student teachers, while a fourth is aimed at making the most of the mutual support that student teachers can give each other. A fifth element seeks to ensure that student teachers are enabled to learn from all the teachers whose classes they teach.

Collaborative planning and teaching

It is not uncommon for student teachers, when observing a teacher in a classroom, to be invited to work with individual pupils or small groups. What is far less common, however, yet considerably more valuable in terms of the student teachers' learning, is for them collaboratively to plan and teach a lesson or series of lessons with their mentor.

The complexity of classroom teaching is such that it is unrealistic to expect student teachers in their first few weeks in school successfully to plan and teach complete lessons on their own. Throwing them into the deep end can lead to both student teachers and pupils drowning. Yet, learner teachers can only acquire the vast range of skills that they need for classroom teaching by trying them out in real classrooms with real pupils. Collaborative planning and teaching reduces the complexity of the teaching task for beginning teachers while at the same time enabling them to try out more ambitious ways of working than would be possible if they were teaching on their own. Above all, it offers the beginning teacher a protected but authentic environment for practice. The many benefits for student teachers are succinctly summed up by Burn (1997: 160):

> Planning with a mentor gives student teachers access to an experienced teacher's methods and insights and impresses upon them the need for rigorous planning. Taking responsibility for parts of a lesson enables student teachers to come to terms with real teaching while remaining in a protected environment. By narrowing the focus and removing some of the panic and confusion, it allows student teachers to approach the task of teaching more rationally, both while engaged in teaching and in analysing it afterwards.

While mentors can experience uncertainty about acceding to beginning teachers' wishes to 'be left to get on with it in the classroom', they are also inclined to be reluctant to 'intrude' by taking part in the beginner's teaching. Sharon Feiman-Nemser, a leading North American authority on mentoring, suggests that seeing mentoring as 'assisted performance' frees the mentor from any such reluctance, providing as it does 'a justification for mentors to participate with novices in the everyday activities of teaching in order to scaffold their learning' (Feiman-Nemser and Beasley 1997: 109). 'Through their joint participation in activities authentic to teaching', they explain, 'the mentor and novice develop shared understandings about the meaning and purposes of these activities, and the novice gradually internalises ways of thinking, problem-solving and acting needed to carry them out' (1997: 108).

This particular approach to practice, modelling and feedback is a very productive way of working at any stage of a beginning teacher's learning, not least because it is such a rich source of different kinds of learning. At first, when planning the lesson together, the mentor will necessarily have a more prominent role than the student teacher. While student teachers' knowledge of the subject may well be equal to or even better than that of their mentors, their pedagogical knowledge will be limited. In the early stages, then, the mentor will have to spell out in detail the wide range of considerations he or she is taking account of, making explicit understandings that, when working alone, would be taken for granted. In the beginning, therefore, the emphasis is on modelling planning. As the student teacher's own craft knowledge develops, the planning will become more truly joint planning, with two professionals sharing ideas. The development of the student teacher's craft knowledge also means that there will be an increasing shared body of knowledge and understanding that can be taken for granted, freeing both to focus more on imaginative lesson design. There are also opportunities for progression in terms of the scope of the planning. In the beginning, the focus will necessarily be on single lessons, whereas later the mentor and student teacher can co-plan a complete module or unit of work, with some lessons taught by the mentor, some by the student teacher and some by them working together in the classroom.

Similarly, in the co-teaching of lessons, mentors can from a very early stage set student teachers progressively more challenging teaching tasks that are important for their learning but that with care they can accomplish successfully. Even after student teachers have reached the stage where they need, and can safely be trusted, to teach lessons on their own, their learning can still be enhanced through the occasional co-teaching of lessons, in which the use of ambitious teaching strategies can be explored. And while the primary concern of this element of the curriculum is the student teacher's learning, there are potential benefits for the pupils too. When two teachers are working together, there are more opportunities for the pupils to learn through engaging in such activities as debating and role play, as well as the likelihood of their receiving more individual attention and support. At the very least, there is no danger of the pupils' learning experience being impaired by a beginner learning to teach on their own through trial and error.

Paired student teaching

Are there advantages to be gained from student teachers working in pairs with the same classes and the same mentors? Our discussion of this idea relies primarily on two contrasting sources. We have direct experience of its use in a secondary school context in the Oxford Internship Scheme, where it has been used from the start in 1987. In that context it involves pairs of student teachers working in the same school subject departments with the same mentors, teaching some classes jointly but spending more time teaching classes individually. Our other main source is the reports of an experiment by Bullough *et al.* (2002, 2003) in two large inner-city elementary schools in the USA, where pairs of student teachers with the same classes and the same mentors were compared with student teachers working individually. What we have learned from both these sources, and from others, leads us unreservedly to commend this idea.

This kind of arrangement brings many advantages for mentors and for their departments. Two student teachers bring twice the financial resources brought by one, but a pair of student teachers does not generally require twice the time required by one. While the individual needs of each do have to be attended to, dealing with a pair presents many opportunities for mentors to use their time more efficiently. And it is not just through greater efficiency that mentors save time. As Bullough and his colleagues found, much of the emotional support for individual student teachers that can take a great deal of mentors' time and energy tends in the paired context to be sought from, and to be very effectively given by, partner student teachers to each other. In other ways, too, some of the pressure seems to be taken off mentors. Where student teachers are teaching a class together, mentors seem to be less anxious about things going wrong – for example, through discipline problems – and to feel more able to adopt a collaborative role rather than an authoritarian one in the planning of lessons.

Student teachers, too, can gain considerably from working in pairs. The emotional support they can give each other is likely to be more readily available, but also fuller, warmer and less complicated by formal responsibilities than that which mentors can give. Bullough *et al.* (2002: 74) reported that 'perhaps the most dramatic difference between partner- and single-placements was the kind and quality of the support available. Partners became friends but also invested in one another's development as teachers'. Paired student teachers provide not only emotional support for each other but also an additional rich source of ideas, of practical help in the classroom and of feedback on each other's teaching. They also provide for each other the very distinctive opportunity of observing the teaching of someone at a comparable stage of development, which can then be analysed, discussed and learned from.

Paired student teaching thus seems to add an extra dimension to the process of student teachers' learning, one that they value considerably. But it may be argued that it is not just the process that is enriched, but also the learning outcomes. Bullough and his colleagues place high value on the fact that paired student teaching allows and encourages student teachers to understand and acquire what Borko and Putnam (1998: 46) call 'a different kind of competence for thoughtful teaching – the ability to draw upon the knowledge and expertise of others and to contribute one's knowledge in productive ways to the group'. Mills (1995) also found that paired student teaching was valuable for the development of such collaborative professional skills.

Other potential beneficiaries from paired student teaching are the school pupils. Indeed, the mentors involved in Bullough *et al.*'s (2003) study saw the greatest benefit as being in the quality of the pupils' learning experiences. The combined advantages of the student teachers being able to share the work of planning and teaching, and also of stimulating and challenging each other's thoughts and efforts, left these teachers in no doubt that their pupils were being offered consistently high-quality learning experiences.

The advantages of paired student teaching depend on it being used flexibly; and in our experience, there is no problem about doing that. It may be useful for a pair of student teachers to be given joint responsibility for one class and perhaps also to collaborate with their mentor in the teaching of another class; but of course they will both need extensive experience of teaching other classes on their own. Similarly, they will benefit from some joint meetings, but also some individual meetings, with their mentor, and from undertaking other tasks in the school or department, some jointly and some individually.

Consulting pupils about classroom teaching and learning

That teachers should consult their pupils about how to improve classroom teaching and learning is an increasingly widely accepted idea, for two very good reasons. The first – articulated, for example, by the 1989 United Nations Convention on the Rights of the Child – is that children should be recognized as full human beings whose views should count in decisions about all aspects of their lives. Second, there is good reason to believe that the quality of teaching and learning in schools can be significantly improved through regular pupil consultation, because pupils have useful ideas to offer and because they find teacher responsiveness to their ideas very motivating (Rudduck and Flutter 2004).

Nonetheless, pupil consultation seems to remain an idea that is quite rarely put into practice, also for understandable reasons. Many teachers are in principle ready to take account of pupil ideas, and good practical advice is available about how to engage in pupil consultation (MacBeath *et al.* 2003); but in practice the idea involves the considerable challenges of finding time to consult pupils, of taking account of big differences among pupils in their classroom experiences (though not in the kinds of teaching they value), and of combining responsiveness to pupils with all the other demands upon teachers (Arnot *et al.* 2004). So, for most practising teachers, pupil consultation seems as yet to be little more than a good innovative idea.

For student teachers, however, pupil consultation is surely an excellent practice, and one which could contribute substantially to all three of the goals we have suggested for ITE. Pupils' insights should be of immediate help to student teachers in developing their competence. Learning how to consult pupils effectively and how to use their ideas should also be of long-term value throughout their careers. And engaging in such consultation should also offer a good opportunity for student teachers to learn to respond constructively but critically to proposed innovations.

Pupil consultation is an excellent example of an idea that is obviously good when considered in generalized academic terms, but much more complex in practice. How to use it effectively has to be the subject of serious practical theorizing. Careful and realistic planning is necessary in order, for example, to help pupils to reflect seriously, possibly for the first time, about the classroom practices that help or hinder their learning, to consult all the pupils in a class effectively and efficiently, and to persuade pupils that all their ideas have been considered seriously, even though only some of them may demonstrably be used. Student teachers also need to consider, with the help of appropriate evidence, the consequences of their consultations for themselves and for the pupils, and the cost-effectiveness of the procedures they have used. They need to reflect on how their initial attempts might be improved, how regularly such consultation might fruitfully be conducted, and how valuable and sustainable such practices are likely to be for them as they become more experienced and acquire greater responsibilities. They need, too, to have good opportunities to discuss the idea and their experiences of it with experienced teachers, some of whom may be sceptical of its value.

For those planning school-based ITE curricula, important decisions need to be made about how much to structure student teachers' work in consulting pupils. On the one hand, they will need a good deal of explicit guidance about the possibilities, since they are probably being asked to go beyond schools' established practices. On the other hand, they are likely to benefit most from being able to try out and to evaluate their own best thoughts about pupil consultation. Another key element in planning for pupil consultation as part of ITE curricula will be, as in the initiative reported in Part B, getting the timing of it right. Premature pupil consultation, before student teachers have acquired some necessary competence and confidence in managing classes, could expose them to morale-sapping criticism. But it would be best for them to start consulting pupils before they begin to establish personal patterns of teaching that exclude such consultation. And a third important consideration in the curriculum planning will be getting the right degree of university involvement. It should certainly be the task of university-based staff to provide helpful syntheses of research-based knowledge about pupil consultation, and to give guidance about potentially fruitful practices and possible problems. But the fruitfulness of this element of the curriculum is likely to depend heavily on the value placed on it by school-based teacher educators and by other practising teachers, and on the extent to which they actively engage with it.

ITE as a shared responsibility of subject or stage teams

School-based ITE is heavily dependent on the willingness of experienced teachers to engage in guiding and supporting the learning of student teachers in schools. This professional activity is commonly referred to as 'mentoring', and few would contest its definition as 'face-to-face, close-to-the-classroom work on teaching undertaken by a more experienced and a less experienced teacher in order to help the latter develop his or her practice' (Feiman-Nemser and Beasley 1997: 108). It is *individual* teachers acting as mentors who have become key figures – perhaps *the* key figures – in school-based ITE. While it is of crucial importance that there should indeed be a 'mentor', the lead teacher educator for any subject or stage context within a school, the opportunities for student teachers' learning can be much enhanced if the activity of 'mentoring' as defined above is distributed among a wider group of teachers.

It is important that student teachers learn from the professional craft knowledge of a number of experienced teachers. It is also important that the teachers with whom they most regularly work should view themselves as a team. This team would most likely be a subject or a stage team; and shared concern within the team for the student teacher's learning would be a highly desirable spin-off from their common concern with their pupils' learning and with their own collective professional learning. Such teams are often, and with some validity, characterized as 'communities of practice', since isolated practice is increasingly giving way to more collaborative ways of working. And, as Sutherland *et al.* (2005: 90) assert, 'one of the challenges of educating pre-service practitioners is to provide them with opportunities for authentic experiences in the communities of practice they are training to join'.

The design and planning of a school-based curriculum for the student teachers in any one school are likely to take place at a number of levels. Outline planning will properly be a whole-school task, undertaken in partnership with the university or college. When it comes to a more detailed planning of the particular elements of the ITE curriculum in relation to classroom teaching and learning, it makes sense for the task to be delegated to the subject or stage teams who both plan and implement that element of the school curriculum. They are the teachers best placed to work out how a beginning teacher might learn how to teach their particular subject or at their particular stage.

With their developed interest in, and understanding of, the processes involved in learning to teach and in guiding and supporting that learning in school, the subject or stage mentor will properly take the lead in both the planning and the implementation of the student teacher's curriculum in relation to classroom teaching. However, the credibility and authenticity of that curriculum depend to a great extent on it being recognized as a shared responsibility of the team. The role of mentor is wide-ranging, but the most important and probably the most challenging aspect of that role is leading a wider team in planning and agreeing an ITE curriculum for which it is prepared to share responsibility.

In carrying out this aspect of their role, mentors need to ensure that everyone in the team:

- understands the nature of the partnership and is clear about the responsibilities of the different members of the partnership, including the student teachers;
- is supported in their work with student teachers and is given every opportunity to develop the skills needed;
- is kept fully informed of the individual student's programme and progress.

It is likely that members of the team will include talk about their work with the student teachers in their regular informal conversations about pupils, lessons, the school managers, and so on. While this is valuable, it is also worth considering a more structured approach to the exchange of information. The mentor may decide to draw up and distribute copies of the student teacher's weekly or fortnightly programme, or to make use of the school intranet so that everyone knows what is happening and can therefore play their part in the student teacher's learning. It is also very helpful if ITE is a regular agenda item for departmental or team meetings. To undertake this aspect of his or her role effectively, it is crucial that the mentor has the strong support of the head of department or team leader.

Progression in feedback and lesson evaluation

The focus of this element is on the formative evaluation of student teachers' teaching. Of all the various aspects of the mentoring role, this is the single most important one, since it is aimed at helping the student teacher not only to become competent as a classroom teacher, but also to learn how to engage in practical theorizing. Our particular interest here is in exploring how this key aspect of the mentor's role develops during the course of an ITE programme.

Observing student teachers' teaching and giving them feedback on their observed teaching is much more than offering short-term support for immediate problems. It is a complex task, so it is necessary to consider what it generally entails before going on to consider issues of progression.

The mentor's role is primarily one of guiding the student teacher's learning and thinking about their teaching. Guided and assisted by their mentor, the student teacher learns to become increasingly competent as a teacher through the identification of specific strengths and weaknesses in their observed teaching and then taking account of these strengths and weaknesses in future planning and teaching. And, at a second level, the student teacher – again guided and assisted by their mentor – learns how to engage in practical theorizing by acquiring the habit of evaluating their own teaching against a wide range of criteria and drawing on a wide range of kinds of knowledge.

Drawing primarily on their own professional craft knowledge, mentors when giving feedback need to:

- articulate that knowledge in analytic, thematic and simplified ways to ensure that it is relevant to the observed lesson and comprehensible to the student teacher;
- take account of the individual student teacher's learning needs at the particular stage of their development;
- draw on other sources of knowledge including, for example, the practice of other teachers and research, especially that which the student teachers will be familiar with through their work at the university.

There are three kinds of progression in the formative evaluation of student teachers' teaching. All three are important, but it is only the third that is discussed more than summarily here.

Progression as coverage of the necessary competences

Part of the mentor's responsibility is to ensure that during the programme, the student teacher acquires the full range of competences that are needed in order to be a competent classroom teacher and practical theorizer. This will involve different rates and patterns of progress for different student teachers.

Progression in gradually learning the complexity of classroom teaching

In terms of the challenges and tasks offered to student teachers, this kind of progression entails moving from the kind of simplicity that is all the student teacher can cope with at the beginning of the programme to dealing eventually with the genuine complexity of classroom teaching (e.g. seeking to attain multiple cognitive, affective and social, short-term and long-term goals; finding the right combination of activities and choices of activities so that all these goals can be attained by each pupil, taking account of their different starting points).

Progression through apprenticeship in practical theorizing

Practical theorizing needs initially to be a social activity, led by the mentor, who provides a model by asking appropriate questions about the observed lesson, using an appropriate range of criteria, and drawing on a range of appropriate sources of evidence. By the end of the programme it needs to be a mental activity in which the beginning teacher engages habitually, competently and fluently.

This will involve a gradual process of change, but three broad stages may be envisaged. At the first stage, the mentor will lead and will model practical theorizing, explicitly drawing the student teacher's attention to this model, including the different kinds of questions, criteria and sources of evidence.

At a second stage, perhaps half-way through the programme, responsibility for asking appropriate questions, and using appropriate criteria and sources, will gradually be given to the student teacher. At this stage, the mentor's role will include the provision of systematic formative feedback on the student teacher's practical theorizing and, as necessary, some continued external feedback on the teaching to complement the student teacher's own self-evaluation.

By the final stage, the student teacher should have internalized the habits of practical theorizing in relation to his or her own teaching. This should extend to the inclusion within lesson plans of significant questions about the assumptions and predictions implicit in these plans. At this stage, while of course continuing to have an overall monitoring role, the mentor's primary role will ideally have become that of research assistant to the student teacher, one who during the observed lesson gathers evidence specified in advance by the student teacher as helpful for the answering of the predefined questions.

Specific suggestions concerned with the content or purposes of parts of the curriculum

The above five suggestions, like that explored in Part B, are all about different processes through which student teachers could usefully learn about classroom teaching. In this section, we offer five more suggestions, concerned with different areas of curriculum content or with specific purposes of the curriculum.

The first of these five elements concerns the crucial need to prepare student teachers to teach effectively pupils from widely diverse cultural backgrounds. We include this element because, on the one hand, we see it as the most important unresolved problem of most national school systems and, on the other, many schools may feel themselves inadequately equipped to deal with this part of the ITE curriculum.

Two of the specific elements that we identify below are focused respectively on the purpose of learning how to deliberately use experience to improve one's teaching and on the purpose of learning to evaluate innovations critically and constructively. While most of what student teachers do in a school-based ITE curriculum should have some relevance to all three of the purposes we have suggested, most of the time their priority concern will be with their immediate competence as teachers and with what they need to learn to become more competent. It is true that in their practical theorizing about any aspect of the work of teaching, they are implicitly developing the expertise they will need throughout their careers for improving their craft knowledge; and often they should implicitly be considering the advantages and problems of introducing innovative ideas. Nonetheless, it is important that some elements of the curriculum should be explicitly focused on these other two purposes; and so we propose these two elements that are specifically of this kind.

The other two specific elements suggested below are included to exemplify the need to plan the content of the school-based curriculum in a balanced way, reflecting the nature of the work that newly qualified teachers are asked to do. The particular elements that we highlight concern the teacher's pastoral role and the work of teachers in collaborating with other adults, including parents. These are well-established elements of university-based ITE curricula, but they are aspects of the teacher's role for which beginning teachers frequently find themselves to be inadequately prepared. It seems probable to us that for these extended elements of the teacher's role – just as for the classroom teaching role, and perhaps even more so – the theoretical discussions in which student teachers tend to engage in universities and the practical experience they are given in schools are just too far apart from each other, thus making each inadequate in isolation from the other. So the need here, too, is for an integrated practical theorizing solution within a school-based curriculum.

Educating teachers for cultural diversity

In the schools where they are learning to teach, student teachers encounter most of the many challenges that face schools and school systems; and they can be helped there to explore ways of thinking about these challenges as well as ways of dealing with them in practice. What happens, however, when the host school does not experience what is recognized as a very important kind of challenge for schools elsewhere? In our view, the most important potential problem of this kind relates to teaching pupils from culturally, materially and linguistically diverse backgrounds. There is overwhelming evidence that within the school systems of virtually every industrially advanced country, many pupils are severely disadvantaged because of their ethnic, linguistic or social class backgrounds. Quite apart from the need to address such evident social injustice, these educational disadvantages represent a major constraint on the overall success of these school systems. So this is an issue that ITE has to take very seriously. But how can that be done within the approach to ITE that we are proposing?

Zeichner (1996) discusses ITE for cultural diversity in an especially thoughtful and well-informed way, and we borrow heavily from him here. He starts by reviewing evidence about what we know of the kind of teaching that is needed to bridge the divide between schools and those many pupils from ethnic, linguistic or social class cultures that schools have generally not served well. Among key characteristics of such teaching, he concludes, are:

- 'the desire and ability of the teacher to learn about the special circumstances of their own students and communities, and the ability to take this knowledge into account in their teaching' (Zeichner 1996a: 139);
- teachers' belief that they are capable of making a difference in their students' learning;
- teachers' belief that all students can succeed and the communication of this belief to their students;
- the creation of personal bonds of trust between teachers and students;
- providing students with an academically demanding curriculum;
- engaging in culturally relevant teaching by providing scaffolding that maintains students' identification and pride in their home culture and uses it as a means to learning the school culture and curriculum;
- recognizing all students as having *individual* strengths, interests, problems and concerns;
- developing strategies for more effective communication with students, their parents and their communities;
- use of a wide variety of teaching strategies;
- having a deep understanding of the subjects being taught;
- creation of collaborative classroom environments;
- avoidance of ability grouping;
- use of flexible assessment practices.

There is, then, Zeichner argues, no lack of established knowledge for sharing with student teachers, or of kinds of expertise that they can usefully be helped to acquire. But how can this most effectively be done? Zeichner emphasizes the benefits of an integrated approach with a focus on cultural diversity pervading whole ITE programmes, but points out that such programmes are rare. He also identifies some specific kinds of university-based study that have proved helpful, but concludes that, valuable as such study can be, 'the necessity of direct intercultural experience ... is universally supported' by experts in this field (Zeichner 1996a: 155): student teachers cannot learn effectively to teach culturally disadvantaged students without extended experience in schools that serve such students. Zeichner describes various such programmes, in some of which school experience is combined with 'intensive cultural immersion experiences in which students live and teach in a minority community and often do extensive community service work' (1996a: 154).

Student teachers should be able to observe teaching that is successfully attuned to developing the learning capacities of disadvantaged students; and they should themselves have the opportunity to try to develop such teaching. Beyond that, the overall approach to school-based ITE advocated in this book should be effective in relation to this specific aspect of the curriculum, provided that:

- there are teachers in the schools whose teaching for cultural diversity is worthy of the attention of student teachers;

- these teachers are able and willing to articulate this aspect of their craft knowledge in order to discuss it with student teachers;
- school-based teacher educators are ready to plan a systematic curriculum to enable student teachers to develop expertise in teaching for cultural diversity.

But how is this generally possible when disadvantaged cultural groups tend to be concentrated in limited geographical areas? To take the case of England, only a small minority of schools have any significant experience of working with, for example, Bangladeshi or African-Caribbean students or communities. This practical problem is related to a more theoretical controversy discussed by Zeichner, that of whether or not it is possible and desirable for student teachers to be educated to teach *specific* identified cultural groups. He concludes that the dangers and difficulties of doing this outweigh any advantages, and that it is much more appropriate for student teachers to develop general ideas, attitudes and abilities for teaching for cultural diversity, which they can then tailor to whatever particular students they find themselves teaching. That seems to us not only to be right but also to provide the solution to our problem. Virtually all state schools work with students from some educationally disadvantaged cultural group, most commonly students from working-class backgrounds; so all such schools should be in a position to address the general principles articulated by Zeichner, and to relate them to their particular context and practices.

Student teachers as classroom action researchers

This element is focused on the purpose of student teachers' learning to improve their own practice. Engaging in classroom action research is one of the most rigorous ways in which practising teachers can set about improving their practice.

A strong international tradition of classroom action research by teachers has been established over the last half-century, stemming from Corey (1953) and, in the UK, from Stenhouse (1975). Within this tradition, Elliott (1991: 25) argued that action research is distinguished by its aim to transform practice:

It focuses on changing practice to make it more consistent with the ideal; it gathers evidence of the extent to which the practice is consistent/inconsistent with the ideal and seeks explanations for inconsistencies by gathering evidence about the operation of contextual factors; it problematises some of the tacit theories which underpin and shape practice ... and it involves practitioners in generating and testing action-hypotheses about how to effect worthwhile change.

It is this conception of action research that should underlie this element of the curriculum. The focal emphasis should be on problematizing one's own practice, on its evidence-based evaluation and on whatever reforms are shown to be necessary for educational improvement, including one's own professional development.

This element needs to come relatively late in ITE courses, because the primary purpose is that student teachers should learn to problematize a particular element of their existing craft knowledge, to ask themselves how they could do something better, or how they could overcome a problem that they have encountered. They need to have established themselves in basic terms as classroom teachers before they can learn to engage in such problematizing and investigation. At the core of action research is a questioning of the preconceptions that are implicit in one's existing practice. The difficulty of doing this is one of the several reasons why collaboration – with a peer, a mentor, and/or one's pupils – can be very valuable in action research.

Asking student teachers to engage in action research is a very well-established practice. Normally, however, it has been an exercise set and supervised by the university; and it is only too easily conceived by student teachers as the kind of thing that university people are keen on, not as something that busy practising teachers do. The significance of it being an element of a school-based curriculum cannot therefore be overemphasized. The emphasis has to be strongly on the practicality of engaging in classroom action research, and on its usefulness for practising teachers.

The practice of action research needs to be conceived primarily as a particular way of engaging in practical theorizing. A realistic approach is to think of it as involving three stages: a stage of formulating and clarifying the goal or the problem, probably involving the identification, gathering and interpretation of relevant evidence; a stage of generating a plan for action and for gathering evidence to examine its consequences, a stage which will certainly involve extended reflection, and can fruitfully involve discussion and reading around the issue; and a third stage, implementing the plan, gathering the relevant evidence, making sense of what has happened and critically learning for the future.

An important part of the university role here is forbearance: it is crucial that the emphasis should be on the usefulness and practicability of action research for teachers as an intelligent but not too demanding way of developing their expertise. So universities' normal concern with research methodology and elegant writing must be kept in check. At the same time, university-based teacher educators can be very useful in working with their school partners to develop helpful guidelines for student teachers and also in providing flexible guidance about useful research-based ideas that might be pursued in student teachers' action research.

Learning to evaluate innovations

One element of the curriculum should focus on the critical evaluation of innovations. In relation to the evaluation of possible innovations, schools (or departments and faculties within schools) and student teachers have complementary needs. If they are to improve, schools inevitably need to innovate; but useful innovations in classroom teaching and learning are very difficult for teachers, because their expertise tends to be so complex, so tacit and so intuitive; and because, until the improvement is achieved, its promise is always uncertain (Fullan 1991). Furthermore, while some government-initiated innovations are virtually obligatory, their educational value depends on schools and teachers working out how to adapt them to make them useful. For student teachers, on the other hand, the problems of classroom innovation are difficult to understand since, although each new teaching strategy they use involves new learning for them, none of that learning involves the unlearning of intuitive and fluent expertise that has been acquired with great effort. If they are to learn about innovating critically, much of their learning needs to be through understanding experienced teachers' perspectives on innovations. Schools should systematically exploit this need by using student teachers as advance guards in trialling innovations.

This element might involve four stages. First, partnership schools (or departments within these schools) should identify, through joint exploration among themselves and their university colleagues, two or three innovations that they believe might contribute to their own improvement. Second, the university-based teacher educators would review research relevant to these proposed innovations and would generate notes of guidance for the schools and the student teachers, based on relevant literature, explaining the merits of the innovation, identifying problems that might need to be overcome, suggesting questions that would need to be investigated, and outlining practical steps that should be taken in the implementation of the innovations. Third, each student teacher would decide in consultation with his or her school which innovation to implement in their teaching of one class, with preferably at least two in each school implementing the same innovation; and, in each school or department, the student teachers would, in implementing the innovation, be guided by the staff's concerns and questions relating to the innovation. The fourth stage, of teachers themselves implementing an innovation, would come – if at all – only after they had studied the student teachers' problems and achievements, discussed the implications, and agreed that, on this preliminary evidence, it would be worthwhile for them to try out the innovation for themselves.

Such projects should offer excellent professional education for student teachers in relation to the processes and problems of innovation. Their learning to think critically about such processes and problems will depend on their having a level of confidence and competence that is unlikely until they are in the later parts of their courses. It will depend heavily, too, on their accepting the role of agent for their host school or department, and so first seeking to understand as fully as possible the hopes, concerns and questions of the teachers. That would then provide an important framework for their trying to implement the innovation successfully and also for evaluating it critically. Such innovative teaching, however, will obviously depend less than other teaching on what student teachers learn from the kinds of expertise already being used in schools, so they will need to rely more on the guidance of university-based teacher educators. One helpful model for this is offered by Wilson (2005), a university-based science teacher educator who, wishing to promote a more constructivist approach to science teaching, first negotiated a teaching role for herself in a partnership school to test and elaborate her ideas within the context of current realities, and so was then able to give credible practical guidance to student teachers exploring a similar approach in similar contexts.

The value and the feasibility of such projects for ITE will depend crucially on schools or departments having the active level of interest in them that would come only from seeing them as potentially contributing to their own improvement. They will depend, too, on very substantial contributions from university teacher educators, who could themselves benefit from the exceptional opportunities these projects will offer them to support and influence innovative practices in schools and also to develop their own research and thinking about such practices. Most of all, the success of these projects will depend on the quality and relevance of the practical theorizing that student teachers do, helped by school-based teacher educators.

Engaging in pastoral roles

In the UK, teachers are *in loco parentis* and so have responsibilities to their pupils that go beyond the teaching of particular subjects. For teachers who work with younger children and are responsible for the same group for all or a large part of each school day, their pastoral role cannot easily be disentangled from other aspects of their class teacher role. For student teachers learning to be primary school teachers, engaging in the pastoral work of teachers will be an integral part of their learning to become classroom teachers.

For secondary student teachers, however, the situation is not quite the same. At a broad level, all secondary classroom teachers are involved in pastoral care with its focus on the well-being and development of the whole child. Also, simply as members of the school community, teachers are involved in promoting pupils' development and fostering positive attitudes. However, as secondary school teaching tends to be organized on a subject basis, pupils may have contact with ten or more teachers during the course of their weekly or fortnightly timetable. Therefore, to ensure that concern with the pupil as a whole person is properly addressed, secondary schools have developed systems, structures and roles specifically for pastoral care. For secondary student teachers, therefore, their learning about pastoral care will take them beyond their learning as a subject teacher.

In planning for the learning of student teachers in relation to pastoral care, it is helpful first to break down what is a very broad concept. Best (1999, 2003) distinguishes among five pastoral tasks that teachers undertake:

1 Pastoral management: the work of the head of house or year in leading, co-ordinating and supporting a team of teachers in their pastoral work.
2 Reactive casework: offering guidance and support on a one-to-one basis to a pupil experiencing problems; the form tutor would normally be the first point of contact, but such work includes referral to specialists in and beyond the school.
3 Proactive, preventive pastoral care: usually carried out with a group, possibly as part of a school's Personal Social and Health Education programme, providing children with learning experiences that will enable them to cope better with predictably important issues and critical times.
4 The developmental pastoral curriculum: planning and delivering a pastoral curriculum, aimed at promoting the individual's personal, social, moral, spiritual and cultural well-being and development.
5 Community building: meeting the needs and observing the rights of pupils as citizens within the whole community.

Academic tutoring, whereby the tutor supports pupils in their academic work, is becoming an increasingly important aspect of the pastoral system in many schools, and may usefully be added to this list.

Not all of the tasks outlined above are of equal importance for student teachers. For example, while they need to understand the pastoral system in their school, and how it is managed, pastoral management is not something at which they need to become competent. They do, however, need to learn how to become skilful form tutors, because of the importance of that role and because it is a role that most student teachers will find themselves taking on in their first posts as qualified teachers.

In order to understand the work of form tutors, and to practise and develop the skills needed, each student teacher needs to become a member of a tutorial team, and to be attached to a tutor group for a sustained period of time.

Lang (2004), in discussing the form tutor's role, helpfully distinguishes 'should be' from 'could be' elements of the role. The former – those that are essential for the functioning of the school's overall system – call for administrative competence and skill in what Earl (2003: 80) calls 'boundary issues, i.e. determining whether the problem is one you can or should deal with, and then determining either how to deal with it yourself or who to refer it on to'. All student teachers need to become competent in these 'should be' elements of the role. They also need to develop their understanding and have experience of the 'could be' elements of the role, defined by Lang (2004: 303) as 'extra undertakings' which will reflect the importance to the teacher of 'pastoral support for pupils'.

As with their subject teaching, student teachers' learning about form tutoring needs to be systematically planned to enable them to develop their competence and identity as form tutors and also to examine critically the thinking underlying their developing practices. Their learning experiences could usefully include:

- study of documents prepared by university-based teacher educators, in consultation with their school-based partners, explaining different aspects of the form tutor's role;
- access to the thinking of a number of form tutors, especially in the context of their practice;
- practice in undertaking the form tutor role themselves, with feedback from form tutors and preferably from their pupils on their efforts;
- practical theorizing tasks, involving them writing about problems and dilemmas encountered during form tutoring.

Learning how to work with other adults

An increasingly important and wide-ranging aspect of teachers' work is with other adults, although probably the most important other adults with whom teachers have to deal are still their pupils' parents and carers. The area of home–school relationships is one over which people with very different ideologies have argued in recent decades, and so it would not be surprising if student teachers' preconceptions about it were widely varied or were quite confused. In the UK, more than in many countries, teachers were for a long time able and content to pay little attention to their pupils' parents, while at the same time being inclined to attribute much of the variation in their pupils' success to their homes; and both of these tendencies remain very strong today. In the 1960s, several major studies, including that conducted for the Plowden Report (Central Advisory Council for Education 1967), showed very clearly that children's educational success varied with the extent to which their homes were in tune with their schools and vice versa, and since then the implications for schools' practice have been hotly debated (e.g. Vincent 1996; Bastiani 2003).

If student teachers are to learn both to work competently with parents in present circumstances, and also to be able to generate, or to respond constructively to, innovative plans for more effective collaboration with parents, they will need quite carefully planned learning opportunities and resources. These could appropriately include:

- access to the thinking of teachers with expertise in working with parents, especially in the context of these teachers writing reports for parents, and meeting with parents;
- practice in themselves writing such reports and meeting with parents, with feedback from their mentors, and ideally from the parents, on their efforts;
- documents prepared by university-based teacher educators, in consultation with their school-based partners, explaining different ideas for home–school relations, and their implications for school policy and practices;
- extended opportunities to meet with volunteer parents (including those of lower-achieving pupils), to practise listening to parents and discovering their perspectives on their children and their schooling;
- structured practical theorizing tasks, involving them writing about desirable kinds of collaboration with parents and about the conditions necessary for such collaboration.

There are also many other kinds of adults with whom teachers need to collaborate. Increasingly, for example, teachers need to work closely with educational psychologists and with social workers. Teaching assistants are an especially important group, because of the rapid increase in their numbers and the UK government's policy of giving them an increasingly important role. Whereas the dominant pattern of school teaching for the last two centuries has been one of teachers working alone in classrooms with their classes, such isolation from other adults is now a thing of the past. Indeed, in 2001, Estelle Morris, the then Secretary of State for Education in England, looked forward to a situation ten years later when classrooms would be 'rich in the number of trained adults available to support teaching' (Morris 2001: 15). But working with teaching assistants is not part of the craft knowledge of most experienced teachers, and few have had any formal opportunity to learn about such work. A survey of its members by the National Union of Teachers in 2002 suggested that less than 2 per cent had had any training in their initial professional education in working with teaching assistants, and only one in seven had received training at any stage for such work. Accordingly, there is enormous variation both in the ways in which the services of teaching assistants are used and in both teachers' and teaching assistants' satisfaction with the collaboration achieved (Lee 2002).

Student teachers' learning about working with teaching assistants will depend heavily, then, on the quality of support they are given with their own practical theorizing. It will be important for university-based teacher educators to introduce them to issues raised by research. The core of their learning will, however, result from their own experience of working with teaching assistants; and so it will be very important for such experience to be preceded by advice from teachers, by conversations with teaching assistants and by careful joint planning with the teaching assistants; and for it to be followed by equally careful joint evaluation.

Overall, the school-based ITE curriculum needs to devote considerably more time to working with other adults, and to provide learning opportunities that are a good deal more structured, than has normally been the case.

Moving towards a realization of the full potential of school-based ITE

This final section will explore some of the considerations and the processes that may be involved in developing the kind of school-based ITE curriculum that we have envisaged. What barriers need to be overcome? What resources are needed? What strategies for promoting this kind of development are likely to be practicable and effective? The answers to such questions will of course depend to some considerable extent on where one is starting from. Some of the changes needed in Scotland or the USA, for example, will be very different from those needed in England, with its already predominantly school-based ITE. But some of the more constructive changes involved in planning and developing new school-based curricula may be quite similar everywhere.

Are the central ideas attractive enough?

The first requirement for any proposed innovation is that the vision it embodies and the central ideas on which it depends are clear, credible and attractive. It is necessary that the innovation should be sufficiently attractive to all those who would be affected by it, and that it should offer all of them opportunities to pursue their own most fundamental agendas with confidence. We hope that we have gone some way towards offering such a vision. We hope and believe that our vision will be attractive for *schools* and for *teachers*, because it:

- recognizes the complexity of classroom teaching;
- recognizes teachers as experts;
- puts teachers at the centre of the task of renewing their profession;
- offers multiple spin-offs, including richer learning opportunities for school students and professional development opportunities for teachers.

We hope and believe that our vision will have attractions for *governments*, because it:

- offers a robust plan for well-prepared teachers who are going to go on learning;
- makes schools and what happens in schools the centre of attention;
- builds (in England) on previous reforms, but overcomes major weaknesses in these reforms;
- contributes to the development of an enhanced professionalism among teachers.

We hope and believe that our vision will have attractions for *universities* and *university-based teacher educators* because it:

- values their expertise;
- gives them a realistic and intellectually challenging role in ITE;
- reduces the tension between their engagement in ITE and their research role;
- may, if anything, enhance their influence over beginning (and other) teachers, by making their ITE role more realistic.

Finally, we hope and believe that our vision will have attractions for *student teachers* because it:

- values above everything else the quality of the support they are given in their practical engagement with the work of schools;
- takes very seriously the ideas and the ideals they espouse as they approach and engage in their initial professional education;
- treats the tasks of teaching and of school-based learning to teach as more intellectually challenging than they generally have been in the past;
- takes seriously as part of the school-based ITE curriculum the problems of developing one's identity as a teacher.

The need to learn

The second basic requirement for any innovation is the need for a very clear recognition that the vision from which one starts, however clear and credible it may be, is nothing more than a starting point. Those who work to realize the vision will necessarily develop and change it as they confront unexpected constraints and possibilities, and as they negotiate their way through the diverse costs and benefits to the different groups affected (cf. Fullan 1991). To emphasize the importance of this we need only remind ourselves of the several kinds of learning we needed to do in the context of the relatively modest experiment that we reported in Part B of this book. These kinds of learning will predictably be necessary on a much larger scale.

There will also be much necessary learning that we cannot at this stage predict. Our vision, we hope, is clear, but at best all it can do is give a clear sense of direction for exploratory initiatives. We would hope to encourage others (in England and internationally) to engage in a range of such initiatives, all of them planned so that not only those involved but also other teacher educators can learn from them. On that basis there could be quite rapid stepwise development over several years. The need is for exploratory innovation and for learning as we go.

A climate for constructive development

The third prerequisite for this innovation to be successful is an appropriate climate. It is true that the English reforms of the early 1990s were successfully imposed through directives from the centre and despite bitter resentment on the part of university-based teacher educators (cf. Gilroy 1992). But these were in a very large measure mechanistic innovations, which owed little to teachers' professional expertise or to research-based understandings, and nothing at all to excitement about new intellectual or professional opportunities. What is being proposed here, in contrast, will depend for its success on the active, intelligent and expert engagement of many teachers and university-based teacher educators, as well as on the constructive support of government agencies. It can succeed only if all these parties are motivated to engage with it creatively and energetically; grudging compliance will not be enough.

The central characteristic of the required climate is mutual trust and respect. Teachers must be able to trust that new government frameworks are constructed primarily for the improvement of education, not primarily to win headlines and votes. And while teachers must accept the need to be held accountable in terms of consensually established standards, they must be able to trust that government frameworks will be there primarily to support them in intelligently using their own professional expertise, not primarily for accountability purposes as in recent years. That implies respect from government for classroom teachers' expertise and professionalism, not an uncritical respect, but a respect and a humility on the part of government that have been strikingly lacking in recent years, and not only in England.

The necessary climate also depends upon similar mutual trust and respect between school-based and university-based teacher educators; and again, that does not mean uncritical or unquestioning trust and respect. Indeed, the quality of ITE partnerships depends fundamentally upon school and university teacher educators establishing relationships in which each can feel confident enough openly to question the claims or assumptions of the other. And the climate will be right only where that openness to questioning operates equally in both directions.

A climate of openness and debate is important for the development of school-based ITE curricula, because such a climate provides the conditions for ongoing experimentation by teacher educators, individually and in groups, and also by student teachers. Confidence in the trust of relevant others, and confidence that they will express their honest opinions, are necessary conditions for experimentation and therefore for thoughtful learning. In such a climate, government frameworks are treated properly as guidelines to be adapted and used as scaffolding to support creative building. In such a climate, also, innovative practices and evidence about them are shared at every level – individual school, partnership, national and international – in the confidence that they will be both respected and honestly criticized. Government agencies, universities and school leaders all have major responsibilities for the creation and maintenance of such climates, both through their positive fostering of experimentation and debate, and through avoiding the imposition of narrow or authoritarian requirements.

Funding

The very low level of funding for ITE in England, and in many other countries, has been a major constraint on the development of high-quality provision. Improved funding is another important condition for the kind of radical improvement in ITE that we are seeking.

In England, ITE has always been poorly funded in comparison to other HEI-based types of vocational education (cf. Robbins 1963). The shift to a partnership approach in the early 1990s brought no increase in funding, although the necessary intensive collaboration required for partnership between institutions inevitably made ITE courses more expensive. The most recent evidence on the adequacy of funding is an independent study for the Department for Education and Skills by JM Consulting (2004), which found that the cost of ITE in England was on average over £1000 per student per annum more than the funding received by institutions for this work. The report notes, too, that no 'extra cost' was included in the calculations to take account of the long hours that staff had to work.

Universities need, then, to subsidize their ITE courses. They respond to this in various ways. Typically, their staff–student ratios for ITE are very poor. Furlong *et al.* (2000) estimated staff–student ratios to be on average 1:21.5. They also noted widespread casualization of ITE staffing, with increased reliance on part-time and temporary staff. Predictably, universities respond also by minimizing the proportion of the available resources that they pass on to schools. JM Consulting (2004) estimated that on average only 12 per cent of universities' ITE costs were for payments to schools (i.e. less than £600 per full-time equivalent student). The consequence is that there is severe understaffing of ITE, both in schools and in universities. The genuine professional dedication and enthusiasm of both school-based and university-based teacher educators can easily give way under the insupportable burden of multiple demands that they cannot find time to meet, despite working many extra unpaid hours each week.

In these circumstances, progress towards the kind of high-quality school-based curricula for ITE that we are proposing is likely at best to be slow and sporadic. Funding is necessary to facilitate, and to provide incentives for, the development of new initiatives for schools working as members of partnerships, and also for the effective implementation of proven good practices developed elsewhere. As we have noted, such funding has already been made available in England to Training Schools, but it needs to be available for all schools engaged in partnership ITE. Funding needs to be gradually increased both to meet the costs of developing new school-based curricula and also for their sustained implementation. Our guess would be that national expenditure on partnership ITE programmes in England needs to be enhanced by 50 per cent per student teacher, and that this would do little more than meet the true current costs of ITE.

Such increased government expenditure is essential; but both schools and universities should also be prepared to contribute to the extra costs involved in the improvements to ITE that we are seeking. It has been clear for many years (cf. McIntyre and Hagger 1992) that the professional development advantages to school staff of involvement in good ITE partnerships are considerable. The much enhanced role for schools now proposed would offer even greater advantages. With large proportions of their staff having some involvement in the planning and provision of effective school-based ITE curricula, and with the professional learning ethos in the schools that such curricula would both need and help to foster, schools could hardly avoid becoming more thoughtful, self-critical and effective learning institutions. The virtuous circle of serious engagement with ITE, generation of a pervasive professional learning ethos, consequent improvements in teaching and in learning opportunities for pupils, leading back to improved ITE, provides benefits for everyone. The costs for schools committing themselves seriously to school-based ITE will be well matched by the benefits to them.

Much the same is true for universities. The *raison d'être* of most university departments of education is to study, understand and support schools, and to help them improve. The opportunity to engage in partnership with schools on school-based ITE curricula is an opportunity not only to do the work of ITE better, but also for building the kinds of professional relationships on which other aspects of their work, in research and scholarship, and in continuing professional development, depend. But for whole universities, too, relationships with schools are of crucial importance. As even the most research-intensive universities are increasingly coming to realize, their capacity to attract the quantity, quality and range of students they want depends heavily on the nature of the reputations that they establish in schools. And it is in the context of their ITE partnerships that universities can do most to develop their reputations in schools. For universities too, therefore, the costs of committing themselves seriously to school-based ITE are well matched by the benefits.

Political will

Even if what we have suggested is the best way forward for ITE, it will not happen unless there is a strong co-ordinated political movement to make it happen. At this moment, it is difficult to see where such a movement would come from. We believe that both governments and their agencies, and also universities, which still have strong vested interests in ITE, can be persuaded of the need for such change; but not that they will take the lead in promoting it. That must be done by those whose interests will best be served by this kind of development – that is, by teachers. When the time is right, we should expect it to be supported by teacher unions, and it would certainly need their support. We believe too that it is a movement that should be actively promoted by national general teaching councils, in England, Scotland and elsewhere. In the first instance, however, those ideas will have to be promoted by those who are best placed to judge them, teacher educators – those who work in universities and especially those who work in schools. Perhaps the time has come to form, in England in the first instance, a national association of teacher educators, to debate and promote ideas for the improvement of teacher education.

References

Allen, D.W. and Ryan, K.A. (1969) *Microteaching*. Reading, MA: Addison-Wesley.

Allexsaht-Snider, M., Deegan, J.G. and White, C.S. (1995) Educational renewal in an alternative teacher education program: evaluation of a school–university partnership. *Teaching and Teacher Education*, 11(5): 519–30.

Argyris, C. and Schön, D. (1974) *Theory in Practice: Increasing Professinal Effectiveness*. San Francisco: Jossey-Bass.

Arnot, M., McIntyre, D., Pedder, D. and Reay, D. (2004) *Consultation in the Classroom*. Cambridge: Pearson Publishing.

Australian Council of Deans of Education Inc. (2003) *Response to the Commonwealth Review of Teaching and Teacher Education*. Canberra: ACDE.

Ball, D.L. and McDiarmid, G.W. (1990) The subject-matter preparation of teachers, in W.R. Houston (ed.) *Handbook of Research on Teacher Education*, pp. 437–49. New York: Macmillan.

Bastiani, J. (2003) *Materials for Schools: Involving Parents, Raising Achievement* (ed. S. White). Department for Education and Skills.

Benton, P. (ed.) (1990) *The Oxford Internship Scheme*. London: Calouste Gulbenkian Foundation.

Berliner, D. (1987) Ways of thinking about students and classrooms by more and less experienced teachers, in J.Calderhead (ed.) *Exploring Teachers' Thinking*. London: Cassell.

Best, R. (1999) The impact on pastoral care of structural, organisational and statutory changes in schooling: some empirical evidence and a discussion. *British Journal of Guidance and Counselling*, 27(1): 55–70.

Best, R. (2003) Citizenship and pastoral care, in L. Gearon (ed.) *Learning to Teach Citizenship in the Secondary School*. London: RoutledgeFalmer.

Booth, M., Furlong, J. and Wilkin, M. (eds) (1990) *Partnership in Initial Teacher Training*. London: Cassell.

Borko, H. and Livingstone, C. (1989) Cognition and improvisation: differentiation in mathematics instruction by expert and novice teachers. *American Educational Research Journal*, 26(4): 473–98.

Borko, H. and Putnam, R.T. (1998) The role of context in teacher learning and teacher education, in K. Howey (ed.) *Contextual Teaching and Learning: Preparing Teachers to Enhance Student Success in the Workplace and Beyond*, pp. 33–66. Columbus, OH: ERIC Clearinghouse on Adult, Career and Vocational Education.

Brisard, E., Menter, I. and Smith, I. (2005) *Models of Partnership in Initial Teacher Education. Full Report of a Systematic Literature Review Commissioned by the General Teaching Council for Scotland*. GTCS Research Publication No. 2, September. Edinburgh: GTCS.

Brophy, J.E. and Good, T.L. (1986) Teacher behaviour and student achievement, in M.C. Wittrock (ed.) *Handbook of Research on Teaching* (3rd edition), pp. 328–75. New York: Macmillan.

Brown, G. (1975) *Microteaching: A Programme of Teaching Skills*. London: Methuen.

Brown, S. and McIntyre, D. (1993) *Making Sense of Teaching*. Buckingham: Open University Press.

Bullough, R.V. Jr., Young, J., Erickson, L., Birrell, J.R., Clark, D.C., Egan, M.W., Berrie, C.F., Hales, V. and Smith, G. (2002) Rethinking field experience: partnership teaching versus single-placement teaching. *Journal of Teacher Education*, 53(1): 68–80.

Bullough, R.V. Jr., Young, J., Birrell, J.R., Clark, D.C., Egan, M.W., Erickson, L., Frankovich, M., Brunetti, J. and Welling, M. (2003) Teaching with a peer: a comparison of two models of student teaching. *Teaching and Teacher Education*, 19: 57–73.

Bullough, R.V. Jr., Draper, R.J., Smith, L. and Birrell, J.R. (2004) Moving beyond collusion: clinical faculty and university/public school partnership. *Teaching and Teacher Education*, 20(5): 505–22.

Burn, K. (1997) Learning to teach: the value of collaborative teaching, in D. McIntyre (ed.) *Teacher Education Research in a New Context: The Oxford Internship Scheme*, pp. 145–61. London: Paul Chapman Publishing.

Burn, K., Hagger, H., Mutton, T. and Everton, T. (2000) Beyond concerns with self: the sophisticated thinking of beginning student teachers. *Journal of Education for Teaching*, 26(3): 259–78.

Calderhead, J. (1996) Teachers' beliefs and knowledge, in D. Berliner and R.C. Calfee (eds) *Handbook of Educational Psychology*. New York: Simon & Schuster Macmillan.

Calderhead, J. and Robson, M. (1991) Images of teaching: student teachers' early conceptions of classroom practice. *Teaching and Teacher Education*, 7(1): 1–8.

Carter, K. (1990) Teachers' knowledge and learning to teach, in W.R. Houston (ed.) *Handbook of Research on Teacher Education*, pp. 291–310. New York: Macmillan.

Carter, K., Cushing, K., Sabers, D., Stein, P. and Berliner, D. (1988) Expert–novice differences in perceiving and processing visual classroom information. *Journal of Teacher Education*, 39: 25–31.

Central Advisory Council for Education (1967) *Children and their Primary Schools*. London: HMSO.

Chapman, J., Toomey, R., Gaff, J., McGilp, J., Walsh, M., Warren, E. and Williams, I. (2003) *Lifelong Learning and Teacher Education*. Canberra: Department for Education, Science and Training.

Chase, W.G. and Simon, H.A. (1973) Perception in chess. *Cognitive Psychology*, 4: 55–81.

Chi, M.T.H., Glaser, R. and Farr, M. (1990) *The Nature of Expertise*. Hillsdale, NJ: Lawrence Erlbaum.

Clandinin, D.J. (1985) *Classroom Practice: Teacher Images in Action*. London: Falmer.

Clandinin, D.J. (ed.) (1993) *Learning to Teach, Teaching to Learn: Stories of Collaboration in Teacher Education*. New York: Teachers College Press.

Clandinin, D.J. and Connelly, F.M. (1986) Rhythms in teaching: the narrative study of teachers' personal practical knowledge of classrooms. *Teaching and Teacher Education*, 2(4): 377–87.

Clark, C. and Peterson, P. (1986) Teachers' thought processes, in M. Wittrock (ed.) *Handbook of Research on Teaching* (3rd edition), pp. 255–96. New York: Macmillan.

Clark, C. and Yinger, R.J. (1987) Teacher planning, in J. Calderhead (ed.) *Exploring Teachers' Thinking*, pp. 84–103. London: Cassell.

Connelly, F.M., Clandinin, D.J. and He, M.F. (1997) Teachers' personal practical knowledge on the professional knowledge landscape. *Teaching and Teacher Education*, 13(7): 665–74.

Conway, P.F. and Clark, C. M. (2003) The journey inward and outward: a re-examination of Fuller's concerns-based model of teacher development. *Teaching and Teacher Education*, 19: 465–82.

Cope, P. and Stephen, C. (2001) A role for practising teachers in initial teacher education. *Teaching and Teacher Education*, 17: 913–24.

Corey, S. (1953) *Action Research to Improve School Practice*. New York: Teachers College, Columbia University.

Darling-Hammond, L. (ed.) (1994) *Professional Development Schools: Schools for a Developing Profession*. New York: Teachers College Press.

Darling-Hammond, L. (1999) The case for university-based teacher education, in R. Roth (ed.) *The Role of the University in the Preparation of Teachers*. London: Falmer.

Department for Education (1993) The initial training of primary school teachers: new criteria for courses (Circular 14/93). London: DFE.

Department for Education and Science (1992) Initial teacher training (secondary phase) (Circular 9/92). London: Department for Education and Science.

Department for Education and Skills (2002) *Qualifying to Teach: Professional Standards for Qualified Teacher Status and Requirements for Initial Teacher Training,*. London: Teacher Training Agency.

Doyle, W. (1980) *Classroom Management*. West Lafayette, IN: Kappa Delta Pi.

Doyle, W. (1986) Classroom organisation and management, in M. Wittrock (ed.) *Handbook of Research on Teaching* (3rd edition), pp. 392–431. New York: Macmillan.

Dreeben, R. (1970) *The Nature of Teaching: Schools and the Work of Teachers*. Glenview, IL: Scott, Foresman.

Dreyfus, H. and Dreyfus, S. (1986) *Mind over Machine*. New York: Free Press.

Earl, M. (2003) Pastoral care and the work of the pastoral tutor, in J. Beck and M. Earl (eds) *Key Issues in Secondary Education* (2nd edition). London: Continuum.

Edmonds, S., Sharp, C. and Benefield, P. (2002) *Recruitment to and Retention on Initial Teacher Training: A Systematic Review*. Slough: National Foundation for Educational Research.

Elliott, J. (1989) Appraisal of performance and appraisal of persons, in H. Simons and J. Elliott (eds) *Rethinking Appraisal and Assessment*. Milton Keynes: Open University Press.

Elliott, J. (1991) *Action Research for Educational Change*. Milton Keynes: Open University Press.

Eraut, M. (1994) *Developing Professional Knowledge and Competence*. London: Falmer Press.

Eraut, M. (2000) Non-formal learning and tacit knowledge in professional work. *British Journal of Educational Psychology*, 70: 113–36.

Feiman-Nemser, S. and Beasley, K. (1997) Mentoring as assisted performance, in V. Richardson (ed.) *Constructivist Teacher Education*, pp. 108–26. London: Falmer.

Feiman-Nemser, S. and Buchmann, M. (1989) Describing teacher education: a framework and illustrative findings from a longitudinal study of six students. *The Elementary School Journal*, 89(3): 365–77.

Fullan, M.G. (1991) *The New Meaning of Educational Change*. New York: Teachers College Press.

Fuller, F. and Bown, O.H. (1975) Becoming a teacher, in K. Ryan (ed.) *Teacher Education, Seventy-Fourth Yearbook of the National Society of Education*. Chicago: University of Chicago Press.

Fuller, F.F. (1969) Concerns of teachers: a developmental characterization. *American Educational Research Journal*, 6: 207–26.

Furlong, J. (2000) *Higher Education and the New Professionalism for Teachers: A Discussion Paper*. London: Committee of Vice-Chancellors and Principals.

Furlong, J. and Maynard, T. (1995) *Mentoring Student Teachers*. London: Routledge.

Furlong, J., Barton, L., Miles, S., Whiting, C. and Whitty, G. (2000) *Teacher Education in Transition*. Buckingham: Open University Press.

Gardner, P. (1993) The early history of school-based teacher training, in D. McIntyre, H. Hagger and M. Wilkin (eds) *Mentoring: Perspectives on School-Based Teacher Education*, pp. 21–36. London: Kogan Page.

Gilroy, D.P. (1992) The political rape of initial teacher training in England and Wales: a JET rebuttal. *Journal of Education for Teaching*, 18: 5–22.

Goodlad, J. (1990) *Teachers for Our Nation's Schools*. San Francisco: Jossey-Bass.

Grant, G.E. (1992) The sources of structural metaphors in teacher knowledge: three cases. *Teaching and Teacher Education*, 8(5/6): 433–40.

Grisham, D.L., Bergeron, B., Brink, B., Farnan, N., Lenski, S.D. and Meyerson, M.J. (1999) Connecting communities of practice through professional development schools. *Journal of Teacher Education*, 50(3): 182–91.

Grossman, P. (1990) *The Making of a Teacher: Teacher Knowledge and Teacher Education*. New York: Teachers College Press.

Haggarty, L. (1997) Readiness among student teachers for learning about classroom management issues, in D. McIntyre (ed.) *Teacher Education Research in a New Context: The Oxford Internship Scheme*, pp. 60–75. London: Paul Chapman Publishing.

Hagger, H. (1997) Enabling student teachers to gain access to the professional craft knowledge of experienced teachers, in D. McIntyre (ed.) *Teacher Education Research in a New Context: The Oxford Internship Scheme*, pp. 99–133. London: Paul Chapman Publishing.

Hagger, H. (2002) Professional knowledge and the beginning teacher. Paper delivered at the inaugural UPSI International Teacher Education Conference, Kuala Lumpur.

Hargreaves, D.H. (1996) *Teaching as a Research-Based Profession: Possibilities and Prospects*. London: Teacher Training Agency.

Hargreaves, D.H., Dowtich, M.G. and Griffin, D.R. (1997) *On-the-Job Training for Surgeons*. London: Royal Society of Medicine Press.

Hart, S., Dixon, A., Drummond, M.J. and McIntyre, D. (2004) *Learning without Limits*. Maidenhead: Open University Press.

Her Majesty's Inspectorate (1982) *The New Teacher in School*. London: HMSO.

Her Majesty's Inspectorate (1988) *The New Teacher in School*. London: HMSO.

Holmes Group (1986) *Tomorrow's Teachers: A report of the Holmes Group*. East Lansing, MI: Holmes Group.

Holmes Group (1990) *Tomorrow's Schools: Principles for the Design of Professional Development Schools: A Report of the Holmes Group*. East Lansing, MI: Holmes Group.

Holmes Group (1995) *Tomorrow's Schools of Education: A Report from the Holmes Group*. East Lansing, MI: Holmes Group.

Horvath, J.A., Sternberg, R.J., Forsythe, E.B., Bullis, R.C., Williams, W.M. and Sweeney, P.J. (1996) Implicit theories of leadership practice. Paper presented at the Annual Meeting of the American Educational Research Association, New York.

Jackson, P.W. (1968) *Life in Classrooms*. New York: Holt, Rinehart and Winston.

JM Consulting Ltd. (2004) *Review of the Unit of Resource for Initial Teacher Training: Study of Provider Costs.* Norwich: HMSO.

Judge, H., Lemoss, M., Paine, L. and Sedlak, M. (1994) *The University and the Teachers: France, the United States, England*, Oxford Studies in Comparative Education. Wallingford: Triangle Books.

Korthagen, F.A.J. in co-operation with J. Kessels, B. Koster, B. Lagerwerf and T. Wubbels (2001) *Linking Practice and Theory: The Pedagogy of Realistic Teacher Education.* Mahwah, NJ: Lawrence Erlbaum Associates.

Kounin, J.S. (1970) *Discipline and Group Management in Classrooms.* New York: Holt, Rinehart and Winston.

Lacey, C. (1977) *The Socialization of Teachers.* London: Methuen.

Lang, P. (2004) Pastoral care and the role of the tutor, in V. Brooks, I. Abbott and L. Bills (eds) *Preparing to Teach in Secondary Schools.* Maidenhead: Open University Press.

Lave, J. and Wenger, E. (1991) *Situated Learning: Legitimate Peripheral Participation.* Cambridge: Cambridge University Press.

Lawlor, S. (1990) *Teachers Mistaught*, Policy Study No. 116. London: Centre for Policy Studies.

Lee, B. (2002) *Teaching Assistants in Schools: The Current State of Play.* Slough: National Foundation for Educational Research.

Leinhardt, G. (1988) Expertise in instructional lessons: an example from fractions, in D.A. Grouws and T.J. Cooney (eds) *Perspectives on Research on Effective Mathematics Teaching*, pp. 47–66. Hillsdale, NJ: Lawrence Erlbaum Associates; Reston, VA: National Association of Teachers of Mathematics.

Lortie, D. (1975) *Schoolteachers: A Sociological Study.* Chicago: University of Chicago Press.

MacBeath, J., Demetriou, H., Rudduck, J. and Myers, K. (2003) *Consulting Pupils: A Toolkit for Teachers.* Cambridge: Pearson Publishing.

McIntyre, D. (1980) The contribution of research to quality in teacher education, in E. Hoyle and J. Megarry (eds) *World Yearbook of Education: Professional Development of Teachers.* London: Kogan Page.

McIntyre, D. (1988) Designing a teacher education curriculum from research and theory on teacher knowledge, in J. Calderhead (ed.) *Teachers' Professional Learning*, pp. 97–114. Lewes: Falmer Press.

McIntyre, D. (1991) The Oxford University model for teacher education, *South Pacific Journal of Teacher Education*, 19(2).

McIntyre, D. (1993) Theory, theorizing and reflection in initial teacher education, in J. Calderhead and P. Gates (eds) *Conceptualizing Reflection in Teacher Development*, pp. 39–52. London: Falmer Press.

McIntyre, D. (ed.) (1997) *Teacher Education Research in a New Context: The Oxford Internship Scheme.* London: Paul Chapman Publishing.

McIntyre, D. and Hagger, H. (1992) Professional development through the Oxford Internship model. *British Journal of Educational Studies*, 40(3): 264–83.

McIntyre, D., Macleod, G. and Griffiths, R. (eds) (1977) *Investigations of Microteaching.* London: Croom Helm.

McNally, J., Cope, P., Inglis, W. and Stronach, I. (1994) Current realities in the student teaching experience: a preliminary enquiry. *Teaching and Teacher Education*, 10(2): 219–30.

McNamara, D. and Desforges, C. (1978) The social sciences, teacher education and the objectification of craft knowledge. *British Journal of Teacher Education*, 4(1): 17–36.

Merseth, K.K. (1996) Cases and case methods in teacher education, in J. Sikula (ed.) *Handbook of Research on Teacher Education* (2nd edition), pp. 722–44. New York: Macmillan.

Mills, J. (1995) Partnership experiences for students. *Mentoring and Tutoring*, 3(2): 39–44.

Moon, B. (1998) *The English Exception? International Perspectives on the Initial Education and Training of Teachers*, Occasional Paper No. 11. London: Universities Council for the Education of Teachers.

Morris, E. (2001) *Professionalism and Trust – The Future of Teachers and Teaching*. London: Department for Education and Skills.

Morrison, A. and McIntyre, D. (1967) Changes in opinions about education during the first year of teaching. *British Journal of Social and Clinical Psychology*, 6: 161–3.

Munby, H. (1986) Metaphor in the thinking of teachers: an exploratory study. *Journal of Curriculum Studies*, 18: 197–209.

National Commission on Excellence in Education (1983) *A Nation at Risk: The Imperative for Educational Reform*. Washington, DC: US Government Printing Office.

Nias, J. (1989) *Primary Teachers Talking: A Study of Teaching as Work*. London: Routledge.

Ofsted (2003) *An Evaluation of the Training Schools Programme*, HMI 1769. London: Office for Standards in Education.

Ofsted (2005) *An Employment-Based Route into Teaching: An Overview of the First Year of the Inspection of Designated Recommending Bodies for the Graduate Teacher Programme 2003/04*, HMI 2406. London: Office for Standards in Education.

O'Hear, A. (1988) *Who Teaches the Teachers?* Research Report No.10. London: Social Affairs Unit.

O'Keefe, D. (1990) Equality and childhood: education and the myths of teacher training, in N.J. Graves (ed.) *Initial Teacher Education: Policies and Progress*. London: Kogan Page.

Olson, J. (1992) *Understanding Teaching*. Milton Keynes: Open University Press.

Pendry, A. (1997) The pedagogical thinking and learning of history student teachers, in D. McIntyre (ed.) *Teacher Education Research in a New Context: The Oxford Internship Scheme*, pp. 76–98. London: Paul Chapman Publishing.

Reynolds, D. (1998) Teacher effectiveness. Address given at the launch of the Teacher Training Agency Corporate Plan (1998–2001).

Reynolds, M.C. (ed.) (1989) *Knowledge Base for the Beginning Teacher*. Oxford: Pergamon Press.

Robbins, L. (1963) *Higher Education*. London: HMSO.

Robinson, W. (2004) *Power to Teach: Learning through Practice*. London: RoutledgeFalmer.

Ross, J.A. (1995) Professional development schools: prospects for institutionalisation. *Teaching and Teacher Education*, 11(2): 195–201.

Rudduck, J. and Flutter, J. (2004) *How to Improve Your School: Giving Pupils a Voice*. London: Continuum.

Russell, T., Munby, H., Spafford, C. and Johnston, P. (1988) Learning the professional knowledge of teaching: metaphors, puzzles and the theory–practice relationship, in P.P. Grimmett and G.L. Erickson (eds) *Reflection in Teacher Education*. New York: Teachers College Press.

Sabers, D.S., Cushing, K.S. and Berliner, D.C. (1991) Differences among teachers in a task characterised by simultaneity, multidimensionality and immediacy. *American Educational Research Journal*, 28(1): 63–88.

Sachs, J. (2003) *The Activist Teaching Profession*. Buckingham: Open University Press.

Scheffler, I (1960) *The Language of Education*. Springfield, IL: Charles C. Thomas.

Schön, D. (1983) *The Reflective Practitioner: How Professionals Think in Action*. New York: Basic Books.

Shulman, L. (1986) Those who understand: knowledge growth in teaching. *Educational Researcher*, 15: 4–14.

Snoek, M. (2003) Scenarios for Dutch teacher education. A trip to Rome: coach, bus company or travel agency? *European Journal of Teacher Education*, 26: 123–35.

Spencer, F.H. (1938) *An Inspector's Testament*. London: English Universities Press.

Stanulis, R.N. (1995) Classroom teachers as mentors: possibilities for participation in a professional development school context. *Teachers and Teacher Education*, 11(4): 331–44.

Stark, M.E.R. (2000) Learning from experience: the contribution of placement to becoming a primary teacher. Unpublished PhD thesis, University of Strathclyde.

Stenhouse, L. (1975) *An Introduction to Curriculum Research and Development*. London: Heinemann.

Stoddart, T. and Floden, R. (1996) Traditional and alternate routes to teacher certification: issues, assumptions and misconceptions, in K. Zeichner, S. Melnick and M.L. Gomez (eds) *Current of Reform in Preservice Teacher Education*, pp. 80–106. New York: Teachers College Press.

Sutherland, L.M., Scanlon, L.A. and Sperring, A. (2005) New directions in preparing professionals: examining issues in engaging students in communities of practice through a school–university partnership. *Teaching and Teacher Education*, 21(1): 79–91.

Tabberer, R. (2005) Teaching as a people business. Unpublished address delivered at the North of England Education Conference.

Tom, A.R. (1984) *Teaching as a Moral Craft*. New York: Longman.

Tom, A.R. and Valli, L. (1990) Professional knowledge for teachers, in W.R. Houston (ed.) *Handbook of Research on Teacher Education*, pp. 373–92. New York: Macmillan.

Tomlinson, P. (1995) *Understanding Mentoring*. Buckingham: Open University Press.

Valli, L., Cooper, C. and Frankes, L. (1997) Professional development schools and equity: a critical analysis of rhetoric and research. *Review of Research in Education*, 22: 251–304.

Vincent, C. (1996) *Parents and Teachers: Power and Participation*. London: Falmer.

Wang, J. and Odell, S.J. (2002) Mentored learning to teach according to standards-based reform: a critical review. *Review of Educational Research*, 72(3): 481–546.

Wideen, M., Mayer-Smith, J. and Moon, B. (1998) A critical analysis of the research on learning to teach: making the case for an ecological perspective on enquiry. *Review of Educational Research*, 68(2): 130–78.

Wilkin, M. (1999) *The Role of Higher Education in Initial Teacher Education*, Occasional paper, No. 12. London: Universities Council for the Education of Teachers.

Wilson, E. (2005) Powerful pedagogical strategies in initial teacher education. *Teachers and Teaching: Theory and Practice*, 11(4): 359–78.

Younger, M., Brindley, S., Pedder, D. and Hagger, H. (2004) Starting points: student teachers' reasons for becoming teachers and their preconceptions of what this will mean. *European Journal of Teacher Education*, 27(3): 245–64.

Zeichner, K. (1996a) Educating teachers for cultural diversity, in K. Zeichner, S. Melnick and M.L. Gomez (eds) *Currents of Reform in Preservice Teacher Education*, pp. 133–75. New York: Teachers College Press.

Zeichner, K. (1996b) Designing educative practicum experiences for prospective teachers, in K. Zeichner, S. Melnick and M.L. Gomez (eds) *Currents of Reform in Preservice Teacher Education*, pp. 215–34. New York: Teachers College Press.

Zeichner, K.M., Tabachnick, B. R. and Densmore, K. (1987) Individual, institutional and cultural influences on the development of teachers' craft knowledge, in J. Calderhead (ed.) *Exploring Teachers' Thinking*, pp. 21–59. London: Cassell.

Index